From Agamben to Žižek

From Agamben To Žižek

Contemporary Critical Theorists

Edited by Jon Simons

Edinburgh University Press

© in this edition Edinburgh University Press, 2010
© in the individual contributions is retained by the authors

Edinburgh University Press Ltd
22 George Square, Edinburgh

www.euppublishing.com

Typeset in ITC New Baskerville
by Servis Filmsetting Ltd, Stockport, Cheshire, and
printed and bound in Great Britain by
CPI Antony Rowe, Chippenham and Eastbourne

A CIP record for this book is available from the British Library

ISBN 978 0 7486 3973 1 (hardback)
ISBN 978 0 7486 3974 8 (paperback)

The right of Jon Simons
to be identified as editor of this work
has been asserted in accordance with
the Copyright, Designs and Patents Act 1988.

Contents

Contents

Acknowledgements

I would like to thank the members of the Critical Theory team at the University of Nottingham, as well as the contributors to the previous volumes in this series, *From Kant to Lévi-Strauss: The Background to Contemporary Critical Theory* (Edinburgh University Press, 2002) and *Contemporary Critical Theorists: From Lacan to Said* (Edinburgh University Press, 2004) for their sage advice about which theorists to include in this volume. I take responsibility, of course, for all the shortcomings of the final selection. I would also like to thank the contributors to this volume for the effort and care that they put into writing their chapters and for their comments on my introduction. Peter Andrews has prepared an excellent index for this volume, as he did for the previous volumes. Jackie Jones of Edinburgh University Press has been a wonderfully supportive editor; her insight and encouragement turned one book proposal into a series of three volumes. James Dale (for the first two volumes) and Eliza Wright (for this volume) served as accomplished desk editors for the series.

I am grateful to the College of Arts and Sciences at Indiana University, Bloomington, for a generous summer fellowship that gave me time to complete most of the editing of this volume.

I am also indebted to all those who, by enraging me, remind me on a daily basis of the absolute need to think critically about the world. The list is too long to include here, but a special mention must go to all the denizens of the American 'conservative echo-chamber'.

Jon Simons
February 2010

Notes on Contributors

John Armitage is Head of the Department of Media at Northumbria University, UK. He is the founder and co-editor, with Ryan Bishop and Douglas Kellner, of the Berg journal *Cultural Politics* and the editor of *Paul Virilio: From Modernism to Hypermodernism and Beyond* (Sage, 2001), *Virilio Live: Selected Interviews* (Sage, 2001) and, with Joanne Roberts, the co-editor of *Living With Cyberspace: Technology & Society in the 21ˢᵗ Century* (Continuum, 2002).

Peter Beilharz is Professor of Sociology and Director of the Thesis Eleven Centre for Cultural Sociology at La Trobe University, Australia. He has written or edited six books on Bauman, including *Zygmunt Bauman – Masters of Social Thought*, 4 vols (Sage, 2002), *The Bauman Reader* (Blackwell, 2001) and *Zygmunt Bauman – Dialectic of Modernity* (Sage, 2000), and is collecting his essays on Bauman for a separate volume.

Arianna Bove currently teaches at Queen Mary College, University of London. She is a developer of <www.generation-online.org> where her research, articles and translations can be found. She has translated many works from Italian and French into English, including texts by Agamben, Althusser, Foucault, Negri, Berardi, Virno and others.

Samuel A. Chambers teaches political theory at Johns Hopkins University. He writes broadly in political theory, including work on language, culture and the politics of gender and sexuality.

He is the author of *Untimely Politics* (Edinburgh University Press, 2003), *The Queer Politics of Television* (IB Tauris, 2009) and co-author, with Terrell Carver, of *Judith Butler and Political Theory* (Routledge, 2008). He is also co-editor, with Terrell Carver, of *William Connolly: Democracy, Pluralism and Political Theory* (2007), *Judith Butler's Precarious Politics* (2008) and *Carole Pateman: Feminism, Democracy, Welfare* (2009).

Ilana Gershon received her PhD in cultural anthropology from the University of Chicago in 2001. An assistant professor in the Department of Communication and Culture at Indiana University, she writes and teaches about disconnections using new media, the anthropology of democracy, indigenous self-representation (specifically Maori politicians and Samoan migrants), diaspora, US ethnic formations, migration, kinship and the anthropology of knowledge. Her research has been published in *American Anthropologist, Current Anthropologist, Anthropological Theory, Social Analysis* and other journals. Her book, *The Breakup 2.0: Disconnecting over New Media* (Cornell, 2010), deploys her long-standing interest in Actor-Network Theory to explore ethnographically how people use different communicative technologies to end romantic relationships.

Paul Hegarty teaches philosophy and cultural studies in the Department of French, University College Cork, Ireland. He has published books on Georges Bataille, Jean Baudrillard, noise and music, Dennis Cooper, and contributed to Andrew Norris (ed.), *Politics, Metaphysics and Death: Essays on Giorgio Agamben's* Homo Sacer (Duke University Press, 2005).

David Huddart is Associate Professor in the Department of English at the Chinese University of Hong Kong, where he teaches literary theory and World Englishes. He is the author of *Homi K. Bhabha* (Routledge, 2006) and *Postcolonial Theory and Autobiography* (Routledge, 2008).

David Kidner worked as a process design engineer in the petroleum industry before turning to social science with a PhD in psychology from London University. For the past three decades he has taught critical social science and environmental philosophy in Britain and the USA, and is currently at Nottingham Trent University. He is the author of *Nature and Psyche: Radical Environmentalism and the Politics of Subjectivity* (SUNY Press, 2001).

Moya Lloyd is Professor of Political Theory at Loughborough University. She has published widely in the areas of contemporary political theory and feminist theory, focusing in particular on the work of Judith Butler. Her most recent books include *Beyond Identity Politics: Feminism, Power and Politics* (Sage, 2005), *Judith Butler: From Norms to Politics* (Polity, 2007); and (with Adrian Little) *The Politics of Radical Democracy* (Edinburgh University Press, 2009). She is currently working on two projects: a text on gender and sexuality and a research monograph entitled 'Who Counts?'

Joan Faber McAlister is an assistant professor of Rhetoric and Communication Studies in the Department for the Study of Culture and Society at Drake University and holds a PhD in Rhetorical Studies from the University of Iowa. Her research interests include aesthetics, materiality, subjectivity, cultural geography, domestic space and queer, feminist and critical theory. Her work has been published in *Liminalities*, *Women's Studies in Communication*, and edited volumes in the field of rhetorical studies.

Stephen Morton is a senior lecturer in English at the University of Southampton. His fields of research include post-colonial literature, critical theory and visual culture. His publications include *Foucault in an Age of Terror* (Palgrave Macmillan, 2008), co-edited with Stephen Bygrave, *Salman Rushdie: Fictions of Postcolonial Modernity* (Palgrave Macmillan, 2007), *Gayatri Spivak: Ethics, Subalternity and the Critique of Postcolonial Reason* (Polity, 2006) and *Gayatri Chakravorty Spivak* (Routledge, 2003); as well as articles in *Textual Practice, Public Culture, New Formations, The Year's Work in Critical and Cultural Theory* and *Interventions: An International Journal of Postcolonial Studies*.

Benjamin Robinson received his PhD in Modern Thought from Stanford University and has been Assistant Professor of German at Indiana University since 2004. He teaches and studies how key works of modernism reformulate earlier understandings of realism. His book, *The Skin of the System: On Germany's Socialist Modernity* (Stanford University Press, 2009), rethinks historical socialism via the paradoxes of radical transformation. His current monograph project, *Out of All Scale*, examines the centrality of a particular semiotic sign, the index, for an era when cultural themes became dramatically disproportionate to the scale of daily life. For the last several years, Robinson has been actively engaged with Alain Badiou's philosophy, organising several multi-day conferences on his work, one attended by Professor Badiou.

Matthew Sharpe is a lecturer in the School of International and Political Studies, Deakin University. He is the author of *Slavoj Žižek: A Little Piece of the Real* (Ashgate, 2004), and coauthor of *Žižek and Politics* (Edinburgh, 2010), *Understanding Psychoanalysis* (Acumen, 2007) and *The Times Will Suit Them: Postmodern Conservatism in Australia* (Allen & Unwin, 2007). He has also authored numerous articles on political philosophy, critical theory and psychoanalysis. Presently, he is working on a new book, *Jacques Lacan and Leo Strauss: The Ancient and the Modern*.

Jon Simons is an associate professor in the Department of Communication and Culture at Indiana University. He has a broad expertise in contemporary critical theory, having directed the MA in Critical Theory at the University of Nottingham from 1995 to 2005. He is the author of *Foucault and the Political* (Routledge, 1995) as well as many journal articles and book chapters on political and cultural theory. He is the editor of and contributor to *From Kant to Lévi-Strauss: The Background to Contemporary Critical Theory* and *Contemporary Critical Theorists: From Lacan to Said* (Edinburgh University Press, 2002 and 2004 respectively).

Simon Tormey is Professor and Head of the School of Social and Political Sciences, University of Sydney. He is the author of *Making Sense of Tyranny: Interpretations of Totalitarianism* (Manchester University Press, 1995), *Politics at the Edge* (co-edited with C. Pierson [Macmillan, 1999]), *Autonomy, Contingency and the Postmodern: The Political Thought of Agnes Heller* (Manchester University Press, 2000), *Anti-Capitalism* (Oneworld, 2004), and *Key Thinkers from Critical Theory to Post-Marxism* (with Jules Townshend [Sage, 2006]), as well as numerous articles and chapters about radical political theory.

Caroline Williams is Lecturer in Politics, Queen Mary College, University of London. She is the author of *Contemporary French Philosophy: Modernity and the Persistence of the Subject* (Continuum, 2001), as well as journal articles and essays on Spinoza, Althusser, and post-structuralism more generally. She is currently working on a book project, *Spinoza and Political Critique: Thinking the Political in the Wake of Althusser*, to be published by University of Wales Press (in the series Political Philosophy Now, edited by Howard Williams).

Introduction

Jon Simons

This volume offers fifteen introductory essays about key contemporary critical theorists. The type and range of 'critical theory' covered in this volume refers to the broad sense of that term as it is used in Anglophone academia as a catch-all phrase for a divergent set of theories that distinguish themselves from conventional or traditional theories. 'Critical theory' designates a range of 'isms' including Marxism and post-Marxism, semiotics and discourse analysis, structuralism and post-structuralism, ideology critique of all varieties, deconstruction, feminism, queer theory, psychoanalysis, postcolonialism, postmodernism, as well as the successors to Frankfurt School Critical Theory. 'Critical theory' in the broader sense is an effect of the appropriation and integration of both Frankfurt School Critical Theory and the various streams of 'French' and other thought into Anglophone academies since the mid-1960s, when a range of theoretical approaches to different branches of the humanities and social sciences began to be adopted on the margins of established disciplinary methodologies. The labels of postmodernism and post-structuralism became the most common, though reductive if not downright inaccurate, handles with which this range of theory was grasped in the heady days of 'high theory'.

The range of critical theorists covered by this book provides an overview of the general field without privileging one particular area of critical theory. These theorists travel across disciplinary boundaries, their work being useful within a wide variety of disciplines as well as in the interdisciplinary work of say, African-American Studies and visual culture studies.

1

This book is intended to provide an introduction to the thought of the critical theorists selected, such that readers have an understanding of their main ideas that is good enough as a basis for further study. For each thinker or pair of thinkers, a chapter offers some biographical and intellectual contextualisation, presents and explains key concepts, outlines some major angles of criticism, indicates areas and ways in which the theories have been applied, and offers suggestions for further reading. On completing each chapter, readers should feel confident that they can make an informed decision about whether to learn more and subsequently to put theories to work. It should go without saying that each of the thinkers is more complex and their work more extensive than can be presented in a chapter. The aim of the chapters is also to present the work of the thinkers in a fair and accurate way, which has left the authors of the chapters with little or no space to present their own interpretations. There has also not been much scope to present criticisms of the theorists, so more information about the standard criticisms of the thinkers in the volume can be found in the suggested further reading. If this book succeeds in its aims, it will have whetted its readers' appetites to read more of the critical theorists it introduces.

The intended readers of the volume are advanced undergraduate and beginning (post)graduate students who are taking classes that are dedicated significantly to contemporary 'theory', whether that be political theory, social theory, cultural theory, literary theory, continental philosophy, or some other variation. The book will also be useful for students who find that across a variety of classes they are reading work by theorists included in the volume. The chapters provide simplified but not reductive accounts of the theorists, so they are also intended to be instructive for scholars not yet familiar with thinkers whose work they come across in their research. The following sections of the introduction discuss the scope of the book, and the pertinence of the volume in an allegedly 'post-theoretical' intellectual environment.

The Scope of this Volume

The range of theorists included in this volume has been shaped to a very large extent by the two volumes about critical theory that have preceded it. The prior volume, *From Lacan to Said*, covered contemporary theorists who had established significant trans-disciplinary reputations in the Anglophone world by 1990, most of whom were born before the Second World War, namely, Lacan, Althusser, Barthes, Kristeva, Derrida, Levinas, Lyotard, Irigaray, Cixous, Deleuze and Guattari, Foucault, Baudrillard, Bourdieu, Habermas, Jameson and Said.[1] As I wrote in the introduction to that volume, the thinkers included there constituted what had by the end of the 1980s become a 'critical canon' established by the first generations of Anglophone academics to disseminate the mostly imported ideas of critical theory. I also argued that the explosion of critical theories by the 1980s had both its significant precursors and successors. The first volume in this trilogy, *From Kant to Lévi-Strauss*, was dedicated to the former, including chapters on Kant, Hegel, Marx, Nietzsche, Weber, Freud, Lukács, Adorno and Horkheimer, Husserl, Heidegger, Gadamer, Wittgenstein, Arendt and Lévi-Strauss.[2] In the introduction to that volume I suggested that the more recent wave of critical theorists had swelled on the deeper waters of a modern 'critical tradition'. By beginning with Kant, but omitting ancient and medieval thinkers from whom contemporary theorists draw inspiration, that volume conceived of a largely Germanophone tradition of critique that laid the way for the subsequent Francophone predominance in critical theory. As the new theorists build on and replenish the work of their predecessors, an understanding of the theoretical canon is necessary when dealing with the most contemporary theory. The thinkers covered in this volume are those who had established significant trans-disciplinary reputations in the Anglophone world since about 1990, though they are likely to have been well known in some circles before then.

There is no clear dividing line between this volume and its predecessor. Table 1.1 lists the thinkers in the preceding volumes who are precursors (though not necessarily direct and positive influences) on the theorists in this volume. Table 1.2 indicates roughly when and with which work the theorists in this volume established reputations in Anglophone academia. The most honest explanation for the omission of some of the theorists from the preceding volume but inclusion here is lack of space, along with an estimation that those who had to wait until this volume had made less of a trans-disciplinary impact than others. That is especially the case for Castoriadis (who belongs in the generation of Lyotard, Deleuze and Foucault, and is the only author included here who has died) and Virilio, whose significance has, however, grown notably since their first 'breakthrough'. Others appear to be the 'followers' of

**Table 1.1 Contemporary critical theorists and the main
influences on them from the critical tradition**

Contemporary theorist	Significant precursors covered in the preceding volumes of this series
Agamben	Derrida, Foucault, Hegel, Heidegger, Kant
Badiou	Hegel, Marx
Bauman	Marx, Weber
Bhabha	Derrida, Foucault, Freud, Lacan, Said
Butler	Althusser, Foucault, Freud, Hegel, Irigaray, Kristeva, Lacan, Nietzsche
Castoriadis	Althusser, Arendt, Freud, Lacan, Marx
Green critical theorists	Heidegger
Haraway	Foucault, Heidegger, Marx
Laclau and Mouffe	Althusser, Arendt (for Mouffe), Derrida, Foucault, Lacan, Marx
Latour	Foucault
Negri	Deleuze and Guattari, Foucault, Marx
Rancière	Althusser, Marx
Spivak	Deleuze and Guattari, Derrida, Foucault, Hegel, Kant, Marx
Virilio	Heidegger, Husserl, Marx
Žižek	Freud, Hegel, Lacan, Marx

**Table 1.2 The Anglophone emergence of theorists included
in this volume**

Theorist(s)	'Breakthrough' date in Anglophone circles	'Breakthrough' work
Agamben	1998	*Homo Sacer*
Badiou	2001	*Ethics*
Bauman	1987	*Legislators and Interpreters*
Bhabha	1994	*Location of Culture*
Butler	1990	*Gender Trouble*
Castoriadis	1987	*Imaginary Institution of Society*
Green theorists	1970s	
Haraway	1985	'Manifesto for Cyborgs'
Laclau and Mouffe	1985	*Hegemony and Socialist Strategy*
Latour	1993	*We Have Never Been Modern*
Negri	2000	*Empire*
Rancière	1998	*Disagreement*
Spivak	1988	'Can the Subaltern Speak?'
Virilio	2002	*Desert Screen*
Žižek	1989	*The Sublime Object of Ideology*

previous theorists. While the innovation of Laclau's and Mouffe's post-Marxism was immediately felt in political and cultural theory, their debt to more groundbreaking post-structuralist theorists such as Derrida and Foucault is also clear. Similarly, as Žižek burst on to the scene as the decade closed, he was taken very clearly as a follower of Lacan. Other theorists, namely, Haraway and Spivak, established themselves more fully with more substantive publications over the 1990s. Latour's transdisciplinary stature also grew over the decade as his writing became known beyond science studies, while Bauman's post-retirement shift to a less academic style might explain his more widespread influence by the 1990s. Green theory, which cannot sensibly be reduced to a 'star' theorist, drew more attention as awareness about global environmental crises grew, yet had already developed its key insights. There are also theorists included in this volume, most notably Agamben, Badiou, Negri and Rancière, who had published significant work before 1990 but which either was not translated until later or the importance of which was only established in the Anglophone critical humanities retrospectively.

Some of the theorists in this volume can be seen as developers and synthesisers of the work of theorists covered in the previous volumes (as well as others), and hence part of a distinctive 'critical tradition'. As 'replenishers' of this critical tradition, many of the theorists discussed in this volume have also taken the tradition in novel and needed directions. Laclau and Mouffe combined Gramscian neo-Marxism with Derridean and Foucauldian post-structuralism to conceptualise a radical democratic politics for the New Left. Negri's Spinozist autonomist Marxism mingled with Foucault's biopolitics and Deleuze's notion of desire provides a framework for understanding global capitalism and anti-capitalist movements. Bhabha and Spivak engaged critically and variously with deconstruction, psychoanalysis and Marxism in their groundbreaking work in postcolonial theory. Butler built on a blend of 'French feminism', psychoanalysis, Foucault and deconstruction to forge a bold direction for queer theory. By contrast, Žižek's Lacanian Marxist analysis of late modern capitalism, nationalism and racism is a deliberate departure from what was a prevailing post-structuralist trend in critical theory.

Yet, taken as a whole, the critical theorists written about in this volume cannot be considered as some sort of 'Theory 2.0' in relation to those who were already well established by 1990. One tendency among this collection of thinkers is to draw consciously on the precursors to the wave of theorists who were to be labelled as post-structuralists and postmodernists. Such a tendency is indicated by Žižek's Hegelian direction through Marx and Lacan on his way back to Lenin. While Agamben's work on language, the law and sovereignty appears to owe much to Derrida and Foucault, his declared debts are to Kant, Hegel, Heidegger, Benjamin and Aristotle. Badiou's truth-directed Marxism harkens back to Plato in a conscious distancing from Nietzschean postmodernism, while Bauman works above all to renew the ethos of Marxist critique, remodelled to fit 'liquid modernity' rather than 'postmodernity'. Castoriadis had no truck with his more fashionable contemporaries, finding his inspiration for a Marxist politics in Freudian rather than Lacanian psychoanalysis as well as Aristotle, Kant and Merleau-Ponty. Green theorists tend to consider themselves at odds with the whole post-Kantian critical tradition's vacillation between technological optimism and anti-Enlightenment scepticism, though Naess, like Deleuze and Negri, refers back to Spinoza. Haraway engages critically with Marx, Derrida and Foucault in her feminist, post-colonial, anti-racist, anti-anthropocentric analysis of the contemporary capitalist and technologised world. She is also critical of her fellow-traveller in science studies, Latour, who shares with her and post-structuralism a penchant for deconstructing binaries, as well as a background in empirical research. Rancière forges his path in political and aesthetic criticism by working with historical archives and pitting himself against Althusser's scientific Marxism and Plato's hierarchical order, also engaging critically with Arendt, Foucault and Marx. Virilio is indebted to Husserl and Heidegger for his departure from Marxism in his critique of the accelerated, technologised and militaristic world.

Another notable line of departure from most of the already canonised critical theorists is an interest in science and, in a somewhat different vein, an embodied materialism and 'new empiricism'. Most obviously, the inclusion of Haraway and Latour from the field of science studies implies a somewhat different focus for critical analysis as well as requiring different theoretical tools. Badiou relies on mathematical set theory in his quest for axiomatic and universal philosophical truth. Green theorists adopt a critical realist position about the environment in contrast to the seeming anthropocentrism of social constructionism. Castoriadis finds his way back to the radical agency of the human subject through a scientific understanding of the creativity of nature, as well as by critiquing the pseudo-scientific nature of structuralism. Negri's reference to Spinoza's ontology similarly posits a world of lively matter. This empiricist and even scientific tendency among these critical theorists indicates something of a waning of the 'linguistic turn', as Richard Rorty put it,[3] that informed the work of many of the 'canonical' theorists, according to which the human world, society, culture, media and the arts, can best be understood and critiqued in the mode of reading a text. The critical theorists in this volume attend as much to 'things' or 'events' as to 'words' or even 'discursively constructed things'. As Latour puts it, what matters to such theory is the complexity of matter.[4]

There is also less of a Francophone emphasis in more recent critical theory, although the presence in this volume of Badiou, Castoriadis, Rancière and Virilio shows that Paris still holds a significant place in contemporary theory, and one might argue that Agamben comes through the same Franco-Germanic intellectual formation. Latour, Actor-Network Theory and science studies do not belong to that formation and Mouffe, who was born in Belgium, has flourished in an Anglophone setting. Agamben, Negri, Bauman and Žižek demonstrate a diversification of influence in Europe. Butler, Haraway and some Green theorists are not the extent of the North American part in contemporary theory, as the Indian-born postcolonial theorists Bhabha and Spivak have both found intellectual homes in American universities. The dynamic whereby American and other Anglophone academia relied on European (and mostly Francophone) imports in order to generate the intellectual phenomenon that is contemporary critical theory has declined as the wealth of American institutions has created centres for the replenishment of theory.

It is inevitable that there are significant omissions in a volume of only fifteen chapters, even taking into account the preceding volumes. Edouard Glissant and the theme of creolisation could have represented the continuing Francophone anti- and postcolonial tradition, begun most notably by Frantz Fanon. Eve Kosofosky Sedgwick's inclusion would extend the range of queer theory, while either or both of bell hooks and Cornel West would have represented African-American critical theory. Paul Gilroy's omission repeats *From Lacan to Said*'s neglect of key figures in Cultural Studies. Similarly, film and media theorists are not included in their own right, thereby leading aside figures ranging from the feminist and queer film theory of Teresa de Lauretis, to the critical sociological analysis of the information age and network society by Manuel Castells, to Régis Debray's 'mediology', to the embodied media theory of Brian Massumi. The coverage of science and technology studies would have benefited from a chapter on Isabelle Stengers, just as that of post-colonial theory would have with a chapter on Trin T. Minh-ha, and contemporary feminism with a chapter on Rosi Braidotti. The decision to include a chapter on Rancière was made consciously in comparison to other French political thinkers such as Jean-Luc Nancy, partly on the grounds of Rancière's great trans-disciplinary impact. Without chapters on figures such as Axel Honneth or Seyla Benhabib, it might seem mistakenly as if the post-Frankfurt School work of Habermas has run its course. And perhaps it is only a matter of time before the trans-disciplinary influence of other contemporary political theorists such as Iris Young and William Connolly are felt. No single volume could encapsulate all of the tendencies, let alone the figures, of contemporary critical theory.

Critical Theory and 'Post-theory'

The proliferation of omitted candidates for inclusion in this volume might point not so much to the flowering and diversification of critical theory than to its frequently noted decline, if the difficulty is in identifying outstandingly original figures. Terry Eagleton, who did a great deal to promote critical literary theory, has declared that 'The Golden Age of cultural theory is long past', referring to the period of theory dominated by the thinkers included in *From Lacan to Said*. 'Not much that has been written since has matched the ambitiousness and originality of these founding mothers and fathers', he says.[5] Paul Bové, writing mostly with critical literary theory in mind as does Eagleton, also remarks that the 'oppositional possibilities' of the critical theory movements from roughly 1964 to 1984 'have been exhausted'.[6] Bruno Latour argues that the critique of social theory has run out of steam.[7] Yet, critical theory has also succeeded in certain ways at the same time as excitement about it has waned, at least for the generation for whom it was a novel discovery rather than the syllabus studied for a 'Theory 101' class.

Ernesto Laclau indicates another reason why theory may seem to have declined, which is that it is no longer a 'distinctive object', remarkable in its own right, but that the '*post*-theoretical age' is characterised as 'a process of mutual contamination between "theory" and "empiria"'. The range and quality of theoretically-informed research across the 'critical humanities', characterised by 'a new sophistication in the analysis of the concrete', commands attention now, not 'theory' itself.[8] Seen in this light, Latour provides less a diagnosis than a prescription for social theory, namely, a '*renewal* of empiricism' that replaces the emphasis on ideological critique of 'prematurely naturalized objectified facts'.[9] As indicated above, the theorists included in this volume are less marked by the linguistic turn, one consequence of which may be that the latest wave of theory may have had less of an impact on literary and other textual studies than on the social sciences.

Ian Hunter correctly advises that any effort to consider the fate of theory historically must consider its trans-disciplinary nature, which means that it cannot be identified by any 'common object or shared language'.[10] Critical theory is often deployed as a critique of traditional disciplines, whether literary study in the humanistic tradition for which, as Eagleton quips, 'it was enough to pronounce Keats delectable or Milton a doughty spirit',[11] or the behaviourist, positivist, quantitative social sciences. Moreover, the traditional disciplines had different manifestations in different national academic contexts and thus so does critical theory. At the same time, while critical theory is an intellectual pursuit largely practised within academia, it is not as Bové remarks, limited to struggles over revising the canon but is also, as Eagleton says, 'the taxing business of trying to grasp what is actually going on', whether in a text or global capitalism.[12] Martin McQuillan and his colleagues assert that 'Theory wants more than anything to be thought of as "Radical"', not only in relation to academic disciplines within which they are embattled but also in the world, as praxis. And while 'the radicality of political praxis and the radicality of Theory might not be of the same order', at least two contexts need to be borne in mind simultaneously, the immediate institutional academic one and the more general political, social context in which universities exist.[13] The radicality of critical theory, which is one measure of its decline or success, varies, perhaps inversely, according to these contexts.

As Eagleton explains, when critical theory exploded into its Golden Age, it did so against the background of the 1960s, the Civil Rights Movement, anti-colonial struggles for independence, the student revolts, the women's movements and the anti-war movement. At that point, universities, or at least certain sectors of them,

9

were no longer 'citadels of disinterested inquiry' but 'cockpits of culture as political struggle'. Theory is the resultant 'critical self-reflection' of the humanities which had broken with their complicity with social authority. But the political radicality of the 1960s met with only partial success, whereas in academia, 'Theory overshot reality, in a kind of intellectual backwash to a tumultuous political era', providing ideas with 'a last, brilliant efflorescence when the conditions which produced them were already disappearing'.[14] Bové similarly suggests that the radical political atmosphere of the 1960s granted radical intellectuals and theory 'a certain real but limited place in the academy', one which has consistently been under attack since the rise in the 1980s of neo-liberalism and its 'institutional cultural equivalents'.[15] Eagleton and Bové are not defending precisely the same sort of theoretical radicalism, as for Eagleton the theory that Bové advocates betrayed its debt to its dialogue with Western Marxism by becoming not so much post-Marxist as post-political. Yet they both ascribe critical theory's decline to the waning of a general political radicality, the decline of the left (old and new).

The political conditions of radical decline, though, can also be thought of as the conditions for theoretical radicality within academia. 'The rise of Theory as an institutional practice is contemporaneous with the "decline" of the political left', and yet 'the radical effects of Theory are greatly undervalued', notably in the ways in which academic disciplines have been refashioned by theory.[16] But the institutional success of theory has come at a price too, precisely as it is institutionalised, turned into reductive doxa that can be taught to undergraduates. This volume, and the two volumes preceding it, is surely part of the phenomena whereby complex theory is packaged in a form amenable to instruction and marketed as a (not very profitable) commodity. Critical theory has found a way to survive and even prosper in universities during the times of neo-liberal educational reforms. In part, critical theorists have participated in the 'dominant practice and ideology' of professionalism, as part of their effort to 'legitimate theory' within 'the university system', even as critical theory has thrived because of its 'distance from capital'.[17] But critical reflection has itself become a 'transferable skill' required by the entrepreneurial denizens of liquid modernity. Critical theory, as Eagleton notes, is in an ambiguous position, both inside and outside the academic institution, a position he says was inherited from the origins, genders and sexualities of many 'French' theorists, but can in turn be considered the continuity of the pariah status of German Jewish intellectuals who made up much of the wave of theory that preceded the 'Golden Age', as I remarked in the introduction to *From Kant to Lévi-Strauss*. As a pariah, critical theory both inhabits the academy and critiques the state of contemporary higher education, as a local manifestation of the broader social, cultural and political processes that are the main target of contemporary critical theorists.

Critical theory, with or without a capital 'T', will continue to replenish itself as it challenges different academic, cultural and political establishments (including its own orthodoxies). It will carry on playing a central role in innovative research in the humanities and qualitative social sciences. Eagleton is clear that there can be no return to 'the pre-theoretical innocence' of literary studies, and Laclau also insists that the 'post-theoretical' universe is not 'a-theoretical'.[18] In another volume whose title appears to herald a post-theoretical turn in film studies, the editors clarify that they mean only the end of 'Grand Theory', demanding that the theorists of *From Lacan to Said* should give way to a fresher wave of 'theor*ies* and the activity of *theorizing*'. Perhaps their alternative of 'middle-range inquiry' that moves from 'bodies of evidence to more general argument' is not critical in the way that 'Grand Theory' is.[19] Yet, their proposed direction is consistent with the empirical and material turn in critical theory discussed above.

Certainly, the world is no less in need of critical theory at the beginning of the twenty-first century than it was in the middle of the twentieth. The world needs Agamben to theorise the on-going 'states of exception' in which sovereign states kill those they consider outside the law; Badiou to theorise those events to which a militant fidelity might lead humanity closer to universal freedom; Bauman to theorise the plight of 'surplus populations' such as refugees in global, 'liquid modernity'; Bhabha to theorise the extension of the colonial past in the hybrid identities and migrant experiences of the post-colonial present; Butler to theorise the oppression of the 'heterosexual matrix' and the resistance to it in queer performativity; Castoriadis to theorise the role of radical imagination in instituting a society that enables autonomy for all; green thinkers to theorise our existence as embodied creatures within our environment; Haraway to theorise the relation between techno-scientific knowledge and the violence of warmaking, global capitalism and environmental destruction; Laclau and Mouffe to theorise the radical democratic alternative to the prevailing liberal capitalist hegemony; Latour to theorise the actor-networks through which agency is attributed to some actants but not to others; Negri to theorise the domination of global capitalism and the autonomy of 'living labour' that struggles to transform it; Rancière to theorise the radical democratic politics of attending to those who do not count in the 'police' ordering of who can be heard and seen; Spivak to theorise the subaltern histories and languages of those post-colonial subjects, especially women, who are excluded in the complex inter-play between local, national and global hierarchies and capitalist inequalities; Virilio to theorise the arts of technology that condemn us to catastrophic, militarised, industrialised, mediated terror; Žižek to theorise the fantasies because of which we persistently engage in consumerism, nationalism and racism. From Agamben to Žižek, we need these theorists because we live in a world that still needs to be theorised critically. We could only afford to be 'post-theoretical' when the world is no longer characterised by globalised oppression, injustice, inequality and environmental destruction.

Notes

1. Jon Simons (ed.), *Contemporary Critical Theorists: From Lacan to Said* (Edinburgh: Edinburgh University Press, 2004).
2. Jon Simons (ed.), *From Kant to Lévi-Strauss: The Background to Contemporary Critical Theory* (Edinburgh: Edinburgh University Press, 2002).
3. Richard Rorty, *Philosophy and the Mirror of Nature* (Princeton: Princeton University Press, 1979), p. 263.
4. Bruno Latour, 'Why Has Critique Run out of Steam? From Matters of Fact to Matters of Concern', *Critical Inquiry*, 30, 2004, pp. 225–48.
5. Terry Eagleton, *After Theory* (New York: Basic Books, 2003), p. 1.
6. Paul Bové, *In the Wake of Theory* (Hanover: Wesleyan University Press, 1992), p. xii.
7. Latour, 'Why Has Critique Run out of Steam?'.
8. Ernesto Laclau, 'Preface', in Martin McQuillan, Graeme Macdonald, Robin Purves and Stephen Thomson (eds), *Post-Theory: New Directions in Criticism* (Edinburgh: Edinburgh University Press, 1999), p. vii.
9. Latour, 'Why Has Critique Run out of Steam?', pp. 231, 227.
10. Ian Hunter, 'The History of Theory', *Critical Inquiry*, 33, 2006, pp. 78–112 (80).
11. Eagleton, *After Theory*, p. 1.
12. Ibid. p. 223.

13. Martin McQuillan, Graeme Macdonald, Robin Purves and Stephen Thomson, 'The Joy of Theory', in *Post-Theory*, p. x.
14. Eagleton, *After Theory*, pp. 25–9.
15. Bové, *Wake of Theory*, pp. 3, ix.
16. McQuillan et al., 'Joy of Theory', p. xi.
17. Bové, *Wake of Theory*, p. 3; and Fredric Jameson, 'How Not to Historicize Theory', *Critical Inquiry*, 34, 2008, pp. 571–2.
18. Eagleton, *After Theory*, p. 1; Laclau, 'Preface', p. vii.
19. David Bordwell and Noël Carroll, 'Introduction', in David Bordwell and Noël Carroll (eds), *Post-Theory: Reconstructing Film Studies* (Madison: University of Wisconsin Press, 1996), pp. xiii–xvii.

1

Giorgio Agamben (1942–)

Paul Hegarty

Agamben is now regarded as a key theorist or, more accurately, political philosopher. His reception has tied him to the wave of 'French' theory in 1960s, but whilst he acknowledges Derrida and uses some parts of Foucault's theories, he associated himself more closely with 'continental philosophy', and primarily those who can be said to have preceded 'French' theory – Martin Heidegger, Walter Benjamin, Kant and Hegel.[1] He maintains a constant interest in Aristotle as a defining figure in Western metaphysics, and has in recent years devoted considerable attention to Carl Schmitt, as part of his ever-expanding and influential work on sovereignty and the limits of the political. Despite his protestations, Agamben belongs in the fold of contemporary critical theory, because his work continually meditates on how it is being produced; it is nearly always deconstructive (without explicitly following Derrida); it is persistently critical at categorical and political levels; it envisages and presents itself as an avant-gardist approach, always seeking to 'move beyond', even if this turns out to be difficult or impossible.

In the belief that the best philosophical understanding of humanity can be attained through a study of language, Agamben's early writings focus directly on language and its limits – where it begins, ends, fails, becomes nothing. Throughout his oeuvre, he has also considered the form and function of aesthetic production, the role of the artist and so on.[2] Above these two areas of interest, though, towers his thought on the limits of what it is to be human – investigated in nearly all of his work since the mid 1990s, but culminating (philosophically) in *Homo Sacer, The State of Exception* and *Remnants of Auschwitz*. In these books, he looks at what happens when all the rules that govern human conduct are seemingly stripped away. The last of these has been enormously important in rethinking the Shoah (Agamben rejects the term Holocaust, arguing it is a massive category mistake, implying a holiness of sacrifice rather than murder on a colossal scale).[3] Beyond those works, he has honed his ideas of ethics, sovereignty and limit situations, where the question of what it is to be human is at stake. His popularity cannot be credited to the accessibility of his writing but to his concern for the larger questions of human life that many theorists seemed to have left behind (at least in Agamben's view).

Coming to Language

In his early books, Agamben probes the meaning of language and its place in the history of metaphysics, as a way of understanding being. The starting point is the absolute role of negativity in creating the human. Hegel systematically conceived of humanity in relation to negativity, in the early nineteenth century. Negativity in this sense is not 'bad', but the idea of being defined by what you are not (that is, I am me because I understand I am not you, or anyone else).[4] This is the only means through which humans come to self-perception. The profound implication of this, as teased out by twentieth-century phenomenology and expanded on by Derrida, notably, is that the self is not present to itself, but only exists as a by-product of something else (or of everything else). Agamben reworks this idea of 'negativity' to render it as an internal part of the things we understand to be present (beings, objects, the world), which becomes internal in and as language.

According to Agamben, the history of metaphysics (he does not specify Western, but that seems to be his sole reference) understands language as the means of attaining or approaching the transcendental. This transcendental (as seen notably in Kant, Hegel, Husserl and Heidegger) is that which is beyond our mundane existence and knowledge, and yet is the profound truth of humanity. Agamben claims in *Infancy and History* that the transcendental is located not beyond, but in, language. To back up this point, he returns to the question of speech as a human phenomenon. The history of philosophy supposes animals to be without speech and humans the speaking animal. Not so, writes Agamben, as animals are in language, whilst humans come to it gradually, acquiring it as something external to them. This discovery of language is what he calls 'infancy'. At first, this refers to human children's acquisition of language, their move from the simple inhabiting of speech of animals, to language and discourse. In so doing, language becomes a way of knowing the world that is other to the subject, and then the means of self-consciousness: 'if language were immediately the voice of man [as it is for animals] . . . he could never experience the taking place of language or the disclosure of being'.[5] The key point, though, is that 'infancy' never goes away: the point of transition is an origin that is permanently maintained and simultaneously this space between speech/vocalising and language is the location of the transcendent. Furthermore, humanity as a whole has this experience, in the shape of history, where cultural origins never go away, even if hidden, rejected or ignored.

This point about history indicates a contradiction in Agamben, for on the one hand, he attempts a version of history inspired by Hegel (where consciousness develops in the form of the history of philosophy), whilst for the most part in his early books on language he makes extravagant claims about 'the human', 'the animal', 'language', 'science' – as if these were timeless phenomena, always and everywhere the same (the unthinking use of 'the animal' is a widespread problem in critical theory of the last few years). Elsewhere, he states explicitly that modernity has privileged access to the thought of language, and thereby completes a journey into language[6] but, ultimately, the biopolitics of modernity make of it a time where the humanity of humans is more lost than ever.

The thought of 'the space of language' as both negative and truly transcendental is more satisfyingly developed in *Language and Death*, which also contains, in germ, ideas that inform the later texts on sovereignty and limit conditions. This time, Agamben works more explicitly with Heidegger, using the model of 'being-for-death' to be found in the latter's *Being and Time*. Heidegger's argument is that authentic existence occurs only in awareness of death, of death as something that will come, and yet, 'I' will not be there when it happens to me. So, the most authentic human experience possible is one of absence. Both Heidegger and Agamben emphasise how the animal cannot have this negative experience. Instead of dying, animals merely cease living. After a long discussion on the specificity of the human voice, Agamben returns to this dying animal, stating that the animal voice 'contains the death of the animal'.[7] This is notable because it acknowledges that history has to include the animal, as surpassed other. The word evolution, with which Heidegger does not concern himself, is never mentioned but is strongly implied. Nonetheless, it still seems arbitrary that voice is what is lost when an animal dies, as opposed to fur, hearing or the capacity to excrete, until we notice that Agamben is now thinking much more deconstructively, and that it is from the human perspective that we identify this as significant, as if it always already was so.

Because of the connectedness of animal and human, Agamben's insight is that the human voice is the loss of animal voice (a loss which only occurs for the animal at death). The idea announced in *Infancy and History* is developed here to add in the notion of human language always containing a meaning it cannot say. This meaning is simply but essentially 'I speak' or 'I mean'. Language cannot convey the most essential truth about it, which is that it must be distant not only from its object and the speaking subject, but also from the truth of language, which is its capacity to exist as language (as opposed to animal sounds). All of language, whether names, or differentiating parts of language, is there to display that language takes place. This is not 'phatic' in the sense of words whose meaning is irrelevant, rather, it is 'the opening of the *ontological* dimension'.[8] In other words, language's workings, in communicating specific meanings, act to cover up the true meaning, which is nothing, but a nothing which holds the rest together, and continually brings it into being, as an origin that never disappears.

This working through of negativity, deriving from death, and the acquisition of language as the means of being-for-death, comes together in what Agamben calls Voice. In the first prefiguring of his later theories, the animal voice becomes 'the voice of a mere sound'.[9] Voice is not the human discursive voice, but the voice that lies between animal voice and discourse; it is 'no longer the experience of sound, and not yet the experience of meaning'. Agamben is continually fascinated by this 'thought of the voice alone'.[10] Having started with Heidegger, Agamben now thinks himself beyond, and what Heidegger calls thrownness (roughly speaking, alienation) of being can be identified as coming from this perpetual borderline language/voice which is where the impossibility of being there for death 'lives'. In other words, human awareness of death is always lost, always deposited in the voice without meaning, and in turn, this voice without meaning is the indicator that Being is bordered and defined by death. In this way, Agamben claims to have brought Heidegger's 'beyond' back into the centre of human existence.

In a way that is logically consistent, yet somehow detached, the closing few pages of *Language and Death* announce his future interests directly. In a way that recalls Levinas, Agamben suggests that this core of nothingness that lets everything else human exist is the basis of ethics, as it makes otherness and the awareness of otherness the core human attribute. At the same time, human culture is a turning away from brute, simple death. He makes this paradoxical situation the core of humanity, and moves on to ask what it would be like to remove the contradiction, what it would mean to prevent Voice from happening: 'perhaps man – the animal who seems not to be encumbered by any specific nature or any specific identity [i.e. the situation animals find themselves in] – must experience this poverty more radically'.[11]

Agamben's recent works maintain his obsession with language, and the argument that language has an other – whether in the political world, the animal world, the human, or even within language itself, where he continues to mine the distinction between signification and processes around it (the performance of signification, and also the performance of voice as simply human voice) that inform sign production and reception. In *The Open*, he further explores 'the animal', and is keen, as always, to explore a clear-cut divide by making the borderline a more messy, paradoxical space. Philosophy and religion have persistently identified the split between animal and human as a defining feature of what makes people human, but, says Agamben, this split occurs first within humanity. Only once humans are separate does the split occur and can be identified as always already having occurred. The human itself is divided, with part of itself identified as animal. The *supposition* of separation brings us into human culture, in the form of biopolitics, as well as ideologies of human value.

Humanity is defined by the possibility of *not* having language. Following Hegel, Agamben writes that 'the definitive annihilation of man in the proper sense, however, must also entail the disappearance of human language, and its substitution by mimetic or sonic signals comparable to the language of bees'.[12] For Hegel this substitution is a form of apotheosis, whereas for Agamben it is both a signal for the beginning and end of the humanity of individual humans. The absence or loss of language is also the necessary possibility that underlies the existence of language. The human is the only animal with discursive language, echoing the self-reflexivity or awareness that only it has, and the essence of that is the transition where language is nothing, where the threat of death is all: 'perhaps not only theology and philosophy but also politics, ethics and juris-prudence are drawn and suspended in the difference between man and animal'.[13]

Agamben's take on 'the animal' is problematic. He acknowl-edges that in differentiating human and animal through use of lan-guage we are only retrospectively justifying a difference based on a presumption, one that requires tricky judgements on 'pre-humans', 'excluding as not (yet) human an already human being from itself, that is by animalizing the human, by isolating the nonhuman within the human'.[14] So far so good, but what is this 'animal' beyond the ape-man? How can we talk of 'the' animal? Agamben does not seem to be bothered by this problem, caught as he is within Heidegger's thoughtworld (in this book). So when he refers to animal cognition and ethology, it is to Jakob von Uexküll, in whom Heidegger was interested. Uexküll argued that animals are unable to get beyond their habitats to understand either habitat or themselves as selves. Agamben also looks at eighteenth- century taxonomies of nature, but his philosophising about 'the animal' does not match the level of eighteenth-century writers like Buffon, or of the early evolution-ists, let alone attempt a contemporary assessment of the question. Despite this, he makes virtually timeless claims about the human/ animal divide (timeless insofar as it applies to all human history).

This is where we arrive at 'the open', with Agamben resolutely tracking Heidegger. Animals are in the open, are open, even, to the openness of nature, but only humans 'can see the open which names the unconcealedness of beings'.[15] Humans are human by virtue of alienation from all that is other to them. They are dis-tanced from themselves as present beings, and therefore capable of understanding that 'I' am a 'self'. The idea of the open is a good one, particularly when thought of in terms where 'the animal is at once open and not open – or, better, it is neither one nor the other: it is *open in a non-disconcealment*'.[16] The end of *The Open* returns to the idea of the contemporary world being increasingly dominated by biopolitics, bare existence and so on, with the complaint that today's world is vacuous, lost in noise and superficiality (a position Agamben has held since his early writings). The conclusion is that to think the human/animal border through language is a way into a resuscitated politics.

Those Who Can be Killed

For Agamben, the problematic of death as other and death as the ultimate truth of humanity (as evidenced in the existence of language) plays out in the world of politics, law and social control. The figure of *homo sacer* appears – he who can be killed, the one outside of society and deprived of humanity. *Homo Sacer* opens up Agamben's long investigation into sovereignty as a limit condition of law, humanity, politics and the subject. The focus is on the idea of 'bare life', of a humanity stripped of nearly all of its defining characteristics, which is at its most denuded in the Nazi concentration camps. Bare life is at its height in the 'biopolitics' of modernity, but, according to Agamben, it can and must be traced back throughout Western culture, to classical Greek and Roman law. Foucault writes of the biopoliticisation of life, notably in the first volume of his *History of Sexuality*.[17] He argues that Western society moves from a regimen where the ruler controls the right over life and death (that is, to wield the power of death), to one where life itself becomes subject to control. Biopolitics governs in bureaucratic, scientific, rule-based ways, ostensibly to improve the health and well-being of citizens. Agamben's gloss on this is that where the ancient Greek polity removed 'bare' (biological) life as irrelevant, Western modernity makes life the subject of control. The exclusion performed in Western societies prior to the seventeenth and eighteenth centuries was not a complete exclusion, but the purposeful exclusion of the biological in order to found the political, juridical or, even, the human. In fact, society is based not on separation from nature but on its exclusion of biology. Sovereignty, then, must be based on biopolitics, while the concentration camp is almost a return to the essence of human society, to its less-than-contractual origin.

The idea of 'bare life' is an extension of Agamben's ruminations on language: 'there is politics because man is the living being who, in language, separates and opposes himself to his own bare life and, at the same time, maintains himself in relation to that bare life in an inclusive exclusion'.[18] Bare life is empty humanity that is neither quite human nor animal, an intermediate state that, even as it appears, is shoved into the background to be made part of a society based on law. Similarly, the 'state of nature', identified by Hobbes as a terrain of total war, is not pure nature, but man emerging from nature, the condition that must be controlled by political society, and therefore always already inside that society. Political life is based on the possibility of punishment, argues Agamben, and specifically the possibility of being killed: 'the first foundation of political life is a life that may be killed, which is politicized through its very capacity to be killed'.[19] Sovereignty is the possibility of doing what is generally excluded – killing – to what is normally excluded – humans as animals. Both the ones who can be killed and the sovereign are outside the Law just as they are at its very core. The sovereign, in the form of a king, for example, is outside and beyond the Law as he is its guarantor. At the same time, he is the concentration of Law. Agamben identifies this situation as the 'exception' – and from which the 'state of exception' can emerge – that is, the suspension of Law. The exception, the suspension of Law, is the moment Law is founded, which is itself neither legitimate nor illegitimate, but violent. The violence of nature is held back to be restructured as the exception that guarantees all else. According to Agamben, this is not merely the mystical beginning of authority but a potential that cannot go away, the perpetual absent part of existing systems.

At the other end of the scale, but just as politically and primordially, lies *homo sacer*, 'a person [who] is simply set outside human jurisidiction without being brought into the realm of divine law'.[20] This person can be killed because their personhood is effectively removed by being placed outside the Law – they can be killed but are not eligible for sacrifice. They have become nothing – but, for all that, they maintain a residue of humanity – they are the ones that can be killed. We can see how this plays out in the killing of the Nazi camps, but inclusion of the word 'sacred' alerts us that it is not only at its most explicit that this form of power occurs. It is at least as likely that one's biology is subject to control through the notion of life being sacred – that is, wherever and whenever attention is primarily to bodily, bare existence.[21]

Agamben adamantly sets himself against ambiguous notions of the sacred that emerged in late nineteenth-century anthropology. Oddly, the only notion of 'sacred' he considers is from Roman law, where the sacred/*sacer* is the one who can be killed, who is outside the Law. We have to imagine that he means to refer to Western society, as it has developed from Judaic, Greek and Roman traditions, even if his view is flawed. On the basis of his text, Agamben dismisses other conceptions of sacrifical sacreds, where evil and good, taboo and transgression play out deconstructively. Leaving aside the questionable basis of his argument,[22] it follows, for Agamben, that 'the sacredness of life' reveals life at its smallest, almost in the same way as mass slaughter. In general, human life has not been throught of as sacred, but medical and legal developments have brought about such a thought. Agamben's point is that to think life as sacred means treating the people involved as only life – as life that must be saved, rather than in their political/judicial contexts. Even 'humanitarian organizations . . . can only grasp human life in the figure of bare or sacred life, and therefore, despite themselves, maintain a secret solidarity with the very powers they ought to fight'.[23]

For Agamben, all of modern life tends toward biopolitics and the reduction to 'bare life' – whether through mass killings, rights and 'saving' people, or medical technology – 'all life becomes sacred and all politics becomes the exception'.[24] The implication is that, increasingly, humans become totally subject to rules and regulations, subject to exclusion, and less and less subject *as subjects* within the realm of law. It is not that law is done away with, rather it becomes the empty form it came from: Law identifying itself as Law, identifying people as bare life, as material for Law.

While this 'pure' state of Law is neither necessarily good nor bad, the place where it is heightened is the concentration camp, where exception becomes the rule, where all become bare life. Agamben turns to this topic in depth in his powerful and best-known work, *Remnants of Auschwitz*.[25] His purpose is to rethink the Nazi concentration camps in a way that refuses the mysticism of the 'unsayable' he sees at work in other theoretical writings: '[W]hy unsayable? Why confer on extermination the prestige of the mystical?'[26] As is often the case, Agamben does not do justice to the position he criticises, adopting a position much like one he earlier misread.[27] The book is also surprisingly insubstantial unless read as part of his *homo sacer* theory, but it does adopt a convincing position from which to account for 'unsayability' as part of a wider situation occurring in the shape of the concentration camp. As in earlier works, humanity's relation to language as a limit condition is in play, as he focuses on the figure of the *Muselmann* (muslim) – the prisoner who gives up and seems to be living a minimal animal existence, bereft of humanity. The *Muselmann* is the true witness of the camp, truer in one way than those who survive with their humanity intact. These two categories interact in Agamben's argument. The *Muselmann* leaves the world of language and sociality behind, becoming a risk to fellow prisoners, shunned by all. They are effectively dead, barely human. It is the 'effectively' and the 'barely' that count here – because they are still some sort of human, 'mark[ing] the threshold in which man passed into non-man'. It is from them that we can begin to understand what Auschwitz does to humans, and what it tells us about 'the human condition' in general: 'in Auschwitz ethics begins precisely at the point where the *Muselmann*, the "complete witness", makes it forever impossible to distinguish between man and non-man'.[28]

Why though is this most lost of humans a witness? The spaces between human and non-human, between language and non-language are always there in language, in human culture, Agamben claims. All language is 'something to which no one has borne witness'.[29] This is the same argument we saw developed in *Language and Death* – the interstitial moment between is the key, the moment where we have pure language – the existence of language without content, of being without being either animal or fully human, fully social (the place of *homo sacer*). The *Muselmann* is the no-one who can be there for the witnessing, through not really being there. He, in turn, requires the witness who survives to become a witness to this impossibility of witnessing that the *Muselmann* is. The peculiar, exceptional circumstance that produces this category of bare life is one that returns us to the totality of being as witnessing, and to language as a permanent witnessing to what lies outside it, to language as such: 'testimony takes place where the speechless one makes the speaking one speak and where the one who speaks bears the impossibility of speaking in his own speech'.[30] The witness is never present, but is always an other, even in the case of someone who recovers from being a *Muselmann* and survives the camps. Witnessing is not only about recounting the horrors of Nazi industrialised mass murder, but is a testimony about what it is to be human. What it is to be human is most profoundly raised as a question when it is stripped down to bare life – to being only an organic human being (Agamben strays into a type of Cartesian thinking whereby the human is divided into essence and biology, but the point here is the human does not become merely animal but merely human).

Witnessing implies surviving, that something remains (translated as 'remnant' in English), and 'survival designates the pure and simple continuation of bare life with respect to truer and more human life [and/or] the person who in fighting against death, has survived the inhuman'.[31] The existence of both categories is essential, as, in surviving, the witness recounts the bare life of the *Muselmann* existence, exposing what it is to be destructible, revealing 'that it is not truly possible to destroy the human, that something always *remains*'.[32]

Agamben has not sought to reveal a truth about the human condition that is timeless, but one that is historical, occurring in specific times, politics and contexts that bring out something primordial but social. The Nazi regime, in which the camps were the most extreme element, turned the 'state of exception' where the normal legal system is suspended into a permanent condition, a return to the pure sovereignty of the state of nature, which can always return. This 'state of nature' is precisely the sovereign creation of society through biopolitics, the bringing of humans into the realm of 'sacredness' where they can be killed. The *Muselmann* is the ultimate exception, the human being taken out of the human, a product of the state of exception that is the camp; that is, the product of the general suspension of law as the sovereign exercise of power from 1933 to 1945.

Agamben returns to the 'state of exception' through a sustained if selective reading of Carl Schmitt's theory of sovereignty, in *State of Exception.* Just as with *Remnants of Auschwitz*, actual political situations are where the apparently abstract thought of Being can be conducted – Guantanamo Bay and the 'exceptionality' of the US Patriot Act are cited early on. Agamben writes a history of the development of actual states of exception or emergency in the nineteenth century and beyond. He argues that it is only with democracy that we get the notion of 'exception',[33] as individual sovereigns simply wielded power without recourse to breaking free of law in a way that required consulting other legally constituted bodies. As the French and American revolutions spread the idea of democratic legitimacy, they also spread the idea of the moment outside of that legitimacy. This moment can be the founding instance, or when the 'system' needs to protect itself as a matter of urgency. The moment of both sovereignty and of exception, according to Schmitt, is when we have to ask 'who is competent to act when the legal system fails to answer the question of competence'.[34] States of emergency are merely the marker of this permanent capacity and *need* for the system to deconstruct itself, underpinning the rest of the juridical and political order. This potential, as hidden, as essence, of a legal system becomes more acute in democratic parliamentary situations. The exception spreads as legislatures give more and more ground to executive sectors of government, because sovereignty occurs when a decision must be made: 'sovereign is he who decides on the exception'.[35] As well as the need and capacity to make a decision, sovereignty establishes when and where rules can be suspended: 'what characterizes an exception is principally unlimited authority, which means the suspension of the entire existing order'.[36]

For all Schmitt's near-deconstruction, sovereign power is still something 'to-hand' that can be used. This is still true for Agamben, but for him sovereignty is not the power to create exception, but is the operating of the exception – so Guantanamo is the space of sovereignty, not the mere effect of the US government's sovereign power. The suspension of Law is Law at its purest, where it becomes only 'force of law' (with law crossed out for Agamben), as in Nazi Germany.[37] What then occurs is 'legalised civil war',[38] with the State waging war against all whom it deems to be opposed to it. The return to exceptionality, this time made into the rule as it becomes more or less permanent, is the essence of Law, but it is supposed to be left only as trace, not to realise itself. Its realisation in actual political situations reveals the previously interred reality of bare life 'subject' to total sovereignty, not as essence, but as biopolitically constructed, through specific actions at specific historical moments.

Conclusion: The End of All Things

In *The Time That Remains*, we see Agamben's fascination with time as paradoxical, grounded and ungrounding. This is one of his strongest and best-written works, where many of his ideas coalesce, through the prism of messianic time. In looking at St Paul, he also extends Benjamin's exploration of the meaning of 'messianic time'. Messianic time is neither only about waiting for the future nor about redemption. It is not even a deconstructive awaiting of something 'to-come'. He who announces or believes in the future messiah inhabits a time in which it is almost impossible to dwell. It is a time where nothing comes to be, but all the past is made present: 'the time that time takes to come to an end'.[39] Time contracts, becoming an endless moment of all time occurring at once, like Nietzsche's eternal return. This means that time does not coincide with itself – a state of exception (moments outside of time) becoming the norm. Law is suspended and replaced by justice.

Rather than simply a beatific idea, this conception of time refers to how Jewish law pertained only to Jews. From Paul onward, the world is not split into Jew and non-Jew, writes Agamben, but Jew and 'non-non-Jew'. The Jews also become this: everyone is defined only through negativities. Those awaiting in messianic time become a *remnant*: neither one thing nor another, neither subject to law nor fully outside, but something less. This remnant is not a numerical portion but a way of thinking 'possibly everyone' in terms of 'not everyone', which then defines the character of those who await and who have the past resuscitated in preparation for judgement. Agamben's political intent here presumes we agree with his mystical theorisation of politics. This book can be read as part of a diptych with *Homo Sacer*: in both humans must come to nothingness and in both variants of the idea there is something Agamben takes to be ontologically, fundamentally true about the non-presence of humans to themselves and how this is structured historically, politically and theologically.

Agamben has been a major inspiration in the theoretical return to the political that, allegedly, theory somehow forgot. In combining a thoroughgoing critique of biopolitical institutions and a phenomenological 'deconstruction' of being at both individual and cultural level, his theoretical project is a powerful tool. Yet, his readings of philosophers are often sketchy, misrepresenting their ideas to better make his own points. He is less likely to be remembered for his work on literature and aesthetics, or his shaky reading of science and its history. Yet the range of his reading and ethical drive makes him a vital part of any self-reflective political philosophy.

Notes

1. Agamben uses Foucault's notion of 'biopolitics' throughout much of his work, and returns explicitly to Foucault in *Signatura rerum*, where he works through the structure of Foucault's *The Archaeology of Knowledge* (New York: Pantheon, 1972), in order to reflect on the time in which knowledge develops.
2. See Agamben, *The Man without Content*.
3. Agamben, *Remnants of Auschwitz*, pp. 28–31.
4. See, in particular Hegel's *Phenomenology of Spirit* (Oxford: Oxford University Press, 1977), especially his early formulation of 'negativity' in the 'master/slave dialectic' (pp. 105–19). See also Alexandre Kojève's *Introduction to the Reading of Hegel* (New York: Basic Books, 1969).
5. Agamben, *Language and Death*, p. 84.
6. Agamben, *Potentialities*, p. 45.
7. Agamben, *Language and Death*, p. 45.
8. Ibid. p. 26.

9. Ibid. p. 35.
10. Ibid. p. 34.
11. Ibid. p. 96.
12. Agamben, *The Open*, p. 10.
13. Ibid. p. 22.
14. Ibid. p. 37.
15. Ibid. p. 58.
16. Ibid. p. 59.
17. Michel Foucault, *History of Sexuality*, vol. 1, trans. Robert Hurley (Harmondsworth: Penguin, 1979).
18. Agamben, *Homo Sacer*, p. 8.
19. Ibid. p. 89.
20. Ibid. p. 82.
21. Ibid. pp. 82–3.
22. For more on this, see Paul Hegarty, 'Supposing the Impossibility of Silence, and of Sound, of Voice: Bataille, Agamben and the Holocaust', in Andrew Norris (ed.), *Politics, Metaphysics and Death*, pp. 222–47.
23. Agamben, *Homo Sacer*, p. 133.
24. Ibid. p. 148.
25. This will come to be known as *Homo Sacer* III, following the publication in 2003 of *State of Exception* (*Homo Sacer* II.1).
26. Agamben, *Remnants of Auschwitz*, p. 32.
27. He is certainly very close to the position Jean-François Lyotard presents in *The Differend: Phrases in Dispute* (Minneapolis: University of Minnesota, 1988).
28. Agamben, *Remnants of Auschwitz*, p. 47.
29. Ibid. p. 38.
30. Ibid. p. 120.
31. Ibid. p. 133.
32. Ibid. pp. 133–4.
33. Agamben, *State of Exception*, pp. 4–5.
34. Schmitt, *Political Theology*, p. 11.
35. Ibid. p. 5.
36. Ibid. p. 12.
37. Agamben, *State of Exception*, pp. 38–9, 51.
38. Ibid. p. 2.
39. Agamben, *The Time That Remains*, p. 67.

Major Works by Agamben

Homo Sacer: Sovereign Power and Bare Life, trans. Daniel Heller-Roazen (Stanford, CA: Stanford University Press, 1998 [1995]).
Idea of Prose, trans. Michael Sullivan and Sam Whitsitt (New York: SUNY Press, 1995 [1985]).

Infancy and History: On the Destruction of Experience, trans. Liz Heron (London: Verso, 1993 [1978]).
Language and Death: The Place of Negativity, trans. Karen E. Hardt and Michael Hardt (Minneapolis and London: University of Minnesota Press, 1991 [1982]).
The Man without Content, trans. Georgia Albert (Stanford, CA: Stanford University Press, 1999 [1994]).
The Open: Man and Animal, trans. Kevin Attell (Stanford, CA: Stanford University Press, 2004 [2002]).
Potentialities: Collected Essays in Philosophy, trans. Daniel Heller-Roazen (Stanford, CA: Stanford University Press, 1999).
Remnants of Auschwitz: The Witness and the Archive, trans. Daniel Heller-Roazen (New York: Zone, 1999).
The Signature of All Things, trans. Luca di Santo and Kevin Attell (New York: Zone, 2009 [2008]).
Stanzas: Word and Phantasm in Western Culture, trans. Ronald L. Martinez (Minneapolis and London: University of Minnesota Press, 1993 [1977]).
The State of Exception, trans. Kevin Attell (Chicago: University of Chicago Press, 2005 [2003]).
The Time That Remains: A Commentary on the Letter to the Romans, trans. Patricia Daley (Stanford, CA: Stanford University Press, 2005 [2000]).

Suggestions for Further Reading

Mills, Catherine, *The Philosophy of Agamben* (Stocksfield: Acumen, 2008). Useful overview of Agamben's oeuvre.
Norris, Andrew (ed.), *Politics, Metaphysics and Death: Essays on Giorgio Agamben's* Homo Sacer (Durham and London: Duke University Press, 2005). Detailed readings, contextualising the book within political and legal philosophy.
Ross, Alison (ed.), *The Agamben Effect, South Atlantic Quarterly*, 107, 1, winter 2008. Wide-ranging, but as a result focus is on exegesis. Excellent essay by Ziarek on race and gender: Ewa Plonowska Ziarek, 'Bare Life on Strike: Notes on the Biopolitics of Race and Gender', pp. 89–105.
Schmitt, Carl, *Political Theology: Four Chapters on the Concept of Sovereignty*, trans. George Schwob (Chicago and London: University of Chicago Press, 2005 [1934]). Essential background to Agamben.
Wall, Thomas Carl, *Radical Passivity: Levinas, Blanchot and Agamben* (New York: SUNY Press, 1999). Advanced, but the comparative approach works well.

2

Alain Badiou (1937–)

Benjamin Robinson

An Odd End

Alain Badiou is an unlikely heir to the tradition of French post-Second World War philosophy and an even more unlikely heir – despite his declared affinity to the radical events of Paris in May 1968 – to the post-structuralist movement that came into its own around then with luminaries such as Deleuze, Foucault and Derrida.[1] While he engages those thinkers, he demonstrates a different set of loves – of truth, universalism, the subject, fidelity and mathematics; and holds a different set of antipathies – to postmodern celebration of irony and consumption, multicultural identity politics and a textual-hermeneutical grounding of existence. Even stylistically, Badiou tends to be indifferent to cultivating the character of his prose. He writes precisely and didactically, with an irreverent, even pugnacious humour, and no pretense of modesty. As a philosopher, his aspiration is to address everyone without exception, regardless of 'identity'. This aspiration is rooted in a commitment to what he calls 'communism in the generic sense', in which 'everyone is equal to everyone else within the multiplicity and diversity of social functions'.[2] At the same time, his eccentric vocabulary of mathematics and ontology can be intimidating in its straightforward application to the familiar topics of politics and ethics. The philosophical habitus, however, is just what Badiou's simultaneously refined and populist turn of thought succeeds in making strange. Key terms from the philosophical encyclopedia with which Badiou might be tagged include: ontology, the infinite and the void, and structure and event. What matters, however, is how these topics, which reach back to philosophy's formal origins in Greek thought, become new again in Badiou's project.

Toward Plato

Since Nietzsche announced his reversal of Plato's effort to grasp being in the pure, non-relational way numbers exist, it seems that philosophy has eagerly swerved onto the new course. After the past century's total wars, genocides and famines, it would seem that not only philosophers have directed us away from Platonism, but the events themselves, issuing from universal reason run amok, have conspired to set us on a corrective course towards sensitivity regarding diverse forms of being other than the mathematical. The collapse of metanarratives, the implosion of Cold War fronts, the rise of global ecologies, all seem to confirm the end of Plato's regime of mathematically revealed truth.

As close as Badiou is to that tradition that goes under the name of reversing Plato in favour of the contingent, material, aesthetic and historical, he embraces Plato as the very philosopher who put truth and universality on the agenda. While Badiou's philosophy shares a post-enlightenment goal of situating itself among the truths of non-philosophers, it maintains, uncharacteristically for its era, that these truths should be grasped *as* truths, in their universal and infinite import, and be made available indifferently to whomsoever might want to commit themselves to truth. Moreover, it is Plato who insisted on the proximity of philosophy to politics. A 'militant philosophy', such as Badiou's, is one that situates itself within the political conflicts of its time.[3] Given all the cataclysms that have issued from modernity – from its Eurocentrism, logicism, egoism, and destructive pretence to universality – how, Badiou invites us to think, does an oppositional political project assert itself in the mode of truth? And who, he asks, is the subject that would bear the truth? In asking such questions, Badiou sets about reclaiming some old-fashioned ideas for a political left that has been exhausted by its retreat into the noisy difference of the everyday.

Infinity as the Fact of the Matter

Badiou's intervention on behalf of old-fashioned verities – like truth, universalism and mathematical knowledge – responds to a set of problems arising from a political programme in modernity that asserts itself in the paired idioms of freedom and necessity, initiative and responsibility, history and transcendence, and event and structure. Insofar as the Platonic *vita contemplativa* underlying philosophy and religion had understood its power as that of a transcendence opposed to the contingencies of life and death, modernity as a *historical* institution of a *universal* programme undermines the age-old opposition. Whether defined in terms of techniques of power and knowledge or cultures of autonomy, modernity does not foreclose the issue of its contingency, but allows the contingent and universal to confront each other on the same plane of decision.

In this sense, Badiou's call to return to a mindset oriented toward the kind of truth one discovers in mathematics – deductively rigorous, and, if not ascetic, then certainly exacting – is a call to think the modern situation as itself based in thought, where thought is that which correlates most painstakingly with reality. In *The Century*, Badiou does not reiterate the Marxist appeal for a unity of theory and practice, because – for better or worse – the unity of acting and thinking is the twentieth-century *achievement*. Contrary to the received view of a century distorted by ideological passion, Badiou holds that the century's distinctive 'passion for the real' drove it beyond satisfaction with the ideological.[4] What the unity of theory and practice does need, however, as the violence and phantasms of the twentieth century demonstrate, are procedures for distinguishing its truth. To put it more technically, what modernity calls for, as the era in which the infinite has been secularised ('infinite alterity is quite simply *what there is*'),[5] is a way and a will to force, wherever the infinite unexpectedly gapes open, a public declaration of its measure.[6] As abstract as such a mathematically inflected language of infinity and measure is, a careful reading of Badiou demonstrates its resemblance to the perennial topics of freedom and invention and of ethical-epistemological responsibility.

Each of Badiou's books orients our intellectual horizons differently. Here I consider two central texts, *Being and Event* and *Saint Paul*, with reference to *Ethics: An Essay on the Understanding of Evil*. My goal is, first, to draw out some of the reasons why interest in Badiou has reached beyond disciplinary specialisation and second, to connect Badiou's relevance to those philosophical questions that persist despite the waxing and waning of their fashion. Badiou's work has both an anti-philosophical, evental nature and a lineage in the philosophical tradition of thinking about the new, contemporary and relevant.

Being and Event – Mathematical Foundations

As his foundational work of philosophy where he establishes the relationship of his guiding concepts to 'the discourse of being as being' (namely, ontology, which for Badiou is mathematics), *Being and Event* invites a reader to think about how philosophy has positioned itself with respect to two mathematical extremes: the *void* (or empty set) and the *infinite*. These are indeed abstract 'things' lacking the reassuringly intuitive characteristics that our familiar world of material objects and fellow humans has. In fitting the void and the infinite into a foundational philosophy, Badiou also addresses philosophy's relationship to what is not philosophical – to what is not thought within any system of representation. What we do not think, and what Badiou chooses as his foundational axiom, is that 'the one is not' and, hence, 'nothing is'.[7] This axiom is unthinkable for the simple reason that no matter how multifaceted and complex some appearance is, we need to discern it as *something* in order to count it as a phenomenon at all.

To take this unthinkable inconsistency (a pure multiplicity that we cannot discern as anything) as a foundation for philosophy means that what exceeds Being (Being as 'being thought', as sufficient reason) is what no philosophical system can contain and secure: the pure, non-presentable *multiple*. This figure of the pure multiple *is* not, but it does *happen*, and it happens right at the void of a situation, right where a situation cannot account for itself. It happens – the pure multiple appears – when someone throws caution to the wind, jumps into the breach, and declares the unaccountability of a situation to be an event worth heeding.

Deciding that 'the one is not' and 'nothing *is*' thus entails a role for the term Badiou conjoins and disjoins from Being in his book title – namely, the *event*. The event supplements Being – it is nothing and everything. It is nothing in the sense indicated above: that if the one is not, then nothing *is*. It is everything, however, to the extent that nothing or the void is the axiomatic choice on which Badiou wagers his philosophical edifice. Understanding this wager brings us to the trickiest part of Badiou's thinking: how is it that something infinitely multiple, the event, comes to be out of no one thing?

Whether Badiou intends it or not, for those first working

through his arguments, his thinking here might look disturbingly similar to the romantic belief in the creative genius, the fascist belief in the organic leader, and the ultra-left belief in revolutionary decisionism.[8] It seems to give too much credence to pure, violent and uninhibited freedom of choice – and moreover to address this unfounded choice not to the sphere of private sentiment but to that of universal truth. To avoid such misunderstanding, Badiou's conceptualisation of 'the event' should be traced through the scope of the term's usage, in all its variety, which suggests its significance as a concept at odds with rational modernity's most cherished reassurances, those of a continuous and law-abiding world of enduring substance and value. Across the range of its semantic registers the event figures as a remainder, a supplement – a something/nothing – that does not fit into any structure.

- In a *political* register, the biggest events are war and revolution. Even in a liberal era with few declared wars what counts as eventful are upsetting election outcomes; sharp inflations or recessions; natural disasters or unprovoked violence. In each of these cases, what becomes a political event is a phenomenon at or outside the boundaries of expectation and legitimacy; one might say, at or outside the boundaries of the nation-state.
- In a *theological* register, events are apocalypses, miracles and conversions. They pertain to occasions without precedent and measure; occasions that are singular, sudden or vast. What Saint John emphasises about the apocalypse is that it is a judgement that, in contrast to Aristotle's 'just mean', occurs without any proportionality or reserve. A miracle, meanwhile, needs its prophets and saints; and conversion is marked by imponderable grace.
- In an *aesthetic* register, events are sublime. They do not have the pleasing scale and interrelation that characterise the beautiful and intuitive. Rather, they are breathtaking natural wonders, terrifying cataracts, or – in the case of the art object – epiphanic moments of transport instead of pleasant contemplation.
- In a *biographical* register, events are turning points. Not religious initiations, they are rites of passage: births, deaths and fallings in love – occasions that ceremonies, solemnities and celebrations seek to reintegrate into the steady order of the community by demarcating their extraordinary nature.
- In the technical sense entertained by *academic philosophy*, events are occurrences marked by verbs, adverbs, adjectives – signs

that do not indicate substances but rather happenings. As grammatically banal as verbs and adverbs are, they are mysterious because, unlike nouns and the things they signify, it is hard to see what constitutes the unity of their referent, their beginning and end, their boundedness. When does 'loving' begin and end and where does it take place? Or, more venally, if someone is injured by a falling wall, when did the event of its fall begin – with its construction years before; when a later addition was added; when a landlord neglected upkeep; when a drought compacted the soil? What is the unity and totality of such falling whereby one could assign it to a cause?

With these examples of the broad but still mysterious persistence of events in a modernity that imagines itself disenchanted, we come closer to understanding why events – resistant as they are to expectation, legitimacy, proportion, intuition, community and substantiality – are so compelling, not as anti-modernist holdouts, but as a consequence of modern structural rigour. A few canonically modern examples of events from Badiou's work help draw us back into *Being and Event.*

The French Revolution, arguably the inaugural event of modernity, is Badiou's most privileged example.[9] There was nothing in France's *ancien régime* that could have anticipated the Revolution as a step in its developmental logic. When in retrospect that which came to be called the Revolution is inserted into its time, we see that it did not follow necessarily from anything: its site was errant and adventurous. If we insist on reducing it to an enumerable set of conditions, those circumstances do not add up to a revolution – the revolution was strictly extra. Qualifying it as a species of mob violence, a momentary frenzy after a rough winter, or an ideologically fanned outburst of resentment, we qualify away anything deserving the term event: as the sum of its parts, we can say of it, as Badiou does, citing Mallarmé, 'nothing took place but the place'. The Revolution will have been an issue of mismanagement, not political possibility. If, on the contrary, we insist that what became the Revolution is an actual event, we refuse to let it be completely historicised. It remains a chance occurrence that is nonetheless unique to its situation. What was hazarded was a universal opportunity – in excess of all historical particularisation. There was a void in any given ordering of the situation, and the Revolution marks that void's brief, haphazard appearance, but only insofar as we remain faithful to the possibility and consequences of its having happened. This relationship of the event to the persons who proclaim fidelity to its universality is, as we shall see, crucial to Badiou's theory of the subject.

Another of Badiou's favourite examples of an event is atonal music. In its development from Haydn through Beethoven and up to Schönberg, classical music rigorously explored the possibilities of tonality to the point where, at least conceptually, only more-or-less refined repetitions were left to be composed.[10] When Schönberg launched his atonal programme he did not do so recognisably *within* the tonal tradition as a development of a latently indicated possibility. Rather, looking back, we discern that the point where atonalism happened was indifferent to tonality, unmarked by necessity or discovery. It appears now to have been a void in the tonal situation from where something truly new – and general – had been launched.

These examples help clarify why Badiou's conception of the event should not be mistaken for 'just anything' that someone more-or-less disinterestedly declares to be new and for which fidelity is demanded. The simplest reason is hinted at already in Badiou's turn to mathematics with its rigorous truth procedures. Setting aside his demonstrations of set theory, the very gesture of equating mathematics with the discourse of being shows how impersonal, general and universal his founding terms are. Set theory founds mathematics on empty sets. That does not mean that foundations are arbitrary – it means that they are without predetermined quality, essence, relation; in short, subtracted of all attributes, they gain their force by being generic, universal and actual. Being is built on the very possibility of being generic, multiple and infinite, of being not one. But it is hard indeed to seize that spot that is not already beholden to established distinctions.

When a commitment to an event commits instead to the advent of *one* thing that determines *all* belonging in particular, that commitment is evil, as Badiou explicates in his short 1993 treatise on *Ethics*.[11] For evil to exist, according to Badiou, there must be truth, because truth is the process of making an animal into a subject, of distinguishing human being from innocent animality. No contempt for animal being is implied – all Badiou argues is that, without regard to truth, animal being proceeds also without reference to good or evil. Animality is mostly our fate as self-interested, opinionated creatures firmly attached to our situations. If we commit ourselves to an event beyond our particular way of being, however, we become subjects. Subject to truth, we are also subject to the distinction between good and evil. The truth of our decision to declare and show fidelity to an unprecedented occurrence, to a fleeting event marking the universal and generic implications of a situational impasse, proves instead disastrous if this truth only seems generic, but remains wed to particulars. If we are conscientious and law abiding, we might feel like enlightened Kantian subjects, but, cleaving to our situations, we are only the most estimable of animals. If we break the law – not here or there, as further animal adventure, but at the site of what appears to be an event – we risk becoming subjects proper. As proper subjects, we are first subject to truth – and if our commitment is false, if it proves to have been in the name of a particular, then our fidelity becomes evil in proportion to its closure, and our universality is a sham.

Badiou's argument inverts Hegel's case against revolutionary terror in *Phenomenology of Spirit*. There, Hegel interprets Robespierre's terror as the real working out of the universal ideal.[12] Such idealistic universalism is bound to see hostility and factionalism in each particular, including in the particular persons who bear the universal message. It is accordingly driven to extirpate everything that exists because to exist is to exist as one, as particular. For Hegel, hostility to animal particularity is the consequence of abstract universalism and calls forth the development of morality as the rights of the concrete individual. For Badiou, by contrast, it is not by tolerating the one and particular, but by according particularity no allegiance, that a subject is able to act truly *sine ire et studio* (without hostility or bias). In other words, terror and disaster come about not via commitment to the universal implications of truth but by imagining that truth might take the form of closure – even, and especially, the closure of idealism, which marches under the banner of a transcendental vision.

The true subject is militant indeed, but the militancy is directed against compromise with any party of particularism. Fighting compromise does not entitle the militant to close off an antagonist from participation in the truth, especially when such exclusion takes the form of extirpation.

> We might fight against the judgments and opinions [an enemy] exchanges with others for the purpose of corrupting every fidelity, but not against his person – which, under the circumstances, is insignificant, and to which, in any case, every truth is ultimately addressed.[13]

36

So it is not the case, as it is for Hegel, that the true universalist hates particularity – the universalist is indifferent to particularity in the relevant situation. It is, rather, the false universalist, imagining truth to have privileged prophets and caring too intently about individual persons, communities and identities, who directs hostility against everyone, against everyone precisely as generic nobodies outside the community of the elect.

While the event forces an accounting, dictating what is relevant to its break and what is not, it follows a generic rigor pertaining strictly to what the void in its situation proposes. In this sense, deciding what is an event and what a pseudo-event may be difficult, but only by being forced to declare one's decision is one called to live in truth. Living in truth, being subject to the force of truth, means being open to eventuality. Committing to the French Revolution – like committing to atonal music, quantum mechanics or true love – remains tolerant with respect to biographies and identities. The force of the commitment comes via the void it opens wherever people remain closed to its effects. The event thus appears – is retrospectively discernible as having been an event – not as a fulfil-ment of an implied destiny but as an open process of making its multiplicity pertain, of working out what its post-evental situation entails. That is, from pure multiplicity – infinite (since it has no boundaries) and void (since it cannot be taken as one) – it becomes an impure multiplicity, a multiplicity with elements and relations transforming (but not destroying) the situation from which it arose. What maintains this multiplicity in its truth, however, is that it is never imagined as the one that henceforth plugs up the void. Its infinity relates to the way it disqualifies without reserve a situation that held no place for it. It does not relate to complete immanence (divine memory) or ultimate transcendence (the timeless beyond) – it is a secular infinity, a constituent of profane being.

Before turning to Badiou's quintessential militant, Saint Paul, a final consideration of set theory is helpful. As a branch of math-ematics, it theorises number without imagining individual numbers as qualities or intuitions 'out there' in the world. Breaking with realist number theory – wherein numbers subsist as representable entities – set theory eloquently serves Badiou's project of under-standing the world as based on blank 'thatness', a set of denotations with no given properties or relations. 'Thatness' simply names a void of meaning – all content is utterly subtracted. From that void, however, set theory is able to group together multiplicities based on minimal axioms and to develop all one needs for a workable system of number. From number, even infinite number, another key element of Badiou's thought follows: the excess of inconsistent multiplicity. This excess arises from the axiom that every set of elements also composes a set of subsets. This second set, however, may exceed the first by an uncountable magnitude, by another order of infinity. A nice example given by Peter Hallward is the set of letters in the alphabet.[14] While twenty-six is easy to count, when one considers arrangements of subsets, there are 2^{26} unrepeating arrangements. If one allows for combinations that repeat letters – such as the set of all utterable sentences – then the number of alphabetic combinations can no longer be counted by real numbers. Without going beyond a countable twenty-six, our few tokens, grouped in their possible arrangements, rapidly exceed measurement. The uncountable excess of subsets over elements points to a constitutional instability in securing once and for all that of which a multiple consists.

For the non-mathematically inclined Badiou's recourse to set theory might seem overly exacting. It accomplishes, however, an elegant clarification of why number – 'the one and many' at the basis of traditional ontology – arises by marshalling order from blank 'thatness' with but a few axioms. This literal *creatio ex nihilo* allows us to see how permeable the order of the world is, based as it is not on immutable essences but on axiomatic arrangements of empty tokens. Rather than fragility, this implies robustness for Badiou: that any fixed set is susceptible to the excess of possible rearrangements. While such susceptibility makes evil an option, via meaningless nihilism, it also enables new truths, so long as rearrangement occurs not under the sign of jealous attachment to a given situation but in the name of universality.

Saint Paul – The Universal Militant

In *Ethics* Badiou writes that 'a subject [who] goes beyond the animal . . . needs something to have happened, something that cannot be reduced to its ordinary inscription in "what there is"'.[15] What we may have taken as philosophy's quarry – truth – turns out to lie beyond our knowledge. While philosophers can traverse diverse knowledges, critiquing what gets inscribed in our books of 'what there is', they are, for better or worse, not initiators, but formalisers of truth. Originary truth belongs rather to those open to the

unthought – indeed, unthinkable – event. In thought's encounter
with an event, in fidelity's encounter with chance, truth is born as
a procedure of keeping alive the prospect that something new has
occurred. Such events do not happen in philosophy but in love, art,
science and politics – which are each what Badiou calls a 'generic
procedure'.[16]

What do those lovers, artists, scientists and politicians look like
who are open to the event and become subjects in fidelity to evental
truth? When Badiou turns to Christian Church Father St Paul to
discover this sort of person, his move is unnerving, marking 'the
greatest step back', 'when a step forward is the order of the day'.[17]
As a gesture saturated with strategic considerations, however,
Badiou's provocation becomes clearer. What Paul presents to the
world, according to Badiou, is the subjective connection between
freedom and chance, on the one side, and law and nature, on the
other. Paul's mode of forging this link is practical militancy, not
the Greek philosophical wisdom or Jewish interpretative authority
of his era. He names and denies the Hebraic and Hellenic dualism
that so inflects the course of European thought. If the mathematicians whose truth procedures traverse *Being and Event* seem remote,
in *St Paul* we glimpse a canonised figure restored to unexpected
radicality: indifferent to the particularising powers of his time, Paul
exhibits the 'invariant' subjectivity of the militant universalist.[18]

Where *Being and Event*'s project is multifarious and philosophical, *Saint Paul*'s is forceful and direct. Badiou holds that Paul
founded a faith explicitly as a universalism and did so – bore, propa-
gated and defended it – in blatant disregard of law and philosophy.
The contemporary force of Badiou's gesture comes from its assault
on enlightened liberal expectations; namely, that the universal can
be thought only as a figure of law and/or reason – the Hebraic
and Hellenic couplet constituting the topography of modern universalism. Against this expectation, Badiou sees Paul as founding
the universal disposition on the basis of two alternate supports – a
generic subject (unqualified human being) and an event (the fleeting chance of an imponderable opportunity). Despite Nietzsche's
association of Paul with slave morality; despite the anticlerical
excoriation of him as the pillar of organised Christianity; despite
a theoretical recovery, via Benjamin, Levinas and Derrida, of the
Jewish messianism Paul left behind – despite such apparent liabili-
ties, Paul stands out for Badiou as exactly the site to theorise how
truth works as an attitude of subjective militancy in the name of an

unprecedented breach in the status quo. Paul appears not as the righteous and imperious (or devious and communal) founder of orthodoxy but as the consummate tactician of revolution. He steers the revolutionary good news clear of the shoals of canonical law, Roman statism, Greek naturalism and the sectarian proprietorship of prophets.

Rather than elaborating a dogma, Paul practises truth by defending a single absurd statement: Christ is resurrected. The statement's force resides not in factual veracity – it is a fable – but in the way it oversteps orthodoxy by spurring conformity. Conformity – in the light of Paul's addressing the news of Christ's resurrection to all – means adhering to particularity, whether that of a community's jurisdiction or reason's essentialism. Paul defends the 'Christ event' against cooptation by denying authority over it to any constituted identity or recognised rule: 'there is neither Jew nor Greek, there is neither slave nor free, there is neither male nor female' (Gal. 3.28). For those squeamish about the apparent irrationalism of Badiou's basing radical subjectivity on unqualified commitment to Christ's resurrection, the proposition is simply that our choices – about love, beauty, freedom, nature – are grounded on nothing but the possibility that we let ourselves be activated (resurrected) by the implications of truth against all claims for the truth having been settled (death). What the force of Badiou's iconoclastic book comes down to, especially when read with and against *Being and Event,* is that, immersed in philosophical and leftist theoretical traditions, Badiou also turns against them, making his book simultaneously an antiphilosophical gesture and a philosophical explication of that gesture: truth arises only as a rigorously strategised persistence in non-conformity vis-à-vis every particularity.

Badiou presents Paul's achievement against the background of the archetypical distinctions of the ancient world – distinctions whose primordial simplicity still organise much of contemporary modernity. Paul becomes Paul on the road to Damascus, on the basis of his insight that there is neither Jew nor Greek. 'By the grace of God I am what I am'.[19] The implication is that true subjectivity is generic not communal. It is founded on grace, which, in this case is generative affiliation with the 'Christ event'. There is nothing else – just grace alone – that summons Paul to himself and his proper name. Paul is not a biological son, nor a son by ethnicity, but one by public loyalty to the grace that gave birth to the name of the saint.

Positively indifferent to biology and ethos, Paul's grace is an affront to Jew as well as Greek. To the 'discourses' of Hebraic and Hellenic, Paul opposes the properly modern discourse of novelty, a novelty marked by the preeminence of being offspring, not ancestor. What is the Jewish discourse? It is the discourse of the law, of the symbolic order and its recourse to the sovereign exception (the power of the father/prophet to judge all contested cases). What is the Greek discourse? It is the discourse of nature and its rational order (the power of the cosmos to demand conformity of desire and aspiration). What Paul demonstrates, according to Badiou, is that the law has no true support, neither historical nor *a priori*. The classic antinomies of 'the good versus the right' and 'communal consensus versus natural law' are derivative of the Hebraic/Hellenic split. The particularism of Hebraic law is rooted in the symbolic sign, over which the prophet has final – ultimately private – authority. The conformism of Greek philosophy is rooted in the iconic figure of nature, fixing the world according to a timeless cosmos.

If Paul relieves us of the laws of nature and the laws of the father, then what does he give us? At first, it seems a paltry recompense: 'weakness, folly and nonbeing'.[20] This tripartite disposition, however, is not a failure of proper plentitude, but an attitude of subtracting oneself from the constituted order of differences, from a cosmos of distinctions rooted in the unity of authority and closed to the freedom of grace – closed, that is, to the possibility of an event, of a generic, uncounted and infinite multiplicity, such as when a universal truth appears in its moment of declaration. Weakness and folly relate to nonbeing as the subtraction of omnipotence and omniscient as predicates of God's perfective Unity – without those attributes God is not One. Not being one, God's nonbeing is that of the pure multiple. Under that sign of multiplicity Paul becomes Paul, without regard to the limited choices, Jew or Greek, slave or free, man or woman, he is offered.

Again, part of the complexity of this otherwise sweepingly elegant argument for non-conformist individualism is that Paul cannot pronounce his belief in Christ's resurrection in the form of a private revelation with no explicit bearing on the public situation. To the extent this connection to the real remains fabulous, it is incumbent upon those seized by an event in the wake of the Pauline gospel to think through the event's unique site – and how it breaks with the reigning situation. Paul theorises the universal break through the idea of the son of God, which Badiou generalises as the son of an event. What such filiation means is that any voluntarism – any pure freedom in the mode of opportunism or adventure – must come back to the eventual site and account for the way it belongs to its situation obscurely, without representation. Faced with authority's blindness to Christ, the first-century militant grasped how declaring his resurrection undermines the hierarchy of received differences, allowing truth to cut across them all. Truth does not arrive as a demand for recognition placed upon the representational order (upon the institutions of state) nor as a sceptical questioning of the logic of that order (for a reformed state); rather, born under the state but ignored by the state, the son declares the state's irrelevance to his life.

A declaration, however, that addresses itself merely to the state of the situation and, brandishing its novelty, cleaves to particular self-interest is a betrayal. If there is an asceticism to Paul (for which Nietzsche reproaches him as a self-denying priest), then it consists not in denying life but in refusing to sacrifice life to convenience. This discipline – which discovers true subjectivity in fidelity to the generically unprecedented – is one that returns hope in an event to the situation that occludes it. Whatever trivial non-conformism may belittle an orientation toward a glorious future, the orientation toward a present that ruthlessly effaces the event is anything but casual. This present orientation is that of the militant's universal address. It expresses a love (*agape*) that refuses to pander its hope (*elpis*) in compromised terms, in terms that are not open in principle to the boundless faith (*pistis*) of all.

Insisting on universal address lends subjective militancy its greatest risk, and so requires its greatest discipline. The risk is that the situation avenge itself on the apostle of the new, that it thwart any hope that the event displace the existing situation. The terminology of folly, scandal and weakness refers not only to the lack of any place in the language of order for expressing the subject's faith. Not just rhetorical defamations, these epithets mark the real animosity of law and order toward the bearer of truth. Exposed in official language as mortal – never to be resurrected from self-interest to openness toward infinite truth – the truth's 'earthen vessel' becomes easy prey for state violence. For the militant subject, body and soul are not distinguished. While such commitment unites theory and practice against the state's intolerance for what does not belong, its indifference often appears more embattled than ecstatic – it is, of course, both.

Conclusion

Embattled and ecstatic: this is the experience of reading Badiou's philosophy and antiphilosophy. The set-theoretical terminology, which grounds Badiou's thinking in the most generic and generative possibilities of ordering and multiplicity, is demanding. Despite Badiou's protestations that his mathematics is elementary, there is no use denying the effort required to leap from mathematical conceptions of what counts to philosophical discourses of Being. At the same time, as the provocation of *St Paul* makes clear, Badiou relishes in gestures that blithely – if sometimes brutally – reorganise expectations about which distinctions a thinker – and activist – needs to defend and which to let scatter like dust in the face of new truths, truths that are not the property of philosophy but available to all who carefully heed them.

Notes

1. Alain Badiou, 'The Adventure of French Philosophy', *New Left Review*, 35, 2005, pp. 67–77.
2. Alain Badiou, '"We Need a Popular Discipline": Contemporary Politics and the Crisis of the Negative', interview by Filippo Del Lucchese and Jason Smith, *Critical Inquiry*, 34, 2008, p. 648.
3. Ibid. pp. 645–59 (646).
4. Badiou, *The Century*, p. 32.
5. Badiou, *Ethics*, p. 25.
6. Badiou, *Being and Event*, p. 148.
7. Ibid. pp. 31–7.
8. In '"We Need a Popular Discipline"', Badiou sees a politics based in negating the state and seizing power as obsolete. Instead of a destructive politics, he proposes a subtractive one, where 'subtractive' refers to opting out of the relations the state proffers for managing politics. Badiou, '"We Need a Popular Discipline"', pp. 652–3.
9. Badiou, *Being and Event*, p. 180.
10. Badiou discusses 'the Schönberg-event' in 'A Musical Variant of the Metaphysics of the Subject', *Parrhesia*, 2, 2007, pp. 29–36. The example of Haydn appears in Badiou, *Ethics*, p. 68.
11. Badiou, *Ethics*, pp. 58–89.
12. G. W. F. Hegel, *Phenomenology of Spirit*, trans. A. V. Miller (Oxford: Oxford University Press, 1979), §§582–95.
13. Badiou, *Ethics*, p. 76.
14. Hallward, *Badiou*, p. 89.
15. Badiou, *Ethics*, p. 41.

16. Badiou, *Being and Event*, p. 16.
17. Badiou, *Saint Paul*, p. 2.
18. Badiou, *Saint Paul*, p. 2. For a discussion of invariant communist subjectivity in Badiou, see Bruno Bosteels, 'The Speculative Left', *South Atlantic Quarterly*, 104, 4, 2005, pp. 753–69.
19. 1 Cor. 15.10; Badiou, *Saint Paul*, p. 17.
20. Ibid. p. 49.

Major Works by Badiou

Being and Event, trans. Oliver Feltham (London: Continuum, 2005 [1988]).
The Century, trans. Alberto Toscano (Cambridge: Polity, 2007 [2005]).
Ethics: An Essay on the Understanding of Evil, trans. Peter Hallward (London: Verso, 2001 [1993]).
Handbook of Inaesthetics, trans. Alberto Toscano (Stanford: Stanford University Press, 2005 [1998]).
Logics of Worlds: Being and Event, Vol. 2, trans. A. Toscano (New York: Continuum, 2009 [2006]).
Saint Paul: The Foundation of Universalism, trans. Ray Brassier (Stanford: Stanford University Press, 2003 [1997]).
Theoretical Writings, ed. and trans. Ray Brassier and Alberto Toscano (London: Continuum, 2004).

Suggestions for Further Reading

Bosteels, Bruno, *Badiou and Politics* (Durham: Duke University Press, forthcoming). Bosteels, who has translated Badiou's *Theory of The Subject* and some of his early Maoist work, highlights the political stakes of Badiou's philosophy.
Feltham, Oliver, *Alain Badiou: Live Theory* (London: Continuum, 2008). A brief introduction to Badiou divided into four periods of his intellectual genesis.
Hallward, Peter, *Badiou: A Subject to Truth* (Minneapolis: University of Minnesota Press, 2003). Hallward is Badiou's most authoritative English-language interpreter.
Hallward, Peter (ed.), *Think Again: Badiou and the Future of Philosophy* (London: Continuum, 2004). Responses to Badiou's work by leading contemporary thinkers from Slavoj Žižek to Ernesto Laclau.

3

Zygmunt Bauman (1925–)

Peter Beilharz

Zygmunt Bauman has an intriguing presence in English-speaking social theory. His influence is ubiquitous, but at the same time it is marginal. Little surprise: neither has he set out to establish a system, a set of operational theoretical tools, nor has he established a school. Across the years his modus operandi has been solitary and idiosyncratic; and his object has moved, though his sensibilities have remained more constant. He still identifies with sociology, as a field, and with socialism, as a norm or utopia.

Now that his work is well known, it is worth remembering that Bauman is not a celebrity. He is not a public intellectual, or at least not a TV-intellectual. But he writes for a public, even if it is an imaginary one, and this is especially true of his work over the last decade. There is a prehistory to this most recent phase of public writing; and there is another prehistory before that. Bauman wrote fifteen books in Polish during his first career when he was living another life that, quite reasonably, he imagined might be his last. Having joined the Polish Army in the Soviet Union in 1941 he was sacked from his rank as Major in 1953. He opened a new door, that to sociology and philosophy at the University of Warsaw, and eventually became one of its leading lights. Then, again (history repeats) he was sacked for the most honorable possible professorial crime – 'misleading the youth' – in the anti-Semitic purge of 1968. Driven out, he finally settled in Yorkshire, where his fields were still socialism and sociology. This, the opening English language phase of his long life, generated at least thirty books, published in at least thirty languages, and covering an extraordinary array of interests, from utopia to hermeneutics, culture to mortality, postmodernity, intellectuals, violence, stigma, love, death and eternity.[1]

How could we characterise this project? Probably the two most influential academic books across this span are *Legislators and Interpreters* and *Modernity and the Holocaust*. But these are clearly scholarly works, works directed primarily to his students and peers, not so explicitly to the public, real or imagined. Yet there is a clear break or change of strategy in his writing and publishing. It coincides with his retirement, in 1990. *Modernity and Ambivalence* is his last powerful monograph, though it is also a text entirely continuous with *Modernity and the Holocaust* – it literally reads like its second part or extension. Several volumes of essays followed – *Intimations of Modernity, Life in Fragments, Postmodernity and Its Discontents* and others. The sea change came with *Globalization* and the works that followed it, especially *Community, Identity* and *Europe* – all little books, keyword studies in brief compass.[2] These were examples of what he called the *Buchlein*, the little book, the strap hanger for the train or bus, no footnotes, or few, rather a condensing image put to work as the pretext for a complaint about the injustices and asymmetries of the world we have constructed.

Along with these, not always in the same format but designed to be user-friendly, was the flurry of work exercising the theme of liquidity, from *Liquid Modernity* to *Liquid Love, Liquid Life* and *Liquid Times*.[3] By this stage, some of Bauman's critics thought that he was fished out, given merely to repetition. Bauman's strategy was to repeat his claims in different ways, using different symbols – globalisation, community, identity, Europe, whatever – to connect the present to the traditions of critical sociology which he inherited, and indeed to repeat himself. For he was no longer thinking of his reader as someone (like me) who would read his entire output serially, awaiting each instalment in a personal scholarly trajectory. His new imaginary reader was rather the strap hanger who might read one book, and next be reading Richard Sennett or Alain de Botton or *Who Weekly* or *The Guardian*. So, for example, we find Bauman's influence acknowledged in a novel like Monica Ali's *In the Kitchen*.[4] This shows that his strategy for the little books has had some success: they are books that might even be read in the kitchen.

So there are now two different audiences, or constituencies, for the work of Zygmunt Bauman. One is popular, curious, tertiary educated but occasional in its encounter with universities. The other (us) has some professional investment in theory, like it or not, will view matters from different perspectives, not always given to democracy or to sharing, looking for clues or pendants with which to legitimise our work and to make it seem different or distinct from that of our competitors. How, amidst all this, do we find a line into this labyrinth?

There are many, already, suggested. Some, like Keith Tester, value the literary aspect of Bauman's work. Others, like Anthony Elliott, want to stress its contemporaneity. My own inclination has been to stress its continuity, for this is the aspect of his work that shouts the loudest at me. Bauman, for me, is still a traditional East European critical theorist. He carries traditions that he takes very seriously, from Simmel, Freud and Weber, as well as many others, including novelists and anthropologists.[5] But the longest lineage for Bauman starts in Trier and ends in the British Museum, not too far from the library of the London School of Economics where he also laboured.

Marx and Surplus Population

In 1867 Karl Marx published *Capital* Volume One. It was to have a major effect on the life and work of Zygmunt Bauman, who had become a communist in Poland during the Second World War. For it contained a world-view, and a critique of capitalist civilisation as well as of political economy; and its frame reflected Marx's exile in the homeland of capitalism, an exile which Bauman was to follow, a century later, when he took up his chair at the University of Leeds, not too far from Engels's Manchester.

The power of *Capital* Volume One can be found in the rigour of its internal logic, the cell-form of the commodity leading to the ghosts of commodity fetishism, in its descent into the purgatory of the labour process, like entering Dante's inferno, in its majestic survey of the struggle over the working day, in its apocalyptic climax in Chapter 32, where Marx's drama finally closes with the expropriation of the expropriators. But the passages which extend most clearly from Marx's project into Bauman's are different. They arrive in Parts Seven and Eight, the last two acts of *Capital.* Part Seven Section 4 addresses 'Different forms of the Relative Surplus Population'. Marx's initial field of concern here is unemployment, though the idea of 'surplus population' is broader and more expansive. It travels across time and space, right through to the present, to Bauman's concern with the lost postmodern souls he calls vagabonds.

Even in his moment Marx understands the importance of partial employment. Regardless of cyclical trends, he tells us, unemployment has three forms, floating, latent and stagnant, liquid metaphors of the human condition that again anticipate Bauman's critique of modernity a hundred years later. Floating unemployment appears mainly in connection with machinery, in great workshops that prefer to employ boys rather than men. The youth whose fate it is to float often float overseas – they are compelled to emigrate, following that part of capital which emigrates. The mechanisation of agriculture likewise compels local and regional migration. This is what Marx calls latent surplus population. Finally, by stagnant relative surplus population Marx designates those workers who are subject to extremely irregular employment. The lowest category of relative surplus population dwells in the sphere of pauperism. 'Exclusive of vagabonds, criminals, prostitutes, in a word, the "dangerous" classes, this layer of society consists of three categories', he tells us: those able to work; orphans and pauper children; and the demoralised and ragged, the mutilated and sickly.[6] In sum total these categories go to make up the industrial reserve army of the unemployed. All this, of course, is the result of progress, development, the further application of capitalist technology.

Marx returns to these issues historically in Chapter 27, on the expropriation of the agricultural population from the land, a theme which still resonates through Southeast Asia and Latin America today. In Thomas More's nightmare, sheep ate men; you can modify the images as you will for the inhabitants of the rainforests in those other lands today. After all, it was the introduction of local laws preventing the 'theft' of wood from the commons which had originally drawn Marx into the field of radical journalism, before he became a marxist.

Capital closes, infamously, with the double ending of Chapters 32 and 33. (Bauman was to introduce his own double ending, modern and postmodern, in *Legislators and Interpreters*). Colonisation, as Marx and Engels had anticipated earlier in *The Communist Manifesto*, would sooner or later expand to cover the planet. There would be nothing outside the rule of capital. Primitive accumulation would extend across the entire globe. And as Bauman would conclude, in his own time, the planet would be full. The connection and affinity between Bauman and his teacher is clear. While Marx's revolutionary choreography culminates in proletarian victory in the penultimate chapter of *Capital*, Chapter 33 opens the door to the world to them, and to the apparent solution to the problem of surplus population proposed by Edward Wakefield, namely, systematic colonisation in Australia. The prospect of migration to the New World provides the safety valve for the Old World. But by our time, and Bauman's own, this idea has been totally exhausted. It was already impossible in Marx's time. The point of connection is an obvious one, which perhaps drops out of sight because it is obvious. The politics of capitalism and of nation states is a geopolitics, a politics of space. Surplus populations will become a major attribute of modern times.

Labour and Modern Capitalism

Marx's work never transcends its labour ontology, or departs from its founding preface, that men and women are suffering, sensuous, creative beings. Bauman's sociology can be characterised in many different ways, as a critique of modernity, as an East European critical theory, as a critique of consumption, whatever. Yet one of its enduring motifs is to be found in the idea of surplus populations, sensuous, suffering, creative beings who are told or compelled to move on. Movement is central to modernity, to power and to culture. Forced movement is one of its central facts of life. This theme can be traced through some of Bauman's most powerful works, from his English language beginning in the 1972 work *Between Class and Elite* to the 1982 classic *Memories of Class*, to the peak of his influence in *Modernity and the Holocaust; Postmodernity and its Discontents; Work, Consumerism and the New Poor;* and *Wasted Lives.*

So let us begin at Bauman's beginning. He had published fifteen books in his native Polish when he was himself driven into exile, like Marx, a political refugee, with all the irony of the great communist experiment: he was too marxist for a putatively marxist regime, so he and his family were harassed and then shown the door, the final exit of the one way visa out of Warsaw via Jerusalem. He had been out before, in moments of authorised scholarly pursuit, not least in the late fifties, when his curiosity took him to Manchester and to the London School of Economics and Bloomsbury, which has meant so much to so many, and Marx's drag as well, from Dean Street and Soho to the splendour of the British Museum. Marx was, as he himself said, a machine condemned to devour books, and also a machine condemned to produce more than his share of them, another characteristic that Bauman was to come to share with him. So it is clear. Zygmunt Bauman was attracted to England for the same reason as Marx was. They would leave you alone, even if they ignored you for a long time; they had the primeval experience of industrialisation, capitalism and modern class struggle; and, by Bauman's time, they had Marx, and they still tolerated marxists.

Its first results appeared in *Between Class and Elite*. It was based on Bauman's earlier work in Polish and was deeply connected to his earlier time and experience in Britain. Bauman is interested in a general theory of labour movements, understood as a prelude to a general theory of social movements. His interest is both in the movements themselves and in their representation. The latter matters, not least because the realities of class and suffering always strain against intellectual self-interest when it comes to the representation of some by others who do not suffer in the same way. Intellectuals always get in the way.

Bauman's curiosity invariably takes him onto the turf dominated by historians, not least of them E. P. Thompson. He contests some of the humanist confidence of Thompson's famous *Making of the English Working Class*, both as regards labour's promethean origins and its present capacity.[7] Bauman views class as a retrospective manner of naming a series of struggles against industrialism. 'Community' matters more than 'proletariat', in the beginning. Thompson, in others words, reads history backwards. The mass worker is a new, twentieth-century phenomenon; the pioneer workers of the industrial revolution still had their heads elsewhere, somewhere before fordism and modernity. But when labour organisation changes, and accommodates itself to capitalism, it does so with a vengeance. In the long run, labour provides the most able lieutenants for capital. Labour develops its own elites, with a thin relationship with those unskilled they actually claim to represent. The organisations of the labour movement became a career escalator.

The Industrial Revolution was a prime mover: it introduced the fact of motion or, as Marx put it, it normalised the possibility of geographical and social mobility. Population density and migration increased dramatically. Movement from the country to the cities became the *Leitmotif* of modernity that it still is. Capitalism's permanent revolution was one of movement. Surplus population constituted a kind of explosion within the old existing social relations and structures. Bauman gestures towards *Capital* as the authoritative source here, but also reminds us of Engels's major contribution in *The Condition of the Working Class in England*.[8] The general sentiment of his analysis, however, is that this was a matter of all that was solid melting. Industrialism normalised change or disintegration before the emergence of the new order was possible. The motif here is exactly the same as that later coined as 'liquid modernity' replacing 'solid modernity'. Estrangement ruled. The least advantaged were the pariahs, the 'navvies', the masterless men.

Having been there first, Edward Thompson pilloried Bauman and his book in *The Guardian* on 28 December 1972. It was bad enough that Bauman was a sociologist, but he also imagined he knew more about socialism than Thompson did. Bauman nevertheless persisted. He returned to Thompson's fields, in company with the unwelcome figure of Michel Foucault, in his major reprise, *Memories of Class: The Prehistory and Afterlife of Class*. Bauman was, in a sense, writing the marxian instalment missing from Foucault's project, where there was Discipline, Power, Hospital, Clinic, Prison – but no Factory.[9] For Marx, for *Capital*, of course, the factory was the characteristic institutional form and core of modernity. And Bauman follows this, until the 1970s, when consumption replaces work or production as the central activity of modernity, and the mall replaces the factory as its institutional embodiment. The factory is the Panopticon.

Here, again, the issue of representation is fundamental. For the new industrial class, the proletariat, there is another, new intellectual class, the helpers, from social workers to trades union leaders and politicians – no Panopticon without Bentham, no reform without its Fabians, no Russian Revolution without Bolsheviks. But it was the rapid erosion of protective institutions which was a major cause of discontent; and again, the obvious echo in Bauman's work is with the dismantling of the welfare state after the decline of the golden age of capitalism after World War Two. Alongside Foucault's *Discipline and Punish* and Thompson's *Making of the English Working Class*, the third pillar of Bauman's thinking is Barrington Moore's *Injustice*.[10] Socialism and the labour movement, on this way of thinking, represent reaction rather than progress, resistance to change rather than its enthusiastic pursuit. The results of industrialisation were unmistakable. The dissipation of locally based paternalistic institutions resulted in a massive production of paupers and beggars, vagrants and vagabonds.

Call it modern capitalism, call it the Industrial Revolution, the most powerful immediate effect of the great transformation was demographic. Now there was the beginning of material abundance.

Together with surplus product and surplus value came surplus population. The historical novelty of the factory system, after its disastrous collapse in the Depression, was in its capacity to absorb labour. This was the exceptional moment of postwar fordism, when producers had been taught to produce and now were able also to consume, before they had to be taught that consumption, alone, was to be the primary source of identity. The factory, in any case, was at least as profoundly a cultural as an economic institution. Its purpose was to make new men, and women, and to bind them into the new order, not merely to generate profit or to extract surplus value.

Throughout the period of its consolidation into the twentieth century, capitalist culture worked through the politics of inclusion and, via inclusion, exploitation. Peasants became proletarians; pariahs eventually became factory fodder. But there remained problems of surplus population, of stigma, of others who did not belong or whose belonging was temporary or contingent. The proletarian was never quite unmarked in his universality; some were more completely included or assimilated than others. Not all were to be welcomed into the Panopticon, or into the Factory. There were other institutions yet to be fully designed and constructed, like those of the gas ovens, anticipated earlier in lightweight canvas form as the camps of the nineteenth century. The bodies of others had also been drilled through the slave trade and plantations, which as Bauman observes may in turn have influenced the formation of factory systems.

In the heartlands of the West, in the meantime, the proletariat had garlanded its chains with flowers. They had been lead actors, along with the bourgeoisie and the new class, in the construction of corporatism, which represented the inclusive moment of postwar capitalism. The outsiders now were those without hope, the postwar *lumpenproletariat.* The 'new victims' of this social arrangement would be those who truly missed out. For there was now, again, a discernable underclass in the cities of the West. And there were others. They might be marginals within these systems, or they might consist of the massed ranks of the dispossessed of the earth, the poor and excluded of the Third World.

Postmodernity and Intellectuals

Two turns follow, in the path of Bauman's work, in 1987 and 1989. The 1987 turn is to the postmodern, famously, in *Legislators and*

Interpreters: On Modernity, Post-Modernity and Intellectuals. The hyphen gives it away – this was a pioneering work on the postmodern in sociology, before the connector became lost and the unitary term, 'postmodern', became naturalised. The title tells more, and less. First, the proper object of Bauman's enquiry is intellectuals; for the postmodern is first and foremost an intellectual preoccupation. Neither proletarian nor bourgeois would be much moved by it, except until the postmodern became a consumer good. But more, Bauman's enthusiasm for the idea of the postmodern was limited, analytical rather than celebratory. Something had changed, since corporatism or fordism or what he would later call solid modernity. And one aspect of this was that intellectuals, who hitherto were keen to step up not only to celebrity but also to power, might now step back, return to more modest claims to interpretation or translation between life-worlds. Second, and more surprisingly, we had met the enemy, and he (she) was us. For the problem in this book was intellectuals, Enlighteners, implicitly all of us would-be improvers, from Fabians to Bolsheviks to postwar social democrats, social engineers all.

While Bauman remained committed both to socialism and to sociology, and had long identified utopia as a norm rather than as a state-of-affairs to be achieved, this was nevertheless a step back or away from his own class. Another significant step came in *Modernity and the Holocaust.* Here, under the influence of Janina Bauman's childhood memoirs of life in and escape from the Warsaw Ghetto, *Winter in the Morning* (London: Virago, 1986), Bauman chose to foreground the Holocaust as a way of seeing modernity. If the victims of the do-gooders in *Legislators and Interpreters* were the masses of ordinary people who were the victims of routine social engineering since the nineteenth century, then the victims of the Holocaust were also apparent. Outsiders, Romany, socialists, deviants, radical Christians, homosexuals, but above all, Jews. Jews, notoriously, had to be stigmatised, culturally alienated before they could be banished or destroyed. Vermin, weeds, dirt, matter out of place; all the most powerful stigmata were applied prior to the mass destruction of the Jews. But why? Because these people represented surplus population. 'Rootless', they could be charged with belonging nowhere, first to be driven to Madagascar, then east, into Poland, for the Final Solution. Nazism was also, fundamentally, a means of dealing with 'surplus population'.

Bauman could not fully articulate the case in this way, because of the pioneering nature of his work. And it is worth remembering that, while it now has been assimilated into social science common-sense, and despite its Amalfi-Prize-winning status, Bauman and his book were originally shunned.[11] Most of his initial reviewers did not welcome this messenger, but dismissed Bauman for blaming moder-nity, rather than the Germans, for this atrocity. Today, Bauman's message is rather accepted, even if as a necessary provocation, and students of Holocaust studies routinely approach their subject in terms of surplus population, viewing Nazism primarily as a massive project in demographic engineering.[12] The Holocaust, like the Enclosure Acts before it, was a topological project. Nazism was primarily a territorial politics, a project which necessarily included the deterritorialisation of others and the reterritorialisation of their spaces as German ground. Anti-Semitism was fundamental to this; but its territorial aspects plainly involved relocating and extermi-nating populations in order to establish the Third Reich in all its spatial grandeur. *Lebensraum* (the German and Nazi drive for more territory) was elemental.

Underneath all this there is a hostility on Bauman's part to the spectre of Faust, the legendary German figure who makes a pact with the devil in return for knowledge, and his children, those who want to set the social and natural world to rights. Faust is happy to cut up the world, as well as to sacrifice others along the way. Hitler's project became a gardening state, seeking out the weeds and their eradication. So the Nazi kind of social engineering also had some-thing to do with the Enlightenment impulse of setting-the-world to rights, even if and as the Nazis hated the Enlightenment. They used its technologies, and those of the industrialism it later licensed. They became Faustian gardeners with a vengeance, cultivators without a precedent. Gardening was a metaphor which Bauman had used in *Legislators and Interpreters*, where he contrasted the zeal of the do-gooders with the gentler ecology of the gamekeepers. Bauman's own temperament has long been apparent, in contrast. He has always been a gamekeeper.[13]

Liquidity

There remains an unavoidable tension in modernity. There are always others who need help. But is it better to help or not to help? Does the welfare state merely reproduce or even increase patterns of dependence? We all depend on others, almost every moment of our waking lives. To turn away is even worse. For there will always be outsiders, strangers in our midst. Bauman returns to these themes in his essays on 'Parvenu and Pariah: The Heroes and Victims of Modernity' and its sequel, 'Tourists and Vagabonds: The Heroes and Victims of Postmodernity'.[14] Here, before the idea of liquid modernity is coined, it is modernity itself which is restless: as Bauman puts it, 'modernity is the impossibility of staying put. To be modern means to be on the move.'[15] This is not a choice. We are driven to move by the disparity between the beauty of the vision and the ugliness of reality. This makes us all nomads, in this sense at least. Nomads are parvenus, *arrivistes, in* but not quite *of.* This is the tragedy of modern culture: we only feel at home in our homelessness and this is an ambivalence beyond cure. The same ambivalence holds true for tourists and vagabonds, even if the latter move by necessity as contrasted to the choice of the former. Tourists have credit cards; and the vagabonds serve them, or can do, carry their bags, hold their doors open, service them sexually. Neither tourists nor vagabonds can be fixed in place, though tourists get closer to fixity by choice (they can choose home) and vagabonds get closer to fixity by circumstance (there is simply nowhere else to go, until further notice). Tourists, as Bauman puts it, in an early exercise of the notion, are the supreme masters of the art of melting the solids and unfixing the fixed. They do not belong, yet they can keep their distance. Tourists move, on this account; they do not arrive. Vagabonds, in contrast, are the *waste* of the world which has dedicated itself to servicing tourists. The background image of vagabonds is as Romany, and again Zygmunt Bauman is working here under the influence of the work of his wife, Janina. Tourists happily evacuate, leave their mess behind for the vagabonds to work over and deal with. Their worlds are attractive. Vagabonds move because they find the world unbearably inhospitable. Tourists travel because they want to, vagabonds because they have no other choice. Their momentary sense of tolerance or 'welcome' can be withdrawn at a moment's notice.

Bauman knows that these are metaphors, rather than concepts; he is not presenting this couplet, tourist/vagabond, as a replacement or updating of, for example, class relations. Nevertheless, he suggests that 'the opposition between the tourists and the vagabonds is the major, principal division of the postmodern society',[16] and it is a global divide, even as it is lived out locally in the metropolis as well. This is an extension of the older, Hegelian dialectic of master and slave. The poor, the dispossessed of the world, become the rubbish bins of the privileged. Vagabonds are trash cans for tourist filth.

Bauman pursues these themes further in *Work, Consumerism and the New Poor*. Here, everything that is old is new again. For the worlds of division and exclusion that we face today still call out earlier images of pauperism and a literature which runs through Disraeli, 'The Two Nations', Carlyle, Gaskell, Ricardo and Mayhew, Bentham and Chadwick. What he here calls modernity phase two, consumer's modernity, however, summons up a different emphasis between production and consumption. For some years, by this point, Bauman had been travelling in company with the kindred spirit of Jeremy Seabrook. Here, in effect, their concerns merge, for there is also a fellow traveller to this 1998 book, which is the little book on *Globalization*, where the effects of displaced peoples is tracked globally, in a complementary dimension to that of the Keynesian welfare state which is the analytical object of *Work, Consumerism and the New Poor*. The point, after Marx, with Keynes, is that capital is not only the vampire which sucks living labour dry; it also expels labour, literally evacuates it from the core institutions of modernity. Capital prices labour out of work, so that there is now a global reserve army of the unemployed, while welfare provision remains local. The underclass, Marx's *Lumpenproletariat*, returns to haunt us. No longer mere victims, they now become demons, moral rather than economic in their primary function, constantly reminding all of us of the horrible fates of outsiders, keeping our noses down and bums up. The figure of the poor person becomes a scarecrow, not only superfluous to economic needs but also scary.

The most powerful condensation of these concerns comes, finally, with *Wasted Lives – Modernity and Its Outcasts*. This is the point at which Bauman connects most powerfully back to the issue of humans as waste posited in *Modernity and the Holocaust*. 'Our planet is full'.[17] Not only full, but bloated, as parts of the planet are rendered unfit for habitation, and the world system of consumption has expanded to the point that there is nothing left outside it, even as its marginal members struggle to survive. The production of 'human waste', more correctly wasted humans, excess souls, surplus population, the redundant, is an inevitable outcome of modernisation. Colonialism no longer offers the outlet for surplus population that it once did. The vast masses of lost humans want in, want in to the cities, most evidently in the megacities of the developing world. We are awash in shit, in the detritus of an economy based on obsolescence of humans and materials alike. Bauman is too polite to use the word, but it is the image of shit, human waste, wasted humans, actual and metaphorical, which holds up this entire book. So Mary Douglas reappears in the text, along with the anthropology of dirt. More, as he puts it,

> Waste is simultaneously divine and satanic. It is the midwife of all creation – and its most formidable obstacle. Waste is sublime: a unique blend of attraction and repulsion arousing an equally unique mixture of awe and fear.[18]

This much across time, but so much inflamed by modernity and its recklessness. Modernity is excess. Surplus population is one of the great externalities of capitalist economy. Prisons become the most expressive of institutions for this dumping of human lives. Refugees become its most stigmatised object.

But in the meantime, at the turn of the millennium, Bauman has posited the idea and the telos of *Liquid Modernity*, and all that which follows – liquid love, liquid fear, liquid times. The primary sociological purpose of the idea of liquid modernity seems to be to clarify the periodisation of twentieth century development outside of the language of postmodernity. Yet postmodernity routinely was used to describe the capitalist world after the 1970s, and liquid modernity indicates the same kind of notional periodisation. Solid modernity is fordism. Liquid modernity is what comes after, fraught with uncertainty, fragility, precariousness. Liquidity, like the postmodern before it, might be an attitude rather than a fixed condition or a fact. If postmodernity was for Bauman a matter of experiencing modernity without illusions, then liquid modernity was a matter of taking on modernity without certainty, safety or security. Life, henceforth, would be even more precarious, especially for those who did not choose this but had it forced rather upon them. Certainly the rate of change seems to be accelerating, and the purpose of liquidity is to capture this mercurial quality of flux, inasmuch as it is open to capture at all. How will all this look later, after the fact, after the immediacy of our moment and its experience? As Bernard Smith is given to remind us, in the company of Hegel, it remains entirely possible that we only understand history after the fact.[19] What looks liquid to my generation, or Bauman's, might well look different to those who are just now entering this world, and experience it as normal. The fact of movement, and the problems of surplus population, will persist, and accelerate further.

The image of liquidity is an intellectual device, not a thing in the world. It is a way of seeing, and Bauman has always been fond of ways of seeing, of the metaphor of past social critique and new. Like its object, modernity, Bauman's critical theory keeps moving on, anchoring interpretation between past critique and new futures. Its fascination rests with this intricate sense of negotiation, where the interpreter represents the present in between. This much we owe to his example.

Notes

1. See for example Peter Beilharz (ed.), *Zygmunt Bauman*; Keith Tester and Michael Hivid Jacobsen, *Bauman before Postmodernity: Invitation, Conversations and Annotated Bibliography 1953–1989* (Aalborg: Aalborg University Press, 2006); Anthony Elliott (ed.), *The Contemporary Bauman*.
2. Zygmunt Bauman, *Community: Seeking Safety in an Insecure World* (Cambridge: Polity, 2002); Zygmunt Bauman, *Identity: Conversations with Benedetto Vecchi* (Cambridge: Polity, 2004); Zygmunt Bauman, *Europe: An Unfinished Adventure* (Cambridge: Polity, 2004).
3. Zygmunt Bauman, *Liquid Love: On the Frailty of Human Bonds* (Cambridge: Polity, 2003); Zygmunt Bauman, *Liquid Life* (Cambridge: Polity, 2005); and Zygmunt Bauman, *Liquid Times: Living in an Age of Uncertainty* (Cambridge: Polity, 2006).
4. Monica Ali, *In the Kitchen* (New York: Doubleday, 2009).
5. Peter Beilharz, 'Another Bauman: The Anthropological Imagination', in M. Davis and K. Tester (eds), *Baumann's Challenge: Sociological Issues for the 21st Century* (Basingstoke: Palgrave Macmillan, 2010), pp. 62–9.
6. Karl Marx, *Capital* Volume One (London: George Allen and Unwin, 1867/1946), p. 659.
7. E. P. Thompson, *The Making of the English Working Class* (London: Victor Gollancz, 1963).
8. Friedrich Engels, *The Condition of the Working Class in England in 1844* (London: Swan Sonnenschein & Co., 1892).
9. See Michel Foucault, *Discipline and Punish: The Birth of the Prison* (New York: Vintage, 1979).
10. Barrington Moore, *Injustice: The Social Bases of Obedience and Revolt* (New York: Random House, 1978).
11. See Beilharz, *Zygmunt Bauman*, Volume 2, Part 3, 'The Holocaust'.
12. Ibid. David Blackbourn, *The Conquest of Nature: Water, Landscape and the Making of Modern Germany* (London: Cape, 2006).
13. John Carroll, 'Zygmunt Bauman – Mortality and Culture', in M. H. Jacobsen, S. Marshman and K. Tester (eds), *Bauman beyond Postmodernity* (Aalborg: Aalborg University Press, 2007).

14. See Bauman, *Postmodernity and Its Discontents.*
15. Ibid. p. 77.
16. Ibid. p. 93.
17. Bauman, *Wasted Lives*, p. 5.
18. Ibid. p. 22.
19. Bernard Smith, *The Formalesque* (Melbourne: Macmillan, 2007).

Major Works by Bauman

Between Class and Elite (Manchester: Manchester University Press, 1972).
Globalization: The Human Consequences (Cambridge: Polity, 1998).
Intimations of Postmodernity (London: Routledge, 1992).
Legislators and Interpreters: On Modernity, Post-Modernity and Intellectuals (Cambridge: Polity, 1987).
Liquid Modernity (Cambridge: Polity, 2000).
Memories of Class: The Prehistory and After-Life of Class (London: Routledge, 1982).
Modernity and Ambivalence (Cambridge: Polity, 1991).
Modernity and the Holocaust (Cambridge: Polity, 1989).
Postmodernity and Its Discontents (Cambridge: Polity, 1997).
Socialism: The Active Utopia (London: Allen and Unwin, 1976).
Wasted Lives: Modernity and Its Outcasts (Cambridge: Polity, 2004).
Work, Consumerism and the New Poor (London: Open University, 1998).

Suggestions for Further Reading

Beilharz, Peter, *Zygmunt Bauman: Dialectic of Modernity* (London: Sage, 2000). One of the first general surveys of Bauman's work.
Beilharz, Peter (ed.), *The Bauman Reader* (Oxford: Blackwell, 2001). The first general collection of Bauman's work, historically focused on themes of culture, socialism and sociology.
Beilharz, Peter (ed.), *Zygmunt Bauman*, Sage Masters of Modern Social Thought, 4 vols (London: Sage, 2002). This collection combines all available critical responses and supplementary materials until 2001.
Elliott, A. (ed.), *The Contemporary Bauman* (London: Routledge, 2007). Brings together more recent views and materials on the 'little books', liquidity and contemporary culture.
Smith, Dennis, *Zygmunt Bauman – Prophet of Postmodernity* (Cambridge: Polity, 2000). A useful early survey of Bauman's work.
Tester, Keith, *The Social Thought of Zygmunt Bauman* (London: Palgrave, now Basingstoke: Palgrave Macmillan, 2004). A major work of interpretation with a significant emphasis on literary and political-philosophical themes.

4

Homi K. Bhabha (1949–)

David Huddart

Introduction

Homi K. Bhabha is best known for his central contribution to the development of post-colonial theory, extending across writing about visual arts, literature in English, and issues relating to human rights and globalisation. Through his work, Bhabha has become one of the so-called Holy Trinity of post-colonial theory, alongside Edward W. Said and Gayatri Chakravorty Spivak, and now teaches at Harvard University.[1] He has been widely discussed and celebrated as a thinker of post-colonial cultures, the importance of which he explores by drawing on the work of Said and Spivak, as well as diverse figures such as Jacques Derrida, Frantz Fanon, Sigmund Freud, Michel Foucault, Anish Kapoor, Jacques Lacan, Albert Memmi, Toni Morrison and V. S. Naipaul. Many critics in various disciplines have taken on board his ideas about the hybridity of cultures, which are particularly significant in the light of ongoing imperialism.

Bhabha brings together many different critical theories, in particular psychoanalysis and deconstruction, in order to explore how the cultures of colonialism are fissured or divided against themselves, despite appearing to be straightforward expressions of authority and dominance. Beginning with the idea that colonial culture is a form of discourse, he stresses the ambivalence and anxiety contained in many of its examples. Bhabha explores this anxiety within the coloniser's authority, juxtaposing it with the active agency of the colonised, seen in strategies of mimicry and 'sly civility'. Together, these two features of colonial discourse also help us understand the hybridity of our post-colonial world, most clearly seen in minority cultures that have to embrace the mutability of cultural identity. Overall, Bhabha encourages us to see that colonialism is still uncannily influential in our post-colonial present, and gives us powerful theoretical models for understanding this ongoing influence.

Although one feature of Bhabha's work is the questioning of fixed or pre-given identity, his background is a useful context for his most influential ideas. Born in what is now Mumbai, Bhabha is a Parsi. The Parsis, a minority with a worldwide population of approximately 160,000, are Zoroastrians who migrated from Persia to India in the eighth century to avoid persecution. However, Bhabha's references to his origins are not declarations of a fixed ethnic identity. Stressing the multilingual and commercial associations of his family and Parsis generally, he makes the following observations:

> Of modernity, the Parsis have a largely transnational experience, at first mediated by British colonialism, and later developed through a spirit of commercial and financial enterprise. On the question of western culture, middle-class Parsis, often called the 'Jews of the East', have emulated the bourgeois ethic of professionalism and philanthropy, and have sought recognition in the high cultures of the West.[2]

Elsewhere, he refers to their 'negotiated cultural identity',[3] an identity negotiated between very different cultural contexts. A principal characteristic of Parsi identity is, then, its cultural/linguistic hybridity, which accompanies an economic mobility and international experience. Bhabha's own educational background demonstrates this mobility: he first studied at the University of Bombay, before moving to the University of Oxford. His teaching career has taken in the University of Sussex in the UK, before Chicago and then Harvard. In his work, Bhabha explores the extent to which hybridity and migrant experiences of many kinds are defining features of modern life. His work also translates art and ideas between different contexts, showing how this translation is in fact transnational and comparable to Parsi culture as Bhabha understands it. In addition, it is arguable that this translation is fundamental to both the cultures in which Bhabha is interested and the methods which he uses to study them; indeed, translation in a general sense helps to explain the ongoing influence of his work, as other critics have sought to translate his ideas to understand their own concerns and contexts.

David Huddart

Interdisciplinary Theory

While Bhabha's influence is clear, he has also been attacked as a representative of 'high theory', which often seems a specifically Western discourse and so quite unsuited for the purposes of post-colonial criticism. Accordingly, it is important to understand Bhabha's commitment to theory, which he conceives as an _interdisciplinary_ enterprise. Questioned by W. J. T. Mitchell about the importance of theory for post-colonial studies, Bhabha distinguishes two forms of interdisciplinarity. The first emphasises the development of joint degrees and teaching in order to widen the pedagogical or research base, juxtaposing disciplines which at the same time retain their solid foundations. The second form of interdisciplinarity acknowledges disciplinary limits, but responds to a crisis of their apparently solid foundations; Bhabha argues that it

> is not an attempt to strengthen one foundation by drawing from another; it is a reaction to the fact that we are living at the real border of our own disciplines, where some of the fundamental ideas of our disciplines are being profoundly shaken. So our interdisciplinary moment is a move of survival – the formulation of knowledges that require our disciplinary scholarship and technique but demand that we abandon disciplinary mastery and surveillance.[4]

Elsewhere, in his central essay 'DissemiNation', Bhabha expands this point to argue that this second form of interdisciplinarity is _necessary_:

> To enter into the interdisciplinarity of cultural texts means that we cannot contextualize the emergent cultural form by locating it in terms of some pre-given discursive causality or origin. We must always keep open a supplementary space for the articulation of cultural knowledges that are adjacent and adjunct but not necessarily accumulative, teleological or dialectical.[5]

As in the foundational work of Said, the significance of interdisciplinarity is not just a question of adequacy to a multifaceted object; as Bhabha indicates, interdisciplinarity also in principle resists transcendent critical judgements that would erase difference in pursuit of an increasingly inclusive total discipline. Disciplines, like cultures, can be understood as effects of efforts at stabilisation, but they are no less real for that. The interdisciplinary post-colonialism envisaged by Bhabha presumes that duplicating the procedures of its object is unlikely to be rewarding: that is Bhabha's most general point about colonial discourse analysis, which on one level works to *categorise* hierarchies of race and culture. For Bhabha, because there is tension between the apparent pre-givenness of culture and the necessity of its ongoing production, this tension must be marked thematically and formally in our critical language. As he argues:

> Interdisciplinarity is the acknowledgement of the emergent sign of cultural difference produced in the ambivalent movement between the pedagogical and performative address. It is never simply the harmonious addition of contents or contexts that augment the positivity of a pre-given disciplinary or symbolic presence.[6]

The interdisciplinary form of his criticism is an attempt to capture the ambivalence of its object.

The Post-Colonial Challenge

Bhabha's interdisciplinary translation of ideas makes them *hybrid*, which is clearly a key term in his work, even if its complexities are not always understood. His ideas about hybridity owe much to postmodern and post-structuralist philosophers and cultural critics, with Bhabha offering a kind of post-colonial supplement to their attempts to question and de-centre the traditional assumptions of Western thought. In the essay 'The Postcolonial and the Postmodern', Bhabha writes the following about the connection between the two terms:

> My growing conviction has been that the encounters and negotiations of differential meanings and values within 'colonial' textuality, its governmental discourses and cultural practices, have anticipated, *avant la lettre*, many of the problematics of signification and judgement that have become current in contemporary theory – aporia, ambivalence, indeterminacy, the question of discursive closure, the threat to agency, the status of intentionality, the challenge to 'totalizing' concepts, to name but a few.[7]

In other words, although postmodernism challenges many traditional assumptions in Western thought, assumptions mainly relating to the stability of meaning, post-colonialism actually anticipates these challenges. If we return to the historical archive, particularly

David Huddart

that of colonialism, it is possible to find a pre-history or pre-text for the philosophical and critical controversies that characterise post-structuralism and its reception. However, Bhabha is not only directing us to return to the historical archive. The term post-colonialism, in this case, does not refer to post-colonial criticism, but instead to the complex of thinkers and movements arising out of colonial contact, anti-colonial activism and post-colonial culture. For Bhabha the post-colonial perspectives derived from these contexts are more radical and challenging than postmodernism.

Bhabha expresses this post-colonial challenge clearly: in the most general terms, his work attempts to account for the ways in which colonialism has been more than a simple expression of one culture's domination over another. In the essays collected in *The Location of Culture*, Bhabha introduces various, sometimes apparently incompatible, critical perspectives to the study of colonial rule, and its ongoing consequences. For example, he draws on the work of Jacques Derrida to explore the way colonial authority and identities were always different and deferred, and therefore never fully as present and authoritative as they appeared. Bhabha also controversially draws on Frantz Fanon's revolutionary psychology, but instead of focusing on the more famous *The Wretched of the Earth*, he emphasises the early *Black Skin, White Masks*, to explore the way the identities of both coloniser and colonised are always partial and in process. Using such diverse writers as Derrida and Fanon leads Bhabha to write a form of inventively hybrid and interdisciplinary criticism. His writings are complex, allusive and fragmented, and therefore can seem rebarbative; they are hybrid in their tangential approach to their sources, using concepts or quotations in a kind of *bricolage* critical form, an approach which has been criticised.

While many readers have found his style needlessly complex, and his conceptual framework difficult to pinpoint, Bhabha's general aims are clear. Throughout his work, although he focuses on different contexts and uses different critical terminology, Bhabha consistently argues the following:

> Our major task now is to probe further the cunning of Western modernity, its historical ironies, its disjunctive temporalities, its much-vaunted crisis of representation. It is important to say that it would change the values of all critical work if the emergence of modernity were given a colonial and postcolonial genealogy. We must never forget that the

64

establishment of colonized space profoundly informs and historically contests the emergence of those so-called post-Enlightenment values associated with the notion of modern stability.[8]

Understanding how the West reached its present state, Bhabha suggests, demands that we look outside the West, principally of course for historical reasons relating to slavery, colonialism and so on. For example, during the colonial period, the violence of colonial Algeria testified to a certain disease at the heart of the French *mission civilisatrice*. The same kind of understanding helps us consider broader histories of colonialism and imperialism, from the British Empire through to present-day neo-colonialism. Fundamentally, Bhabha believes that in the contemporary moment the post-colonial perspective has a privileged role in rethinking global and local cultural relations. The post-colonial perspective comes from the margins, but cannot remain there if it is to play this role. Indeed, the post-colonial perspective is necessarily part of the metropolitan centre, through the hybrid qualities of modern cultures that are a consequence of increased migration in its many forms.

Hybridity and Hybridisation

Hybridity is a central category in Bhabha's work, being neither a simple description of cultures as mixed-up nor referring to a phase of history in which cultures have come increasingly into contact. While it could certainly be argued that we have entered a phase of globalisation that is distinct from earlier comparable phases owing to specific historical events and technological developments, that is not Bhabha's point. He has resisted narratives that either celebrate *or* dismiss global simultaneity, preferring instead to investigate forms of slowness or 'time-lag'. The impetus behind his concept of hybridity can be seen in an interview from *Art in America*, in which Bhabha summarises his own project:

> The postcolonial perspective resists attempts at holistic forms of social explanation. I question the traditional liberal attempt to negotiate a coming together of minorities on the basis of what they have in common and what is consensual. In my writing, I've been arguing against the multiculturalist notion that you can put together harmoniously any number of cultures in a pretty mosaic. You cannot just solder together different cultural traditions to produce some brave new cultural totality. The current phase of economic and social history makes

you aware of cultural difference not at the celebratory level of diversity but always at the point of conflict or crisis.[9]

While calling the perspective outlined here 'the' post-colonial perspective is controversial, this passage does give a clear sense of Bhabha's own perspective. He rejects totalising explanatory schemes, associating such schemes with one idea of multicultural-ism that imagines its goal is to bring disparate cultures together into harmonious wholes, rendering difference largely irrelevant, if not erasing it. This version of multiculturalism is not so far away from an assimilationist perspective, in that consensus or harmony are taken to be goals that are achievable, so long as we can overcome practical obstacles. However, in terms of Bhabha's work, the key point comes in the last sentence: he argues that those disparate cultures are not pre-existent, but instead are an *effect* of historical change, specifi-cally of colonialism and post-colonialism (this is what is implied by the 'point of conflict or crisis').

From Bhabha's perspective, cultural hybridity is neither abso-lutely general nor equivalent to cultural diversity. Hybridity may appear to be a category applicable to all cultures, and indeed in one way it is. Bhabha cautions against a concept of hybridity that blurs all difference into indifference, consequently making all hybridity appear equivalent. He warns that finding examples of ambivalence in (for example) Hong Kong or Mexico is merely to transmit a theory without translating it.[10] Hybridisation is a process that takes place continually, with cultures in their different forms the result of that process, each time requiring specific contex-tualisation. Cultural difference, likewise, is simply what we find ourselves within, while cultural diversity is a misleading category insofar as it implies that the diverse cultures have coherent and static identities that coexist in a bounded national space. In short, Bhabha's theory of hybridity denies that there were cultures already in existence that later became hybrid: hybridity is less important than hybridisation.

Bhabha believes that this process of hybridisation is central to the discourses of colonialism, which he argues form 'an apparatus that turns on the recognition and disavowal of racial/cultural/historical differences'.[11] In the essay 'The Other Question', he pays particular attention to the operation of colonial stereotypes and the way they are undermined by forms of psychical resistance. Drawing on the pioneering work of Said, particularly *Orientalism*,

Bhabha is interested in the ways that European discourses tend to stereotype the Other; unlike Said (in *Orientalism* at least), Bhabha focuses on the necessary failure of this stereotyping. Bhabha argues that stereotypical knowledges are understood by the coloniser to be stereotypes with the function of maintaining control, and are therefore kept separate from the 'civilising' justifications of the colonial project. However, Bhabha further argues that the two are necessarily inseparable, with the *phantasy* world of the stereotype always undermining the coloniser's civilising narrative. We usually think the problem with a stereotype is that it fixes identities, denying groups their own sense of identity and presuming to understand them on the basis of prior, usually defective and often racist knowledge. This problem would certainly be found in colonial discourse, which wants stereotypes to be fixed, in order that relationships of domination can be justified. In turn, traditional criticism of such colonial stereotypes assumes them to be fixed. Against this assumption, Bhabha argues that this fixity is coexistent with disorder, which the apparatuses of colonial power recognise and desperately guard against.

Analyses of colonial discourse that subject colonial stereotypes to normalising judgements make the same assumptions as colonial discourse itself: in other words, these analyses assume that there exists a prior normality, this time a positive one, next to which stereotypes can be seen for their simplifications and racism. Bhabha insists that all forms of identification must be understood as 'modes of differentiation, realized as multiple, cross-cutting determinations, polymorphous and perverse, always demanding a specific calculation of their effects'.[12] Accordingly, every time we come across a stereotype, we need to see it as a singular instance rather than merely another example of general patterns that we can so easily dismiss.

Agency of the Colonised

Bhabha's analysis of stereotypes is extended to consider the agency of the colonised, particularly through the process of mimicry, which he analyses in 'Of Mimicry and Man'. According to him, the colonial desire for similarity with difference leads to inevitable instability in identity.

> Colonial mimicry is the desire for a reformed, recognizable Other, as a subject of difference that is almost the same, but not quite. Which is

to say, that the discourse of mimicry is constructed around an ambivalence; in order to be effective, mimicry must continually produce its slippage, its excess, its difference.[13]

Colonial discourse directs the colonised to be like, yet not identical with, the coloniser: if there were equivalence between the two, then the ideologies justifying colonial rule could not operate, because they assume a structural non-equivalence that explains how any one group might dominate another. The colonised is also marked by mimicry, with Bhabha arguing that it 'does not merely "rupture" the discourse, but becomes transformed into an uncertainty which fixes the colonial subject as a "partial" presence'. The oscillation between equivalence and excess makes the colonised both reassuringly similar and also terrifying: 'mimicry is at once resemblance and menace'.[14] The colonised therefore seems to be engaged in an act of resistance through this menace.

However, it is not clear that this resistance really can be compared to the anti-colonial resistance that is such an important precondition of post-colonial thought. Some critics have responded to Bhabha's analysis by suggesting that, in adapting Said's work, he has introduced new conceptual and political problems. For example, Michael Pickering suggests that Bhabha adopts a 'textualist' approach which leads to 'a unitary conception of the psychic economy of the stereotype and the colonial discourse in which it operates'.[15] For Pickering, Bhabha's model does not pay enough attention to differences in colonial contexts, partly because it is a textual model. Bhabha could respond that his account should not be abstracted and applied without translation to other contexts. A more serious criticism is elaborated by Anne McClintock who suggests that, even in the context he analyses, Bhabha's theory of the stereotype is seriously deficient, in that his analysis of the colonial context successfully emphasises the position of race but ignores the significance of class and gender. Bhabha theorises 'an ungendered mimicry' and so, in his analysis of the colonial stereotype and colonised resistance, 'masculinity becomes the invisible norm of post-colonial discourse'.[16] Women, McClintock argues, are 'an elided shadow'[17] in Bhabha's work, a claim which seriously undermines his understanding of the colonial situation. Caroline Rooney has suggested that Bhabha's work actually *does* contain the outlines of a more thorough analysis: 'somewhat implicit in Homi Bhabha's Lacanian theorization of the colonized is an understanding of the colonized as feminized inasmuch as his analyses of mimicry and fetishism could co-implicate a phantasmatic femininity'.[18] Nonetheless, his work certainly lacks an *explicit* theory of how stereotyping and class/gender interact in the colonial context.

Furthermore, the question of the colonised's agency remains controversial: even though Bhabha implies that if recognised as a form of agency this mimicry could become a strategy of resistance, the entire psychical structure necessarily operates *unconsciously*. Despite the apparent shift to the colonised, it seems that mimicry remains on the level of the coloniser, just as the term 'post-colonial' seems to make the experience of colonialism too definitive: mimicry indeed is something in which the colonised cannot avoid becoming involved. Bhabha suggests that the partiality of presence in colonial discourse leads to a drive towards authenticity: this means authentically British, although this could always blur into being more British than the British. Bhabha writes that, 'The desire to emerge as "authentic" through mimicry – through a process of writing and repetition – is the final irony of partial representation.'[19] The more partial an identity is recognised to be, the more we strive to solidify it and draw a clear boundary around it. This desire is not only that of the colonised but also that of the coloniser: colonial discourse at once demands both similarity and difference in the figures of the colonised, but additionally colonial discourse's ambivalence has the strange effect of making the British feel not quite British, alienated from what they must believe is their true identity. Colonial power shows concern about its ability to draw boundaries around its identity: it presents itself as serenely self-confident and stable, but is actually anxiously ambivalent. This is the structure of mimicry, and it is clearly far removed from the anti-colonial activism that played such an important role in ending colonial rule in different countries.

Nations and Globalisation

Despite critics' concerns, the basic position advanced in Bhabha's work on colonial discourse is clear: colonial power is hardly as authoritative or self-identical as it portrays itself to be. This insight is something that informs all Bhabha's work, and can be seen as a reaction to one understanding of Said's *Orientalism*. Bhabha draws further on such arguments questioning the stability of authoritative identity, particularly in his analysis of modern nations. This analysis is found in the edited collection *Nation and Narration*, and expressed most clearly in the essay 'DissemiNation', also included in *The Location of Culture*. Bhabha draws upon the well-known work of Benedict Anderson,[20] who has examined the imagined but very real power of national identities. Bhabha's central point in 'DissemiNation' is that 'the space of the modern nation-people is never simply horizontal'.[21] In this he is using Roman Jakobson's characterisation of metaphor operating 'horizontally' (selection according to similarity) and metonymy operating 'vertically' (combination through contiguity).[22] With industrialisation and globalisation, there has been a loss of simple community identity; according to Bhabha, 'The nation fills the void left in the uprooting of communities and kin, and turns that loss into the language of metaphor.'[23] Given this emphasis, Bhabha is less interested in nationalism, which is on the side of metaphor, and therefore has a kind of 'contexture deficiency'. Instead, he is more interested in the unending ambivalent vertical shifts of metonymy: these shifts remind us that while national identity is an achievement, it is an ambivalent one, often excluding those to whom the nation owes much. Instead of progressing serenely and horizontally through what Walter Benjamin calls 'calendrical time', nations are inevitably beset by vertical instabilities. Bhabha's fundamental point about nations is that they are structured by an ambivalent temporality: 'The language of culture and community is poised on the fissures of the present becoming the rhetorical figures of a national past.' Bhabha refers to 'the disjunctive time of the nation's modernity', suggesting that we are caught 'between the shreds and patches of cultural signification and the certainties of a nationalist pedagogy'.[24] National identities are *both* pedagogical and performative: the nation is something that is *taught* as a stable entity but is *lived* as a constantly changing process.

Such a critical perspective on the nation has led Bhabha to increasing engagement with ideas about the transnational elements of contemporary culture. In this he comes into conflict with particular critics who argue that post-colonial theory, including that associated with his work, is no longer appropriate for an age that has been transformed through technology. For example, Michael Hardt and Antonio Negri focus on Bhabha's work as an example of an earlier phase of progressive thought that valorised difference in opposition to dominant forces of the same.[25] They argue that as global capitalism itself now embraces difference and relativity, progressive thinkers must grasp the challenge of the same or simultaneity, which increasingly is enabled by developments in communications technology. From this perspective, technology now enables a potential simultaneity of global revolution. With his emphasis on hybridity, we might expect Bhabha to celebrate the transnational and the cosmopolitan, but also the kinds of technology that increasingly (and increasingly quickly) enable new forms of cosmopolitanism. However, despite the arguments of writers like Hardt and Negri, for Bhabha matters are not so simple; in the context of comments on Jacques Derrida, Bhabha expresses reservations about what we could call the *digital technological imaginary*:

> If the virtual community shares the essential *temporal* structure of the modern national-form and its social imaginary, then what will prevent the reproduction on the Net of the worst excesses of nationalism and xenophobia? the agonisms of center and periphery? the travails of majoritarianism and minoritarianism? Although cyberspace communities do not have the territorial imperatives of nationalism, it is interesting how active xenophobic nationalists are on the Web, often in the cause of nations to which they no longer belong, but to which they now turn to justify their fundamentalist aspirations.[26]

There is nothing inherently transnational about communications technology: even if its form seems so clearly suited for the creation of bonds beyond the nation state, its content can so easily fall back into simplistic homogeneity. Bhabha is suspicious of the ideologies of digital capitalism, because those ideologies obscure homologies of temporality quite in keeping with the reproduction and extension of modernity's worst features.

In stressing temporality, however, Bhabha is not simply dismissing these ideologies. 'We' may all be digital nomads in some sense, but there is a great deal of diversity and conflict and therefore multiple nomadic identities to be scrutinised: not all culture travels easily, or quickly, and some of the time at least culture simply *stops*. Bhabha does not consider 'the' exile to be a normative identity, and he certainly does not assume that all exiles are cosmopolitans like himself; indeed, he has written dismissively of 'a doctrinal espousal of global nomadism or transnationalism'.[27] Elsewhere, responding to the historian of anthropology James Clifford, he emphasises 'the place of a lack of movement and fixity in a politics of movement and a theory of travel', paying attention to those 'people caught in that margin of nonmovement within an economy of movement'.[28] Process and circulation, attributes that Bhabha wants to reintroduce to the identity of nation states (and which minorities necessarily if controversially reintroduce), actually come to a halt for many different reasons. National myths may desire a return to a 'golden age' that of course never existed, and so such myths can be criticised for their damaging effects. Refugees, by contrast, hold onto fixed symbols for their *survival,* and as a consequence hybridisation and stability come together.

Accordingly, whatever the ideologists of digital capitalism might argue, Bhabha has recently developed an emphasis on *slowness,* something that can help us understand the stability of certain symbols of cultural survival. This slowness is positioned specifically as a counterweight to what he calls the 'digital impulse of acceleration and immediacy – the split-second, virtual transmission of messages, money, and meaning'.[29] Writing in tribute to Said, Bhabha criticises what he calls 'telegraphic forms whose rapidity renders the world one-dimensional and homogeneous'.[30] Describing Said's critical practice as based upon a 'philological imperative' demanding close reading, Bhabha suggests that rapidity (or even simultaneity) has a tendency to totalise and therefore be uncritical. By contrast, when we slow down our reading and thinking, we can be truly critical and attend to the decisions and omissions that necessarily structure our knowledge but that cannot be allowed to go unconsidered and unremembered. Bhabha writes that 'The slow pace of critical reflection resists processes of totalisation – analytic, aesthetic, or political – because they are prone to making "transitionless leaps" into realms of transcendental value, and such claims must be severely scrutinized.'[31] Such leaps must be interrogated all the more when they occur in the context of well-intentioned attempts to right past wrongs and defend the rights of the greatest number. Bhabha's more recent work has explicitly applied his understanding of cultural identity and process to various connected contemporary contexts.

In particular, Bhabha has written on vernacular cosmopolitanism, global citizenship and human rights discourses, drawing out the implications of his ideas about colonial discourse for contemporary culture. In 'On Writing Rights', he has argued that international human rights discourses must be adapted to encompass those peoples without nationality as such, because as they stand such discourses too easily assume the centrality of stable, coherent national cultures. This position follows directly from Bhabha's suspicion of simple and fixed cultural identities, questioning the extent to which international discourses necessarily begin from the perspective of nations. In an essay on W. E. B DuBois, Bhabha makes the same point in the particular context of the Universal Declaration of Human Rights, Article 27, which defends *cultural* rights: 'a strong preference for cultural "holism" prevents Article 27 from envisaging, or providing protection for, new and affiliative forms of minoritarian agents and institutions that do not necessarily choose to signify their lifeworlds in the *political forms of nation-ness and nationalisms*'.[32] He further argues that the adaptation of such discourses will only become more important as various kinds of migration and displacement become increasingly common. Many attempts to conceptualise the transnational have so far translated awkwardly into legal and political realms, which have been understandably slow to shake off the fundamental category of the nation. Nonetheless, it is already vital that new concepts of transnational and minoritarian culture are developed, and to do this Bhabha looks to central figures who were very much part of nation states but already imagined categories beyond them. For example, adapting DuBois and Albert Memmi, Bhabha imagines a 'transnational gathering of the "quasi-colonial" not as a racial or ethnic community but as a "community of *condition*"'.[33] Discussing DuBois's novel *Dark Princess*, Bhabha focuses on its pessimistic criticism of the superficiality of 'spontaneous solidarity', claiming its central theme is the way minorities that share histories of oppression are yet drawn into conflict and betrayal. All of these recent writings develop in some way from the earlier analysis of colonial discourse, and the connections will no doubt become clearer when Bhabha publishes his next two books, *The Measure of Dwelling* and *The Right to Narrate*, which systematically explore his ideas about global citizenship, vernacular cosmopolitanism, human rights and transnational cultures.

Conclusion

The recent expansion of Bhabha's focus follows from the impact of his work beyond literary and cultural criticism. His writing has been very influential and is discussed by a large number of writers in colonial discourse analysis and post-colonial theory, as well as related fields relating to contemporary literature and culture. Bhabha has been invited to lecture around the world: he delivered the Clarendon Lectures at the University of Oxford, the Wellek Library Lectures at the University of California Irvine, the Presidential Lecture at Stanford University, the Richard Wright Lectures at the University of Pennsylvania, and the W. E. B. DuBois Lectures at Harvard University. However, his influence has also been evident beyond the university: for example, he was a central participant and writer of the manifesto for the 1997 British Council conference on 'Re-inventing Britain', a keynote speaker at the UNESCO Forum on Higher Education, Research and Knowledge Colloquium, and was faculty advisor to the DAVOS World Economic Forum. Nonetheless, in terms of critical evaluation, Bhabha's work has never been less than controversial, with writers such as Benita Parry and Aijaz Ahmad questioning its historical accuracy and pertinence.[34] There has been a persistent charge that Bhabha's work applies its theoretical influences without sufficient attention to the specific details of time and place. This inattention, it might be said, concurs with the generalised qualities of the term 'post-colonial', which groups together so many disparate cultures and experiences. However, it can be argued that, with its stress on translation, Bhabha's work inevitably appropriates historical, cultural and theoretical examples, re-contextualising them productively. It is this translation that catches the attention of critics and artists from so many different lifeworlds, and that will continue to make Bhabha's work fire the imagination of new communities large and small.

Notes

1. Robert J.C. Young, *Colonial Desire*, p. 163.
2. 'Joking Aside', p. xv.
3. 'Translator Translated', p. 81.
4. Ibid. p. 118.
5. *The Location of Culture*, p. 163.
6. Ibid. p. 163.
7. Ibid. p. 173.
8. Ibid. p. 64.
9. 'Art and National Identity: A Critics' Symposium', p. 82.
10. 'Translator Translated', p. 83.
11. *The Location of Culture*, p. 70.
12. Ibid. p. 67.
13. Ibid. p. 86.
14. Ibid. p. 86.
15. Michael Pickering, *Stereotyping: The Politics of Representation* (London: Palgrave, now Basingstoke: Palgrave Macmillan, 2001), p. 159.

16. Anne McClintock, *Imperial Leather: Race, Gender, and Sexuality in the Colonial Contest* (London: Routledge, 1995), pp. 64–5.

17. Ibid. p. 363.

18. Caroline Rooney, *African Literature, Animism and Politics* (London: Routledge, 2006), p. 104.

19. *The Location of Culture*, p. 88.

20. Benedict Anderson, *Imagined Communities: Reflections on the Origin and Spread of Nationalism*, 3rd edn (London: Verso, 2006).

21. *The Location of Culture*, p. 141.

22. Roman Jakobson and Morris Halle, *Fundamentals of Language*, 2nd edn (The Hague: Mouton de Gruyter, 1971).

23. *The Location of Culture*, p. 139.

24. Ibid. p. 142.

25. Michael Hardt and Antonio Negri, *Empire* (Cambridge, MA: Harvard University Press, 2000), pp. 143–6.

26. 'Arrivals and Departures', p. ix.

27. 'Another Country', p. 34.

28 Bhabha, citing James Clifford, 'Traveling Cultures', in Lawrence Grossberg, Cary Nelson, Paula A. Treichler (eds), *Cultural Studies* (London: Routledge, 1997), pp. 96–116.

29. 'Another Country', p. 30.

30. 'Adagio', p. 11.

31. Ibid. pp. 12–13.

32. 'The Black Savant and the Dark Princess', p. 57.

33. Ibid. p. 58.

34. Benita Parry, *Postcolonial Studies: A Materialist Critique* (London: Routledge, 2004); and Aijaz Ahmad, 'The Politics of Literary Postcoloniality', *Race and Class* 36, 3, 1995, pp. 1–20.

Major Works by Bhabha

'Adagio', in Homi Bhabha and W. J. T. Mitchell (eds), *Edward Said: Continuing the Conversation* (Chicago: University of Chicago Press, 2005), pp. 7–16.

'Another Country', in Fereshteh Daftari (ed.), *Without Boundary: Seventeen Ways of Looking* (New York: The Museum of Modern Art, 2006), pp. 30–5.

'Arrivals and Departures', in H. Naficy (ed.), *Home, Exile, Homeland: Film, Media, and the Politics of Place* (London: Routledge, 1999), pp. vii–xii.

'Art and National Identity: A Critics' Symposium', *Art in America*, 79, 9, 1991, p. 82.

'The Black Savant and the Dark Princess', in H. Trivedi (ed.), *The Nation across the World: Postcolonial Literary Representations* (New Delhi: Oxford University Press, 2007), pp. 41–62.

'"Caliban speaks to Prospero": Cultural Identity and the Crisis of Representation', in P. Mariani (ed.), *Critical Fiction: The Politics of Imaginative Writing* (Seattle: Bay Press, 1991), pp. 62–5.
'Democracy De-realized', *Diogenes*, 50, 1, 2003, pp. 27–35.
'Joking Aside: The Idea of a Self-Critical Community', in Bryan Cheyette and Laura Marcus (eds), *Modernity, Culture and 'the Jew'* (Cambridge: Polity Press, 1998), pp. xv–xx.
The Location of Culture (London: Routledge, 1994).
Nation and Narration, ed. Homi Bhabha (London: Routledge, 1990).
'On Writing Rights', in Matthew J. Gibney (ed.), *Globalizing Rights: The Oxford Amnesty Lectures 1999* (Oxford: Oxford University Press, 2003), pp. 162–83.
'Re-inventing Britain: A Manifesto', *British Studies Now*, 9, 1997, pp. 9–10.
'Translator Translated: W. J. T. Mitchell Talks with Homi Bhabha', *Artforum* 33, 7, 1995, pp. 80–3.

Suggestions for Further Reading

Fanon, Frantz, *Black Skin, White Masks*, trans. Charles Lam Markmann (New York: Grove Press, 1967 [1953]). Necessary for understanding Bhabha's interpretation of the colonial psyche, which Bhabha reinterprets powerfully if controversially.
Huddart, David. *Homi K. Bhabha* (London: Routledge, 2006). Systematic reconstruction of Bhabha's arguments, drawing in his many theoretical influences, and using literary examples for illustration.
Moore-Gilbert, Bart, *Postcolonial Theory: Contexts, Practices, Politics* (London: Verso, 1997). Patiently reconstructs post-colonial theory's arguments, putting Bhabha alongside thinkers like Wilson Harris to suggest that post-colonial theory has many connections with traditions that it seemingly displaces.
Said, Edward W., *Orientalism: Western Conceptions of the Orient* (New York: Pantheon Books, 1978). Necessary in order to understand post-colonial theory in general, but Bhabha's early work on stereotypes in particular.
Young, Robert J. C., *Colonial Desire: Hybridity in Theory, Culture and Race* (London: Routledge, 1995). A text that often discusses Bhabha explicitly, and throughout shows the influence of his psychoanalytic approach to colonialism and post-colonialism.
Young, Robert J. C., *White Mythologies: Writing History and the West*, 2nd edn (London: Routledge, 2004). Considers Bhabha as part of a lineage of post-structuralist thought that has sought to decentre Western constructions of knowledge.

5

Judith Butler (1956–)

Moya Lloyd

Born in Cleveland, Ohio, Judith Butler first came to academic prominence with the publication of *Gender Trouble* in 1990, a book now regarded as foundational to the development of queer theory and as a classic of feminist theory. Currently a professor of rhetoric and comparative literature at the University of California, Berkeley, and renowned for the inter-disciplinarity of her work, Butler trained as a philosopher. Her rabbi tutored her in Spinoza, existential theology, and German Idealism and its relation to Nazism (all topics she had chosen herself).[1] This career, principally in continental philosophy (phenomenology, existentialism, hermeneutics and the Frankfurt School, with forays into German Idealism) included a spell studying with Hans-Georg Gadamer at Heidelberg University in Germany. Yet, Butler has been keen to maintain some distance from the 'institutionalised life' of philosophy.[2]

It is significant that Butler's formal philosophical training began in the context of a Jewish education conditioned by ethical questions raised by the Holocaust. It marked her writing both methodologically (her mode of engagement with texts is arguably informed by Talmudic scholarship) and thematically (the emphasis on negativity, the idea of life as precarious, questions of mourning, the notion of Otherness, not to mention the Spinozan desire for existence). It made her resistant, initially, to reading Nietzsche (a fact that might surprise those familiar with her work); produced both fascination and yet revulsion at the ideas of deconstructionist Paul de Man; and cultivated a concern for politics and, later, ethics (specifically an ethics of responsiveness to the Other). Significantly, it also appears to have underpinned her enduring interest in and engagement with Hegel, the philosopher, *par excellence,* of alterity (on whom she wrote her doctoral thesis) and whose ideas on recognition inflect all her major texts to date.

Not all Butler's intellectual endeavours can be construed in the light of her Jewish education, however. Butler published her thesis as *Subjects of Desire: Hegelian Reflections in Twentieth-Century France.* It contained a new final section on the 'post-Hegelian' ideas of Jacques Derrida, Michel Foucault, Jacques Lacan, Gilles Deleuze and Julia Kristeva. Although she quickly dropped Deleuze and became increasingly critical of Kristeva, this engagement with French theory came to be regarded as one of the hallmarks of her work.

Butler's interest in gender and sexuality developed at the same time, through reading Simone de Beauvoir, Michel Foucault and French feminist theorist, Monique Wittig. A participant in the famous 'Towards a Politics of Sexuality' conference held at Barnard College in 1982, she signed its petition to counter attempts within the women's movement to restrict feminist discussions of sexuality and wrote a report on the conference for *Gay Community News,* a radical gay and lesbian periodical of the time.[3] This conference was important for at least two reasons: first, because it argued the need for feminists to *theorise* sexuality; and, second, because the theoretical framework favoured by many at the conference was social constructionism, namely, one that rejected the 'naturalness' of sex and sexuality.[4] Since then, Butler has been active in gay and lesbian human rights campaigns, chairing the International Gay and Lesbian Human Rights Commission; protested about affirmative action; and spoken out against gay marriage. Her ongoing political involvement has not been limited to queer or feminist issues, however. Butler has also been critical of US involvement in the Iraq War, of events at both Guantanamo Bay and Abu Ghraib, as well as intervening in debates on Zionism and on the Palestinian-Israeli conflict. As such, the caricature of her as the apolitical theorist that some critics draw is clearly ill deserved.

Sex/Gender/Sexuality as Performative

The idea for which Butler is best known is undoubtedly that of gender performativity, which is given its most extensive treatment in her second book *Gender Trouble.* The term performativity derives from the ordinary language philosophy of J. L. Austin, where it is used to denote an utterance that is also an enactment; where, that is, saying something is also its doing (as in 'I promise'). As used by Butler in *Gender Trouble*, however, performativity is conceived less as a linguistic phenomenon (a speech act) than a form of corporeal enactment.

One of the goals of *Gender Trouble* is to problematise feminist understandings of the relation between sex and gender and, in particular, the emphasis of 'French Feminism' on sexual difference.[5] Developed initially to contest the idea of biology as destiny, the distinction between sex and gender allowed feminists to contend that whereas sex (the biological differences between men and women) is fixed gender is not. Because it is culturally constructed, it can be altered. This, in turn, means that gender hierarchies (the patriarchal privileging of men) can be assailed. Butler accepted the argument that gender is cultural but, controversially, challenged the ideas central to other feminist accounts that sex is natural and that sex both temporally and logically precedes gender. Or, to put it the other way round, Butler denied that gender is built on sex.

If gender is only 'the cultural meaning that the sexed body assumes' rather than being determined by sex then it follows that there is no necessary connection between maleness and masculinity or between femaleness and femininity.[6] If such a connection exists, by implication, it must be because gender is the apparatus through which binary sex is produced. Inspired by Foucault's argument in *The History of Sexuality* that sex is constituted by a specific regime of sexuality, by Wittig's idea of the 'heterosexual contract', as well as the notion of 'compulsory heterosexuality' developed by both Gayle Rubin and Adrienne Rich, Butler argues that sex is not merely an effect of gender norms but rather that sex, gender and sexuality are constituted within a 'heterosexual matrix', which she defines as 'that grid of cultural intelligibility through which bodies, genders and desires are naturalized' as heterosexual.[7] This matrix generates a set of ideal relations between sex, gender and desire where each is said to be implicated in the other. Thus, femaleness entails femininity, which is expressed in sexual desire for a man and so 'intelligible' (that is, normalised heterosexual) subjects are produced. Where sex, gender and sexuality align in a different way, say where a masculine woman desires another woman, both the relation and the person are normatively unintelligible. Butler's reputation as a queer theorist rests on her focus on heteronormativity (that is, the normativity of heterosexuality) and her critique of the sex–gender relation.

The notion of performativity is developed through Butler's changing interpretations of Beauvoir's idea that 'one is not born, but rather becomes, a woman'.[8] When she begins theorising about Beauvoir, Butler's goal is to develop a phenomenological account of gender. This entails understanding how the body (conceived as a historical idea) acquires its gendered form. Her reading of Beauvoir leads Butler to the idea that gendering is a process – a '*stylized repetition of acts*'.[9] Becoming a woman involves, in other words, reiterating a series of 'bodily gestures, movements, and enactments of various kinds'.[10] From this Butler deduces that it is the *doing* of gender that constitutes the gendered body and subject. In *Gender Trouble*, Butler distances herself from Beauvoir and phenomenology, recasting her ideas in Nietzschean terms as 'there is no "being" behind doing . . . the deed is everything'. In terms of gender, this means '[t]here is no gender identity behind expressions of gender; that identity is performatively constituted by the very "expressions" that are said to be its results'.[11] Gender is an effect created by the reiteration of a corporeal lexicon. It exists, that is, *only* in the acts that constitute it.

Critics were divided by Butler's radical account of gender. Some discerned in her work the potential for a new gender politics generated through the performative reconfiguration of gender norms (that is, through doing them differently – 'parodically' as Butler notes in *Gender Trouble*), which would validate already existing, though presently unintelligible, forms of sex, gender and sexuality. Others, however, worried about its voluntaristic assumptions, taking performativity to imply that one could change one's gender at will, simply by acting or dressing differently. It did not help that drag was Butler's example of how the enactment of a determinate set of practices creates the impression of a specific gender identity. In demonstrating the fictive nature of all gender it appeared to confirm the idea of gender politics as performance, a mode of dressing-up/ cross-dressing. Partly to allay concerns such as these, Butler sought to clarify the concept of performativity in her next book, *Bodies That Matter*, by exploring Derrida's ideas about iterability and citationality as he elaborated them in response to Austin.[12]

Butler focused on Derrida's objection to Austin's attempt to differentiate between authentic speech-acts (those that are serious, intentional and singular) and parasitic speech-acts (such as those said by a stage-actor and which, are thus, citations). Refusing the distinction, Derrida contends instead that all performative utterances are already citations. They succeed because they 'repeat a "coded" or iterable utterance'.[13] Although dependent on prior uses, meaning is not necessarily fixed; in certain situations words may be recited in ways that shift their meaning. According to Butler, gender has the same citational structure as language. It too is 'coded': behaviour is identifiable as masculine, namely, because it recites normative practices that have, over time, come to signify masculinity. Apprehended thus performativity is 'neither free play nor theatrical self-presentation' but rather the 'regularized and constrained repetition of norms'.[14] Even as there is scope to repeat gender norms in such a way *potentially* as to challenge heteronormativity – there is always the risk that non-normative performances of gender might, in fact, reinforce it – norms have to be reiterated. Performativity as a 'process of iterability' (or ritualised repetition) is the very condition of possibility for the subject's existence. As such, it is both constraining (it must be done) and enabling (it might be done differently).

Citationality and 'Talking-back'

During the 1980s and 1990s in the USA, a group of feminists and critical race theorists began to argue that pornography and racially assaultive speech, respectively, should be removed from the protection of the First Amendment, which defends freedom of speech. Their argument was that words (and images) wound and, as such, should be prosecutable under law. In *Excitable Speech*, Butler sets out to debunk their claims by invoking the performative power of language. At stake in this debate is how the relation between speech and conduct is theorised. In short, those arguing for censorship charge that assaultive speech is simultaneously both speech *and* assault. Hate-speech and pornography harm *directly* by subordinating those against whom they are directed. They performatively produce the very inequality and abuse they name. Butler is unsympathetic to this line of argument, arguing instead that the pro-censorship lobby has misunderstood the relation between speech and action.

Butler pins her case on a distinction Austin draws between illocutionary and perlocutionary utterances. The former refer to utterances that do something, like a warning; the latter, by contrast, bring something about as a consequence, such as convincing someone to buy something. The two are, Austin suggests, differentiated both by their temporal sequence – illocutionary speech-acts rely on a simultaneous saying and doing whereas perlocutionary speech-acts involve consequences following from the utterance – and by the fact that illocutionary utterances rely on convention.[15] Butler rejects Austin's argument, claiming that the *force* of both kinds of utterance stems from convention, which means logically they both share the same temporal structure. If *any* performative succeeds, she argues, it does so because 'that action echoes prior actions, and *accumulates the force of authority through the repetition or citation of a prior and authoritative set of practices*';[16] a view already familiar from her discussion of gender performativity. Every iteration, in other words, is always a *re*-iteration. The force of hate-speech (its capacity to subordinate) derives, therefore, from the fact that it recycles terms (or images, in the case of pornography) that have already become offensive. Butler does not explain, however, how instances of hate-speech have gathered this wounding force in the first place.

The contention that there is always a gap between speech and conduct, although challenging the argument of pro-censorship advocates, does not in itself undermine the argument for the legal regulation of hate-speech. To justify this claim, Butler focuses on the 'excitability' of language: the fact that a speaker is never fully in control of the language they use, thereby contesting both the idea of sovereign performatives (speech that is always efficacious) and sovereign subjects (those that originate speech).[17] Two consequences follow from this: that hate-speech might fail to wound – it might be inefficacious – and, in an argument derived from Derrida, that because such failure is not only possible but is intrinsic to speech itself, that potentially hateful words can always be deployed in non-hateful ways. Hate-speech (like all speech, in Butler's view) is citational and thus can be resignified. The term 'queer' is, she avers, a case in point: it was resignified from a shaming, stigmatising name into an affirmative, politically defiant one.[18] There is thus no need for the legal regulation of hate-speech. All terms, even the most contaminated and odious, can be cited – or rather *re*-cited – in ways that escape their established connotations. Hence 'talking back' is a more effective strategy than censorship.

There is, however, a second reason Butler advocates a resignificatory politics. She is deeply wary of the state. In *Excitable Speech,* she documents some of the ways that the courts have acted in partial fashion, seemingly countenancing racist hate-speech while being more disposed to prosecute cases of obscenity (particularly those involving representations of homosexuality or rap music, with its sexually explicit lyrics). Allowing the state to censor speech permits the state to establish what counts as publically acceptable speech and, by extension, what counts as offensive speech. The state does not merely censor hate-speech but *'produces hate-speech'*.[19] Hate-speech does not exist, in other words, prior to judicial intervention; the intervention performatively enacts it. As a consequence, the state sets the racial and sexual norms it then deploys actively to police its subjects – an argument that is reprised in slightly different form in her discussions of gay marriage and of the politics of kinship.[20] This is one reason why, throughout her work, Butler favours civil society, and especially the reshaping of 'daily social relations',[21] as the primary locus of political activity: because the state is not neutral in its adjudications.

The Body

One issue that came to the fore because of Butler's discussion of gender performativity was her conceptualisation of the body. The (sexed) body is a central concern of feminism; most notably because it is taken to be one of, if not the, principal sites upon which *gender* differences are erected. Underpinning this claim is the assumption that sex difference itself is immutable and because of this female biology, particularly reproductive capacity, inevitably affects women's lives. Butler's contention that the notion of a natural body wrongly ontologises what is, in fact, a culturally instituted phenomenon is a clear challenge to this view. In *Gender Trouble*, Butler does not merely subscribe to Foucault's Nietzschean view that the body is shaped or disciplined by power; she criticises Foucault for 'maintaining a body prior to its cultural inscription' for the material body, as she conceives of it, is nothing other than the *effect* of specific signifying practices.[22] Unsurprisingly, some of her feminist readers baulked at this conceptualisation, accusing Butler both of denying the 'reality' of women's bodies and of going too far in her denaturalisation of the body.[23]

What perplexed Butler's critics was that she appeared not to subscribe to a belief in the body as a material entity with any innate functions. When she remarks, in the preface to *Bodies That Matter*, that 'surely bodies live and die; eat and sleep; feel pain, pleasure; endure illness and violence', Butler appears to concede that the body does indeed have an extra- or pre-discursive existence. Almost immediately, however, she qualifies this remark when she notes that the body cannot be understood outside culture. It can only be apprehended, she continues, through 'constructions' representing 'that "without which" we could not think at all'.[24] Specifically, the body cannot be thought – or, indeed, lived – except within particular normalising schema (such as heteronormativity), which determine the matter of bodies.

Yet, Butler does not maintain that the body is crafted entirely from language or is a linguistic construction. Like phenomenologists such as Beauvoir, Butler believes this (excessive) body to be itself unknowable. What is amenable to knowledge is just the body 'as an imaginary formation'[25] – the material body as represented or categorised in discourse. This is arguably why, when Butler refers to the matter of bodies, she does so in such a distinctive way: not as a substance but as '*a process of materialization that stabilizes over time to produce the effect of boundary, fixity, and surface we call matter*'.[26] Matter, in this sense, has a dual meaning for Butler: as both mattering (having value) and materialisation.[27] The (sexed) bodies that matter are those that have been rendered intelligible (materialised) by a particular regulatory regime.

Critics might charge, and with some warrant, that in once again stressing the constituted nature of sex in *Bodies That Matter* Butler has not explicitly demonstrated that anatomical sex, though a discursive construct, is nevertheless lived as real, that sex is lived, in other words, as constraint: as a source of anguish, a site of medical intervention, or a fleshy incarnation that is always less-than-human.[28] Certainly the emphasis changes in later works. In *The Psychic Life of Power*, Butler begins to develop the idea of corporeal vulnerability, which is amplified in *Undoing Gender* and *Precarious Life*. Her argument begins with a claim concerning primary human dependency: that all infants rely on others to survive. This reliance reveals a basic fact about the body: it is inherently vulnerable, mortal. Without care, the helpless infant will surely die. This dependency, according to Butler, does not end when the subject is able to take care of itself practically; it continues in perpetuity. The 'skin and the flesh expose us to the gaze of others but also to touch and to violence'.[29] The body is the medium though which we encounter others: be that through love, passion, anger, guilt, mourning, hatred, cruelty or killing. To 'be a body is to be given over to others'.[30] Willingly or not, the body is always already communal: open and susceptible to others; affecting and impacting on others.

84

Cultural (Un)intelligibility, the Human and Normative Violence

Hand in hand with Butler's growing attention to the precariousness of embodied life, there has also been a more explicit focus on something she calls a 'livable life'. The concept of a livable life brings together a series of ideas that have become more explicit in her work in recent times: namely, normative violence, cultural unintelligibility and the human. A livable life is a life that is viable within the dominant normative order. In terms of sex and gender, therefore, a feminine woman who desires masculine men has a greater prospect of being able to live her life with ease than a feminine woman who desires other women. The option of a livable life rests on cultural intelligibility, that is, on the possibility of a particular person being recognised as a subject. For the subject 'is the linguistic occasion for the individual to achieve and reproduce intelligibility, the linguistic occasion of its existence and agency'.[31] Its continued existence hinges on its intelligibility – on its conformity to dominant norms. But what of those who are in some sense 'outside the norm'?[32]

Normative violence is the term Butler gives to the operation of norms in determining who counts as a subject. This is the violence performed by 'ideal morphologies of sex' in designating certain bodies as normal and others as anomalous;[33] it is the violence that occurs when heterosexuality is naturalised and all other forms of sexuality are rendered unreal and, thus, unintelligible. It is the violence at work when a particular racial frame is deployed that serves to render certain populations less than human: be that Arab-Americans at the height of the 'War on Terror' or the '200,000 Iraqi children . . . killed during the Gulf War and its aftermath'.[34] Norms of gender and race are to be understood thus as apparatuses generating and naturalising particular bodies and persons and which have the capacity to constrain how humanity is defined. If livability depends on conforming to norms, then, 'struggle with the norm' defines attempts to extend livability to those made unintelligible by them.[35]

As Butler observes in *Frames of War*, the 'frames' operating to differentiate intelligible from unintelligible life set up specific 'ontologies of the subject'.[36] Breaking with the traditional conception of ontology as revealing fundamental universal truths about the world, Butler conceives of ontologies as contingent, historical and hence political. They are constituted by norms. For a person to be recognisable as human, therefore, she or he has to fit a particular

85

conception of the human; she or he has to be intelligible as human. Intelligibility precedes and conditions recognisability. To suggest that the unintelligible are not yet human, that not all who presently live and breathe qualify as such, is to argue that the 'human' is a site of normative struggle. The political implications that follow from this are significant. Countering unintelligibility cannot be done by assimilating the excluded to current normative standards, by for instance extending to them exactly the same rights extended to intelligible citizens. It requires no less than 'an insurrection at the level of ontology'[37] or a remaking of the category of the human. Given that the frames defining the human have to be reiterated in order to be sustained, such remaking is always possible. Just as there is a risk inherent in language that it may be redeployed, so too there is a risk with normative frames. To bring about the ontological revolution identified by Butler, however, this remaking must produce subject positions that enable the unintelligible to occupy the site of the human. This alone can render them intelligible.

Ethics

Although the initial prompt for Butler's exploration of ethical responsibility in *Precarious Life* was the events of September 11 2001, in many other respects it is the natural culmination of several lines of thought pursued in prior work. The conception of corporeal vulnerability outlined earlier grows out of arguments begun in *The Psychic Life of Power*, and underpins her concern with how experiences such as grief, love, mourning and anger might become resources used to extend what constitutes a livable life. Her enduring interest in questions of recognition, Hegel's bequest, is linked inextricably to Butler's exploration of the connections between intelligibility and *recognisability* – the general conditions under which acts of recognition occur. For, before an act of recognition can occur – before someone's life might be accepted as livable or they might be acknowledged as human – those involved have to be (or become) recognisable to the other as a subject. An additional element which is central to the kind of ethics Butler advances is the self's opacity to itself. It is this 'foreignness to myself' that, in *Giving an Account of Oneself*, she claims is 'the source of my ethical connection with others'[38] and which also indicated the depth of her debt to psychoanalysis.

Throughout her work, from *Subjects of Desire* onwards, Butler has engaged with and drawn on psychoanalysis, particularly the work of Sigmund Freud and Jacques Lacan. When challenged by her critics that, in *Gender Trouble*, she had denied the performative subject any interiority whatsoever, she retorted, in *Bodies That Matter*, that there is, in fact, a psychic dimension to performativity insofar as what the subject performs functions to hide what is opaque or unconscious to it. Specifically, what the psychic subject cannot avow is a form of gender melancholia. In brief, Butler borrows from Freud the idea of melancholia as an ungrieved loss which results in identification with that lost object. (A person loses a lover and so in order to keep them alive psychically he or she takes on certain of their character-istics.) In terms of gender, she interprets this to mean that at the heart of normative heterosexuality there is both disavowed loss of and identification with homosexual desire.

Ethically, that the formation of the subject rests on attachments of which the subject is unconscious matters more than gender melancholia *per se*, for it implies a subject who is not transparent to itself. Butler spots in this notion of non-transparency, when allied with the fact of primary dependency, the possibility for an ethics of responsibility – but an ethics of a very particular kind. Because in some fundamental sense, subjects are opaque to themselves, they are never able to have full knowledge of themselves: of their actions, their desires or their prejudices. Ethically, this means that the subject is not fully accountable or responsible for what it does as many ethical theories assume. The norms conditioning its behav-iour are not of the subject's own choosing and its conscience is actively shaped by 'norms of social regulation' that it interiorises.[39] If responsibility is to mean anything, in ethical terms, then it has to be rethought in such a way as to take into consideration human interdependence, both psychic and corporeal, and opacity. It has, that is, to be reconceptualised as part and parcel of the process of subject formation.

Butler is preceded in this line of thinking by Emmanuel Levinas, a philosopher whose work she has recourse to in the development of her own argument. Butler calls, above all, on his idea that an ethical relation is established at the moment the subject is summoned into existence by the unwilled address of the other. Responsibility is thus an effect of that relation, a relation established 'prior to any possibility of action or choice' and prior to 'the formation of "I"'.[40] The ethical subject is thus never an autonomous subject, as is often contended. From the outset, instead, for both Levinas and Butler, subjects are ethically enmeshed with, and impinged on by, one another.

It is the subject's susceptibility, therefore, to the other – its capacity to be 'undone' by them – that is both the basis of its vulnerability to injury and of its ethical responsibilities. At times of such undoing or 'dispossession' – when, for instance, someone dies – the foreignness to the self noted earlier is revealed.[41] When bereavement occurs, the subject loses not only the person who dies but also something of themselves. The possibility of ethical responsibility to the other, Butler suggests, arises exactly at these instants of unknowingness; when, for example, those who have suffered violence react not with more violence but in order to defend nameless others, including perhaps so-called enemies, from similar violence. At such times, the prospect surfaces of reconfiguring the norms defining who counts as defendable; in essence, who counts as human. It is only by actively cultivating such ethical responsiveness to the other, therefore, that it is possible to protect and support precarious life. In this regard, the fact of being-with others is not a limitation on the subject's capacity for ethical action. Instead, it is the very condition of possibility for its ethical response.

Butler's Influence

To say that Butler's work has had a significant impact on feminism or queer theory is scarcely contentious: *Gender Trouble* alone has been translated into over twenty languages and has spawned responses, commentaries and refutations aplenty. To focus on this one book alone, however, is to underestimate the range of Butler's academic influence. Her work in general is cited routinely in disciplines as varied as philosophy, geography, performance studies, design, sociology, politics and literature (among many others). Butler's idea of performativity has been drawn on not only to illuminate further the relation between sex, gender and sexuality but also the performativity of race. The concept of life's precariousness has been influential in recent international relations theory. Her understanding of subjectivity had been used in film interpretation, while the idea of cultural unintelligibility has been borrowed to explore questions of immigration and asylum. Volumes have been published examining Butler's politics, the influence of her ideas on the study of religion and her contribution to the study of law. In addition, several special issues of journals have also appeared, exploring the impact of her work on the sociology of education, as well as on, for example, feminist and queer studies. Extracts from her writings are found in most readers on feminist or queer theory, and in many on the body. Scholars have recently begun to explore her contribution to radical democratic theory.

It is fair to say, however, that for all their influence Butler's ideas have divided her critics. Some responses have been positively vitriolic. Others have drawn attention in a more measured fashion to perceived limitations with her ideas. Her interpretations of other thinkers, from Beauvoir, through Foucault, to Catharine MacKinnon, have troubled several scholars, who have challenged her for being idiosyncratic, partial, even for distorting the writing with which she is engaging. She has been criticised for failing to stipulate normative criteria against which to measure 'good' performances from 'bad' and 'good' norms from 'bad' norms, taken to task for failing to deal with the 'realities' of (women's) oppression and condemned for her 'hip quietism'.[42] At the same time, however, still others have found questions in her work, undoubtedly, but also insight.

From the outset, Butler has responded to her critics – though not always by directly engaging with them. *Bodies That Matter* endeavours to resolve issues generated by *Gender Trouble*. *The Psychic Life of Power* develops the psychoanalytic dimensions of her thought in ways hinted at, though not always amplified, in her earlier work. *Excitable Speech* takes the theory of performativity in another direction while *Undoing Gender* returns to questions raised in *Gender Trouble* and offers yet another take on them. Questions of kinship touched on in *Bodies That Matter* are given centre stage in *Antigone's Claim*. *Precarious Life* reprises the theme of mourning found in the last text at the same time as it signals something of a shift in direction, with its more explicitly political orientation and overt concern with ethics. These themes are, as already noted, picked up in different ways in *Giving an Account of Oneself* and *Frames of War*. It is this perpetual restaging of earlier arguments that explains both the ripeness of Butler's work for appropriation by others and some of the frustrations her readers feel in attempting to pin her down. For although there are certain ideas that are emblematic of her work, what is also emblematic of it is the way that it is, itself, reiterative, that is, invested with different meanings in different contexts.

Notes

1. Judith Butler, 'Afterword', in Ellen T. Armour and Susan M. St. Ville (eds), *Bodily Citations: Religion and Judith Butler* (New York: Columbia University Press, 2006), p. 277.
2. *Undoing Gender*, p. 234.
3. Carole S. Vance (ed.), *Pleasure and Danger: Exploring Female Sexuality* (London: Pandora Press, 1989 [1984]), p. 452.
4. See ibid., pp. 8–9; and Lynn Comella, 'Looking Backward: Barnard and Its Legacies', *The Communication Review*, 11, 2008, pp. 202–11.
5. 'French Feminism' is used to refer to the work of three thinkers – Hélène Cixous, Luce Irigaray and Julia Kristeva – none of whom is French and only one of whom calls herself a feminist.
6. *Gender Trouble*, p. 10.
7. Ibid. p. 194 n. 6.
8 Simone de Beauvoir, *The Second Sex*, trans. H. M. Parshley (Harmondsworth: Penguin Books, 1972 [1949]), p. 301.
9. 'Performative Acts', p. 519; but see also *Gender Trouble*, p. 179.
10. Ibid. p. 519.
11. *Gender Trouble*, p. 33.
12. Jacques Derrida, 'Signature Event Context', in Peggy Kamuf (ed.), *A Derrida Reader: Between the Blinds* (New York and London: Harvester Wheatsheaf, 1991), pp. 80–111.
13. Ibid. p. 104.
14. *Bodies That Matter*, p. 95.
15. J. L. Austin, *How to Do Things with Words*, 2nd edn (Oxford: Oxford University Press, 1976).
16. *Excitable Speech*, p. 51, original emphasis.
17. Ibid. p. 15.
18. See, for instance, *Bodies That Matter*, p. 226; and 'Changing the Subject', p. 351.
19. *Excitable Speech*, p. 77.
20. *Antigone's Claim*.
21. *Contingency, Hegemony, Universality*, p. 14.
22. *Gender Trouble*, p. 166; see also p. 177.
23. For the former position see Susan Bordo, *Unbearable Weight: Feminism, Western Culture, and the Body* (Berkeley, CA: University of California Press, 1993), p. 38; and Martha Nussbaum, 'Professor of Parody', <http://www.md.ucl.ac.be/ebim/scientif/Recherche/GenreBioethique/Nussbaum_NRO.htm> (accessed 23 January 2007); and for the latter see Carole Bigwood, 'Renaturalizing the Body (with the Help of Merleau-Ponty)', in Donn Welton (ed.), *Body and Flesh: A Philosophical Reader* (Oxford: Blackwell, 1998), pp. 99–114.
24. *Bodies That Matter*, p. xi.

25. Ibid. p. 66.
26. Ibid. p. 9. On the idea of bodily substance see Vicky Kirkby, 'When All That Is Solid Melts into Language: Judith Butler and the Question of Matter', *International Journal of Sexuality and Gender Studies*, 7, 4, 2002, pp. 265–80.
27. *Bodies That Matter*, p. 32.
28. See Samuel A. Chambers and Terrell Carver, *Judith Butler and Political Theory: Troubling Politics* (London: Routledge, 2008), Chapter 3.
29. *Undoing Gender*, p. 21; and *Precarious Life*, p. 26.
30. *Undoing Gender*, p. 20.
31. *Psychic Life of Power*, p. 11.
32. *Undoing Gender*, p. 42.
33. *Gender Trouble*, p. xx.
34. *Precarious Life*, p. 34.
35. *Undoing Gender*, p. 13.
36. *Frames of War*, p. 3.
37. *Precarious Life*, p. 33.
38. *Giving an Account of Oneself*, p. 84.
39. *Psychic Life of Power*, p. 171.
40. *Giving an Account*, p. 88; *Precarious Life*, p. 31.
41. *Precarious Life*, p. 28.
42. Nussbaum, 'Professor of Parody'.

Key Works by Butler

Antigone's Claim: Kinship between Life and Death (New York: Columbia University Press, 2000).
Bodies That Matter: On the Discursive Limits of 'Sex' (London: Routledge, 1993).
'Changing the Subject: Judith Butler's Politics of Radical Resignification', in Sarah Salih (with Judith Butler) (eds), *The Judith Butler Reader* (Oxford: Blackwell, 2004), pp. 326–56.
Contingency, Hegemony, Universality: Contemporary Dialogues on the Left, with Ernesto Laclau and Slavoj Žižek (London: Verso, 2000).
Excitable Speech: The Politics of the Performative (London: Routledge, 1997).
Frames of War: When Is Life Grievable? (London: Verso, 2009).
Gender Trouble: Feminism and the Subversion of Identity, Tenth Anniversary Edition (London: Routledge, 1999 [1990]).
Giving an Account of Oneself (New York: Fordham University Press, 2005).
'Performative Acts and Gender Constitution: An Essay in Phenomenology and Feminist Theory', *Theatre Journal*, 40, 4, 1988, pp. 519–31.
Precarious Life: The Powers of Mourning and Violence (London: Verso, 2000).
The Psychic Life of Power: Theories in Subjection (Stanford, CA: Stanford University Press, 1997).

Subjects of Desire: Hegelian Reflections in Twentieth-Century France (New York: Columbia University Press, 1987).
Undoing Gender (London: Routledge, 2004).

Suggestions for Further Reading

Carver, Terrell, and Samuel Chambers (eds), *Judith Butler's Precarious Politics: Critical Encounters* (London: Routledge, 2008). This is an excellent but challenging volume of essays, which is organised thematically and covers most aspects of Butler's work.
Chambers, Samuel, and Terrell Carver, *Judith Butler and Political Theory: Troubling Politics* (London: Routledge, 2008). This useful and wide-ranging book focuses on Butler's theory of the political.
Lloyd, Moya, *Judith Butler: From Norms to Politics* (Cambridge: Polity, 2007). This book offers a comprehensive and critical examination of Butler's work that focuses in particular on its impact on feminism.
Loizidou, Elena, *Judith Butler: Ethics, Law, Politics* (Abingdon: Routledge-Cavendish, 2007). A challenging book examining the themes of law, ethics and politics, which explores the potential contribution of Butler's work for critical legal scholarship.
Salih, Sara, *Judith Butler* (London: Routledge, 2002). This is a short, accessible introduction to Butler's work up to *Antigone's Claim*. It stresses, in particular, its significance for literary studies.
Salih, Sara (with Judith Butler), *The Judith Butler Reader* (Oxford: Blackwell, 2004). This volume contains a selection of Butler's writings (essays, extracts from books, and interviews), along with a comprehensive introduction and additional editorial material provided by Salih. It is an excellent resource.

6

Cornelius Castoriadis (1922–97)

Caroline Williams

Thinker of a World in Fragments

Cornelius Castoriadis does not figure often among the French philosophers most cited and utilised by critical theorists in the Anglophone world. His vast and varied oeuvre of almost fifty years spans philosophy, psychoanalysis, politics, literature, science and mathematics. But it has developed largely in the margins of contemporary critical thought. Indeed, his thought defies easy classification. It does not sit neatly within a category such as 'post-structuralism' which might act as a somewhat bare label to mark out the thought of many of the thinkers considered in this volume. The very few references made by Castoriadis to prominent French post-structuralist thinkers such as Foucault, Derrida and Deleuze tend to be pejorative and lack sustained engagement, even though it might be argued that there are grounds for interesting dialogue with some, notably with Deleuze's views on science and politics. To the extent that post-structuralism is mediated via an engagement with Nietzsche, such perspectivism could only be, for Castoriadis, a symptom of the cultural conformism of contemporary Western society from which he wished to detach his thought. At a time when the political bearings of structuralism and post-structuralism appeared lost and the primacy of the human subject was being challenged by the disciplines of philosophy, linguistics, politics and psychoanalysis, Castoriadis claimed that the so-called 'death of the subject' was an evasion of political responsibility. His own response to this crisis of philosophy and politics was a novel reworking of the

93

Marxist project as a project of autonomy expressed in the model of a radical, participatory democracy that drew sustenance from a deep engagement with Classical Greek philosophy and Freudian psychoanalysis.

Castoriadis was a heterodox thinker. He was born in Athens where he began reading philosophy at an early age and joined the Communist Youth. He later moved to France and formed the legendary political group Socialisme ou Barbarie, which contained among its membership Nicos Poulantzas, Claude Lefort and Jean-François Lyotard and exerted a significant impact upon the events of May 1968. It was from within this group that Castoriadis began writing the pamphlets and essays that offered a trenchant critique of the rigid, bureaucratic nature of communist regimes with their totalisation of economy and society.[1] The project of social change, he argued, could no longer be conceived in terms of workers' self-management of production but must extend to the collective self-management of society.[2] In his orbituary of this enigmatic figure, Axel Honneth describes Castoriadis as 'the last great representative of the tradition of Western Marxism' whose theory is comparable in originality and scope to that of Merleau-Ponty (whom Castoriadis read closely) and Herbert Marcuse.[3] In common with these two, Castoriadis embarked upon an *immanent critique* of Marxism designed to push open and renew its theoretical framework. This is encapsulated in his central work, *The Imaginary Institution of Society*.

The form of this critique of Marxism is also inseparable from a number of other aspects of Castoriadis's intellectual development, not least his formal training as a psychoanalyst. Beginning his training under the auspices of the Lacanian school, Castoriadis, along with Luce Irigaray, was to break in 1969 with the École Freudienne, forming the post-Lacanian Quatriame Groupe. Lacan's controversial model of analysis, its structural logic and the accompanying conception of the subject as a signifier were understood by Castoriadis to jettison the specificity of the *radical imagination* as an individual and collective form of self-alteration and creation, a concept that would become central to his project of autonomy. Together with the many interventions within contemporary scientific discourse (especially with the biological theory of Francisco Varela) this psychoanalytical approach gives rise to a nuanced conception of the living being as a self-constituting or auto-poietic mode of being. As we shall see in the discussion below, if Castoriadis may be understood as reclaiming (in a qualified form) the reflective and deliberative attributes of the *human* subject against the dominant tendencies of contemporary critical thought, this must nonetheless be viewed also as a *non-human* quality of *physis* or nature. In this sense, aspects of Castoriadis's thought might invite dialogue with Bruno Latour. Indeed, as one commentator has recently argued, there is a clear shift in the later Castoriadis from a regard with a regional ontology of being established with the formation of the human individual in *The Imaginary Institution of Society* to a transregional ontology of *physis* itself as governed by creative emergence.[4]

If it is within the broad context of Marxist theory that Castoriadis's thought may be placed, then the shadow of structuralist Marxism must also be mentioned. The discourse of structuralism certainly organised if not dominated debates in the 1960s across a wide range of disciplines from feminism and philosophy to anthropology and politics. The scepticism with which Castoriadis viewed post-structuralism and postmodernism must also be extended to structuralism, which he saw as little more than a pseudo-science. There can be no structure or law that can predetermine and account for the contents of a given society because there is a *productive* element within every societal structure which remains *ungraspable.* Structuralist attempts to extrapolate a comprehensive system based upon the differences and relations between elements comprising it, such as that developed by Louis Althusser, appear to rely upon an ontology of determinacy. In other words, as a systematic theory seeking an underlying truth or a rational understanding of the object of society, and as a largely ahistorical or at least transhistorical and formal account of that object's ontological emergence, structuralism remains closed in upon itself and is unable to account for the impurities and particularities that form part of its very composition. It is against the elision of the undetermined in this synchronic (or structuralist) view of time and history that Castoriadis develops a view of history as the emergence of new figures and forms. Thus he notes, 'What is given in and through history is not the determined sequence of the determined but the emergence of radical otherness, immanent creation, non-trivial novelty.'[5] It is the recognition of this irreducible moment of novelty that leads Castoriadis to formulate a view of the social world as a *process* of institution, where we understand the term 'institution' not merely as an object (namely, social institutions) but rather as a dynamic state of being of the social-historical world. Let us turn now to reconfigure and evaluate the central concepts of Castoriadis' thought implied by this new philosophy of time and history, and this ontology of genesis, before moving to consider some of the terms of its critical appraisal, and assess the originality of his perspective.

The Imaginary Institution of Society: Towards an Ontology of Creation

The Imaginary Institution of Society offers responses to an important series of questions that continue to preoccupy critical theory today. Such questions include the following. How might we theorise the emergence of social, political, and indeed all living forms? To what extent do power relations shape the individual subject and construct social identity? How can agency be theorised in the wake of the questioning of metaphysical foundations that previously have shaped the conception of the active subject? How might we account for the effect of the unconscious within social life, or the role of contingency *vis-à-vis* social structure? In the wake of the many challenges to foundationalism and the universal status of truth-claims, how might we theorise an 'open' form of knowledge (or science) without presuppositions, and move forward with a viable, transformatory political project? All of these questions – and more – concerned Castoriadis throughout his life.

We have already seen that he is reluctant to attribute *any* model, rationale, teleology, or logic of final causes to human life, instead drawing attention to the multiple and intertwining conditions of emergence of social forms and individuality. It may be possible to identify some common properties of society, namely, that it must provide a system of meaning for (the waking life of) its members. Such a system of meaning must offer a series of norms and values and a shared language; it must establish ways of making and doing, ways of forming social relationships, patterns of gender, recognised forms of desire, and so on, but these can never be the basis of a model or totalising theory. No two societies are ever the same and beyond this need for bare meaning, *social imaginary significations*, as Castoriadis describes them, create individuals in a multitude of different ways (for example, as monogamous, polygamous, monotheistic, pagan or pacific). Indeed, in a society that recognises its *self*-institution, that is conscious of its historicity and perpetual genesis (after all, systems of meaning are always in the process of configuration), there may be a democratic interrogation of norms by autonomous individuals in a political (public) space where the

96

laws and norms, the *nomos* of a society, is subject to rational deliberation and revision. It is the presentation of this double-birth of philosophy and politics that Castoriadis locates in the Greek *polis*.[6] However, modern and contemporary societies have tended to rationalise and manipulate, solidify and fix the mobility of images available to subjects. In this way, both subject and social world appear as already instituted, timeless, exhausted and heteronomous states of being, and the creative, organising, meaning-giving form that is radical imagination is suppressed and covered over. What, then, is the status and function of radical imagination, and how does Castoriadis propose to theorise it?

Radical Imagination: Understanding the Subjective and Anonymous Fields of Creativity

Significantly, Castoriadis posits imagination as having two related modes of being. The first is the singular human being, existing as part of the Soul or *psyche*; its operations permit the very possibility of individuality and social identity. It is therefore theorised primarily in relation to Freud and largely against Lacan. In both the history of philosophy and psychoanalysis itself, radical imagination has been undertheorised and sometimes occluded in positions that emphasise the linguistic structure and presentation of the unconscious. The second mode of being is the collective, anonymous *social-historical* field and here, claims Castoriadis, its occlusion is absolute since no thinker has tried to understand or actualise the dynamic temporal life of society itself as radical imagination. It is first and foremost in *The Imaginary Institution of Society* that the modalities of this concept of radical imagination are elaborated.

For Castoriadis, radical imagination departs from those negative formulations which view it as the other of reason. If in the seventeenth century imagination was tied to an understanding of the passions or emotions (in particular, their passivity/activity or *intensity*), this was often to domesticate and transcend its power rather than to acknowledge its productivity and constitutive role in the creation of form or *eidos*. Imagination is not a figment or delusion and its role is not corruptive of reason. It is neither fictive in structure nor opposed to the real presentations of the intellect. Castoriadis traces a selective genealogy of the radical imagination finding but two transitory historical examples of it in the philosophies of Aristotle and Kant. The former philosopher, in *De Anima*, identifies an elementary coherence of imagination as a movement of thought identified as *phantasia*, a working up *ex nihilo* not simply of images (which are its secondary outcomes) but of *eidos* itself. The latter develops the transcendental imagination, which in *The Critique of Judgement* enjoys an expansive creative power, particularly in the form of genius. In both thinkers, however, imagination is ultimately domesticated between sensation and intellect (in Aristotle) and overruled by Reason (in Kant).[7] One might add to this genealogy the philosophy of Spinoza who likewise develops an account of imagination that prioritises its productive elements as well as its transindividual, impersonal structure. In this example too, imagination is not an illusion; it is a powerful force that circulates *between* composite bodies (be they subject, mass or multitude). For Spinoza, imagination acts as a fulcrum or conductor for the process of identification, creating relations of agreement and possibility between bodies to enhance their activity and power. Indeed, this radical *potentia* of Spinozist imagination has been theorised to great political effect in the work of Michael Hardt and Antonio Negri, and may suggest the value of a comparative study of these thinkers on imagination.[8]

Building upon the philosophical innovations of Aristotle and Kant, Castoriadis resurrects the 'scandal of imagination'[9] as a Heraclitean flux of figure and meaning giving rise to differentiation, distinction and representation. This surging forth of new forms and determinations (always with spacings, gaps, extensions and hence *under*determined) is irreducible to what *already* exists and brings into being something radically Other. As Castoriadis notes, 'It destroys the thesis on being that underlines Greco-Western philosophy from beginning to end, according to which being is considered as determinacy'.[10] Representation has often been reduced to perception but in relation to imagination it is something quite different:

> Representation is perpetual presentation, the incessant flux in and through which anything can be given. It does not belong *to the* subject, it *is*, to begin with, the subject . . . [It] is precisely that by which this 'us' can never be closed in upon itself, that by which it overflows on all sides, constantly makes itself other than it 'is', posits itself in and through the positing of figures and exceeds every given figure . . . Representation is not tracing out the spectacle of the world, it is that in and through which at a given moment a world arises.[11]

This contestation of the unity and foundation of the subject leads Castoriadis to psychoanalytic theory for the development and qualification of imagination, and we will proceed to investigate the basis of this theoretical relation below. It is also of crucial importance, nonetheless, to underscore the sense in which the function and formal activity of imagination described above takes much more than a subjective form; it is not solely a corporeal imagination. If radical imagination also deploys itself in a second, rather more anonymous modality as society, as the social-historical, then it is also that mode of self-alteration which *brings itself into being* as instituted society and as social imaginary. This formulation creates a bone of contention about Castoriadis's ontology of creation, a point of critique not missed by several commentators on his work, in particular Habermas, who finds in his account some unexplained source of vital agency: 'the world-devouring praxis of the social demiurge' as self-instituting society that merely *replaces* the self-positing subject of modern philosophy.[12] How can Castoriadis account for beginnings? What is the *origin* of creativity?

Thinking Beginnings: Conceptualising the Magma

This question of origins is fully recognised and answered by its author, however, who explains it as follows: the social-historical is *at once* instituted *and* instituting; it is the given structures and materialised institutions, *and* that which structures, materialises and institutes. Thus: 'In and through its own creation, society creates the individual as such, and the individuals in and through which alone it can exist.'[13] Castoriadis searches for a number of formulations to express the consubstantiality and interdependence implied here. In particular, this dynamic relation is described in terms of the mutual *inherence* of psyche and society, or the *leaning* of the social *upon* a primary substratum. This primary stratum in its basic form is nature or *physis*, but we must be careful not to think of it as a homogeneous or monolithic Nature as Substance from which the world simply emanates or which we can transcend. As the metaphor of leaning upon makes clear, there is no clear division between natural and cultural, biological and social realities. The striving toward such a division Castoriadis views merely as the 'incoherent fantasy of a certain stage of Western science'.[14] Instead, we might better think about these realities on the model of a continuum, of the becoming culture of nature, or, following Deleuze, as the virtual field of the socio-political. This metaphor also affords a much more *sticky* and intrinsically immanent connection/relation to describe the means

99

whereby myths, symbols or any other figures of social meaning are organised by the social-historical into imaginary significations and, of course, materialised in institutions.

Nature is not to be understood in a determinist fashion as a univocal cause from which life and being emerge as its logical and local effects. Nor is it, as Habermas presents it, a new theodicy where 'the personification of society as a poetic demiurge releases ever new world-types from itself'.[15] How, then, are we to think about the source of this creative power (as imagination)? In order to explain this field of *organisable* potentiality, Castoriadis is inspired not by the history of philosophy but by the contemporary crisis in mathematics (which is also a crucial source for Badiou), the aporias of contemporary physics (such as chaos theory) and problems regarding the emergence and organisation of living beings in biology (how should we understand the biological closure of systems of life?). Engaging, often forcefully and always in an interrogatory manner, he invents a new concept able to give content to the relation of interdependence or inherence expressed above.[16] The originary upsurge of imagination proceeds from a total *in*determination. There is no Essence or Being to ground the productivity of imagination. Similarly there is no primary Cause and thus no straightforward sense of agency behind this creative praxis. Rather there is a *magma*, which can only be described as plural, undifferentiated and indefinite, an 'ontological heterogeneity'[17] or a groundless abyss from which emerge an inexhaustible series of possibilities to stratify, compose and organise the genesis of forms.[18] Nature is, therefore an excessive living Being, an infinitely organisable set of compossibilities, or an irregularly stratified form which, through perpetual self-alteration (that is, creation) presents, *contra* Habermas's view, the absent ground for the emergence of new forms. In order to simplify this inescapably complex description of the role of magma as the undecidable origin of stratified or instituted worlds, let us briefly take an oft-cited example from Castoriadis's writings where he engages with the ground-breaking biological theory of Francisco Varela who introduced (with Humberto Maturana) the idea of *autopoiesis* to define the self-productive activity that brings into being a living being as an autonomous system.[19]

According to Varela, the living being is a self-organising, self-asserting, sense-making system exhibiting an important quality of autonomy. It is in constant exchange with its environment such that what is 'outside' is always constituted internally, and must have meaning *for* the metabolic existence of the system itself. Like the quality of inherence discussed above, this formulation upsets all distinctions between inside and outside, instead suggesting the idea of an informational 'loop'.[20] Varela suggests that autonomy is represented by the on-going maintenance of organisational closure and conservation of the system as a unity, while its disintegration signals a loss of identity and partial or complete death for the system. Varela's work establishes important developments within theories of creative evolution and might refine our understanding of the emergence of *non-human* as well as *human* living systems (an eco-system or a socially constituted individual, for example). While it is evident that Castoriadis draws creatively upon Varela's theory of *autopoiesis,* he is at pains to emphasise a more specific aspect of autonomy against the organisational closure of Varela's theory which leads, for Castoriadis, to paradoxical results.[21] It implies that even a society whose system of world and institution is totally closed and rigid might be considered self-maintaining and, therefore, autonomous. In the context of the project of autonomy developed by Castoriadis, such a political system, be it archaic or authoritarian, fosters not autonomy but only heteronomy. By replacing the focus upon self-organisation with one of self-constitution, Castoriadis transforms the focus from autonomy as biological closure to one of opening. He writes:

> It is ontological opening, since to go beyond this closure signifies alter-ing the already existing cognitive and organizational 'system', *therefore* constituting one's world and one's self according to *other* laws, *therefore* creating a new ontological *eidos,* another self in another world.[22]

Thus the living being *creates* life, as well as the infinity of ways of existing socially and the myriad of laws and norms that pertain to this or another form of life. Furthermore, it is because there is an inexhaustible and indefinite series of possibilities (described above as a *magma*-like horizon of representations, ready for symbolisation and communication) that autonomy exists as a political project and a political activity. It is, he writes, 'the term *nomos* that gives full meaning to the term and project of autonomy' where the subject becomes the explicit author of form.[23] Can the individual become an autonomous being, one who acts deliberatively to modify its law? How might the radical imagination as self-alteration (and the novelty implied by its mode of social-historical being) bring into being new ways of existing politically and socially? In order to answer these questions concerning the 'politics of the subject' we need first to return briefly to psychoanalytic theory.

Psyche and Subject, Autonomy and Democracy

All this points clearly to the sense in which the psyche is *inherently* social, both in terms of the relations it will form (as a living, autopoietic system), and its social existence, given that the mechanisms for the sublimation of its expressions are always socially instituted in the transindividual realm of the social-historical. Castoriadis thus politicises psychoanalysis from the very beginning, and marks out his own project from that of the dominant Lacanian school. He also arguably sets his position against those thinkers who have utilised, albeit critically, some formulation of the Lacanian imaginary (for example, those who follow in the wake of the Althusserian/Lacanian matrix of thought, notably Butler, Žižek and Laclau).

Within both his training as a psychoanalyst, as well as in his writings upon psychoanalytic theory (early and late), Castoriadis has sought to theorise and understand the distinctiveness of the psyche as radical imagination. This, he argues, has been flattened into a purely specular form by the Lacanian imaginary where unconscious images, affects and representations are reduced to the form of a linguistic signifier, and the practico-poetic activity of the subject as 'a ceaseless emergence of representations' is down-played.[24] Since it is haunted by a 'vulgar ontology of reflection'[25] that privileges vision as a measure for designating the constitution of the subject, the act of perceiving itself as an imaginary object is taken as the metaphysical source of the ontological status of the subject as split or fractured (*Spaltung*). It is this condition that renders it a subject of *lack* or an experience of alienation from which there appears to be no possible escape. For Castoriadis (and Merleau-Ponty, upon whom he draws here), perception already implies 'a cutting up of what is lived into discontinuous acts'.[26] In other words and as we have argued above, the mode of *appearance* for and *organisation* of representing and doing and the ways we participate in them are always socially instituted. There is no subject *of* representation and Castoriadis aims to show us a scene of the subject and of imagination other than that offered by Lacan.

A number of commentators, most recently Yannis Stavrakakis, have suggested that a more sustained dialogue is necessary between Lacanian psychoanalysis and Castoriadis. Stavrakakis claims that the latter's work may act as an 'external frontier' since it points to some professed limits regarding creativity in Lacan (that are ultimately misplaced, in his view). Stavrakakis argues that Castoriadis idealises autonomy since he ignores the alienating dimension of creativity, and the way in which desire always emerges from the field of the Other. Since he does not focus strongly on the undifferentiated feature of the magma, Stavrakakis (and Žižek too) tend to reduce Castoriadis's conception of the subject to an essentialist, solipsistic and voluntarist form.[27]

Castoriadis describes the natural stratum of the subject as a 'monadic core' that only *initially* refers solely to itself: it is 'an indissociable unity of figure, meaning and pleasure'[28] where subject, object and other are without distinction. The psyche produces perpetually a flux of images and affects; it is, as we have seen in relation to Aristotle's *phantasia* above, form creating. The subject cannot be assigned the role of predicate or origin here:

> There can be no question of separating, even 'partially,' the subject and the flux. . . The subject is not the possessor of 'its representations,' 'its affects,' and 'its intentions': the subject *is* that: representational-affective-intentional flux in which has emerged the permanent possibility of reflections . . . and in which the raw (*brute*) spontaneity of the radical imagination has in part converted itself into reflected spontaneity.[29]

According to Castoriadis, Freud never thematised the imagination; for him it is the drive that becomes the carrier of representations. Castoriadis reactivates the Freudian legacy, particularly the latter's concept of phantasy, by positioning the radical imagination at the fulcrum of the psyche as that which permits a drive or an affect to have an *ambassador* in the psyche.[30] In this sense, the unconscious becomes part of the magmatic flux of representations and affects described above, and Freudianism is rescued from an association between primal phantasies and phylogenetic explanations such as those described in *Totem or Taboo*. This primary monadic core is modified – or sublimated – with the social imaginary creation (or institution) of the subject as a social individual. But the birth of the subject is also the work of the radical imagination since the psyche has to abandon its own monadic world and, via social imaginary significations, cathect and create new social objects and meanings. Through the social-historical, these significations create a social world and shape the psyche. They create a *drive* for society and a *mood* or cluster of affects; the drive and mood instituting a Christian society is very different from that creating a classical Greek *polis*: the Christian and the Athenian individual are instituted in quite different ways.[31]

In his essay 'The State of the Subject Today' and in the wake of the many theoretical challenges (for example, deconstruction and structuralism) to the philosophy of the subject, Castoriadis draws attention to the subject's capacity for deliberate activity understood as the reflective dimension of imagination as a source of creation.[32] Reflective deliberation here refers to an ability to both challenge and alter itself and the law. While such a project of subjectivity concerns the practico-poetic task of psychoanalysis, which will always remain unfinished, it is also a social-historical project and one which has emerged twice with different modalities in Greece and Western Europe. Castoriadis does not mythologise and romanticise the Greek *polis* as some of his critics have suggested. He draws attention to the qualities of *parrhesia* (speaking one's mind, publicly) and *isegoria* (an equal right to this act of free speech) in ways that recall the writings of the late Foucault on the hermeneutics of the subject. But he also notes on several occasions the restrictive conditions and exclusions that appear *necessary* to the form of the Greek *polis*. Like Arendt too, with whom his thought has certain affinities, and upon whom he often draws in these discussions regarding the public space of democracy, the Greeks must be viewed as a kind of *germ* since they never stopped asking the question: what is it that the institutions of society ought to achieve?[33]

Castoriadis supplements this germ of autonomy by also arguing that one cannot will autonomy without willing it for all. Politics is, then, the *collective* project of autonomy. In this way, Castoriadis's political thought elicits conceptions of social equality and social justice in forms compatible with Marxist views. Nonetheless, democracy is a self-limiting political system without presupposition which can rely on no foundational or extrasocial guarantee outside its own laws (there is a metacontingency of meaning, and democracy is the domain of political reflexivity *par excellence*). Democracy is, therefore, a fundamentally *tragic* political regime. Castoriadis often refers to the centrality of the agonistic element in Greek life, and in his later essays explored this through the Greek poets.[34] This tragic element is connected both to human mortality and to the contingency of foundations: nothing is given once and for all, and the history of the Greco-Western world is the history of the perpetual struggle between heteronomy and autonomy. Thus he writes:

> Democracy is the sole regime that *takes risks*, that faces openly the possibility of its self-destruction . . . [T]his amounts to saying that democracy thrusts aside the sacred, or that – and this is the same thing – human beings finally accept what they have never, until now, truly wanted to accept: that they are mortal, that nothing lies 'beyond'.[35]

This view of politics, and the ontology accompanying it, puts Castoriadis's thought up against a common series of problems that we find in other thinkers too, notably Arendt and Badiou. Castoriadis's unswerving attention to the genesis of creation in imagination, Arendt's conception of natality as the capacity of beginning something anew and Badiou's evanescent event as the chance-like invention that breaks with the prevailing state of affairs, each recognises the abyssal or ungrounded nature of inaugural emergence, and the sense in which creation might also entail destruction as part of this emergence. Viewed in the context of a democratic structure called for by Castoriadis, it is unsurprising that critics such as Habermas and Honneth worry about the political risks of metacontingency, and of how one may arrive at claims of validity and justification for emerging political forms. Of interest in this context is the dialogue established between Castoriadis's more flexible and multifaceted concept of autonomy and theories of deliberative democracy by Andrea Kalyvas.[36]

Conclusion: Charting the Labyrinth of Thought

In comparison with that of his contemporaries in French philosophy, Castoriadis's thought remains somewhat under-explored. Many areas of debate remain uncharted and lines of engagement with his thought undeveloped. Certainly, Castoriadis responds, as we have seen above, to many of the dominant questions of his and our time. At times utopian, his vision offers a refreshing antidote to both the more determinist accounts of politics and state offered by some Marxist positions, and the ultimately liberal postmodern celebrations of difference. His reconceptualisation of the subject brings a novel approach to ontological questions, underscoring the ways in which these are also inescapably political in content and form.

In the Introduction to *Crossroads in the Labyrinth* Castoriadis writes that to think 'is to make be and appear a Labyrinth . . . where things are no longer simply juxtaposed . . . and we no longer know whether there is a centre, what the centre is'.[37] But it is also to take up a position against some background or figure, 'to tear apart the given horizon' and 'to shake up the perceptual institution of the world and society'.[38] In this sense creation is not *in nihilo* but *ex nihilo*; it takes place *against* the constraints of a given world.[39] It is therefore important to consider the ontology of creation and radical imagination developed by Castoriadis in his many writings as a profound challenge to the political present. This occludes the existence of creation and hence threatens the radical imagination with extinction. By redeploying the category of the subject as imagination and deliberative reflection, Castoriadis sought not to return us to a form of existentialism or political idealism but to reinvigorate a radical politics. Positions that allude, in various ways, to the world-disclosing power of imagination or some original presence of the subject to itself tend, unfortunately, to foreclose the political force of the undecidability and radical heterogeneity of imagination in its two key modalities.

Notes

1. See Castoriadis, *Political and Social Writings*, 3 vols.
2. See Castoriadis, *Imaginary Institution*, Part 1.
3. See Axel Honneth, 'Symposium on Castoriadis', *Radical Philosophy*, 90, 1998, pp. 2–8.
4. See Suzi Adams, 'Castoriadis' Shift towards *Physis*', *Thesis Eleven*, 74, 2003, pp. 105–12.
5. *Imaginary Institution*, p. 184. It must be noted that such a view of structuralism begs further questioning. One must surely note the thesis of overdetermination as well as Althusser's later reflections on aleatory materialism since both unravel the rigidity of structure, as Castoriadis views it. See the essays in Louis Althusser, *For Marx* (London: Verso, 1990) and *Philosophy of the Encounter: Later Writings 1978–1987* (London: Verso, 2006).
6. For elaboration, see 'The Greek *Polis* and the Creation of Democracy', in Castoriadis, *Philosophy, Politics, Autonomy*.
7. On Aristotle and Kant, see 'The Discovery of Imagination', in Castoriadis, *World in Fragments*; 'Radical Imagination and the Social Instituting Imaginary', in *The Castoriadis Reader*.

8. For Spinoza on imagination, see G. Lloyd and M. Gatens, *Collective Imaginings: Spinoza, Past and Present* (London: Routledge, 1999); C. Williams, 'Thinking the Political in the Wake of Spinoza: Power, Affect and Imagination in the *Ethics*', *Contemporary Political Theory*, 6, 2007, pp. 349–69.
9. Castoriadis, *World in Fragments*, p. 245.
10. Castoriadis, *Imaginary Institution*, p. 330.
11. Ibid. p. 331.
12. See Jürgen Habermas, *The Philosophical Discourse of Modernity*, trans. F. Lawrence (Cambridge: Polity Press, 1987), p. 332.
13. Castoriadis, *Philosophy, Politics, Autonomy*, p. 145.
14. Castoriadis, *Imaginary Institution*, p. 231.
15. Habermas, *Philosophical Discourse*, p. 333.
16. For an excellent discussion, see 'Modern Science and Philosophical Interrogation', in Castoriadis, *Crossroads*.
17. Castoriadis, *World in Fragments*, p. 353.
18. Castoriadis, *Imaginary Institution*, p. 112.
19. See Humberto Maturana and Francisco Varela, *Autopoiesis and Cognition: The Realization of the Living* (Dordrecht: D. Reidel, 1973). Their work has also been a great stimulus for discussions around the creativity of science in Bergson, Deleuze and DeLanda, among others.
20. See in this context the book by contemporary cognitive scientist Douglas Hofstadter, *I Am a Strange Loop* (New York: Basic Books, 2007).
21. See 'Logic of Magmas', in *The Castoriadis Reader*, pp. 308–10; '*Physis* and Autonomy', in Castoriadis, *World in Fragments*, p. 337.
22. 'Logic of Magmas', p. 310.
23. Castoriadis, *World in Fragments*, p. 332.
24. Castoriadis, *Crossroads*, p. 22.
25. Castoriadis, *Imaginary Institution*, p. 291.
26. Maurice Merleau-Ponty, *The Visible and the Invisible*, trans. A. Lingis (Evanston: Northwestern University Press, 1968). For Castoriadis's discussion, see *Crossroads*, pp. 329–39.
27. See Yannis Stavrakakis, *The Lacanian Left* (Edinburgh: Edinburgh University Press, 2007), Chapter 1; Slavoj Žižek, *The Ticklish Subject* (London: Verso, 1999), p. 24.
28. Castoriadis, *Imaginary Institution*, pp. 300–1.
29. Castoriadis, *World in Fragments*, p. 283.
30. Ibid. p. 254.
31. See Castoriadis, *Imaginary Institution*, pp. 332–7.
32. Castoriadis, *World in Fragments*, p. 160.
33. Castoriadis, *Philosophy, Politics, Autonomy*, p. 123. For a comparison of Castoriadis and Arendt, see Linda Zerilli, 'Castoriadis, Arendt and the Problem of the New', *Constellations*, 9, 2002, pp. 540–53.

34. See the essays under '*Poiesis*' in *Figures of the Thinkable*.
35. *The Castoriadis Reader*, p. 316.
36. See Kalyvas's 'Norm and Critique in Castoriadis' Theory of Autonomy', *Constellations*, 5, 1998, pp. 161–82, and 'The Politics of Autonomy and the Challenge to Deliberation: Castoriadis Contra Habermas', *Thesis Eleven*, 64, 2001, pp. 1–19.
37. Castoriadis, *Crossroads*, pp. ix–x.
38. Ibid. p. xxv.
39. See *Castoriadis Reader*, pp. 332–6 for Castoriadis's account of these myriad constraints. This aspect of the text also represents an indirect response to some critics.

Major Works by Castoriadis (in English)

The Castoriadis Reader (Oxford; Cambridge, MA: Blackwell, 1997).

Crossroads in the Labyrinth, trans. M. Ryle and K. Soper (Brighton: Harvester and Cambridge, MA: MIT, 1984 [1978]).

Figures of the Thinkable, trans. H. Arnold (Stanford, CA: Stanford University Press, 2007).

The Imaginary Institution of Society, trans. K. Blamey (Oxford: Polity; Cambridge, MA: MIT, 1987 [1975]).

On Plato's 'Statesman', trans. D. Curtis (Stanford, CA: Stanford University Press, 2002).

Philosophy, Politics, Autonomy, ed. D. Curtis (New York and Oxford: Oxford University Press, 1991).

Political and Social Writings, Volumes 1 and 2 (Minneapolis: University of Minnesota Press, 1988).

Political and Social Writings, Volume 3 (Minneapolis: University of Minnesota Press, 1993).

World in Fragments, trans. D. Curtis (Stanford, CA: Stanford University Press, 1997).

Suggestions for Further Reading

Adams, Suzi, 'Castoriadis and Autopoiesis', *Thesis Eleven*, 88, 2007, pp. 76–91. This discussion considers the idea of *auto-poiesis* and its relation to the project of autonomy.

Busino, B. (ed.), *Autonomie et autotransformation de la société: la philosophie militante de Cornelius Castoriadis* (Genève: Droz, 1989). This is a multilingual *Festschrift* for Castoriadis and contains a valuable range of critical perspectives on his work (including the pieces by Honneth and Habermas mentioned in this chapter). Castoriadis responds in 'Done and to Be Done', in *The Castoriadis Reader*.

108

Ciaramelli, Fabio, 'Castoriadis', in S. Critchley and W. R. Schroeder (eds), *A Companion to Continental Philosophy* (Oxford: Blackwell, 1999). A nuanced introduction to the thinker.

Klooger, Jeff, *Castoriadis: Psyche, Society, Autonomy* (Leiden and Boston: Brill, 2009). A monograph offering an accessible and uptodate overview of Castoriadis's theory, with an excellent bibliography.

McNay, Lois, *Gender and Agency: Reconfiguring the Subject in Feminist and Social Theory* (Oxford: Polity Press, 2000). An interesting application of Castoriadis to feminist theory.

Thesis Eleven, 49, 1997. A helpful and wide-ranging special issue on Castoriadis, including an excellent piece by Fabio Ciaramelli, 'The Self-Presupposition of the Origin: Homage to Castoriadis', pp. 45–67.

Urribarri, Fernando, 'Castoriadis: The Radical Imagination and the Post-Lacanian Unconscious', *Thesis Eleven*, 71, 2002, pp. 40–51. This article expertly negotiates the differences and relations between Castoriadis, Freud and Lacan.

7

Green Critical Theorists

David Kidner

Introduction

Although green critical theory has only developed over the past three decades, its antecedents can be traced to much earlier eras. In this chapter, I will outline only a few of the more important sources, which generally involve some sort of reaction or challenge to the increasing domination of society by technological and economic considerations, as well as protest against the narrowing of subjectivity that accompanies this domination. Various green writers have argued that rational argument is, by itself, too narrow a framework for articulating what they want to say, and that we need to draw *also* on intuition, empathy and embodied sensing. Edward O. Wilson's 'biophilia hypothesis',[1] for example, suggests that humans are innately drawn to natural entities; and John Livingston has written that rational argument 'is not only inappropriate to our subject matter but may also be destructive of it. There is no "logic" in feeling, in experiencing, in states of being. Yet these same phenomena appear to be the prerequisite for wildlife preservation'.[2] Green writing, then, like green practice, is a heartfelt activity, stemming from our embodiment as a particular sort of animal within a community of other such animals, inherently challenging the split between body and mind which has often been the assumed basis of philosophies since Descartes.

So the conservation of wilderness, for example, is not merely a calculated policy advocated for climatic reasons or to protect 'useful' plants such as the rosy periwinkle. For Edward Abbey

– whose books express the green critical spirit as well as anyone – wilderness cannot be defined simply as 'a minimum of not less than 5000 contiguous acres of roadless area'. Rather,

> the word suggests the past and the unknown, the womb of earth from which we all emerged. It means something lost and something still present, something remote and at the same time intimate, something buried in our blood and nerves, something beyond us and without limit . . . The romantic view, while not the whole of truth, is a necessary part of the whole truth.[3]

Around a century after Descartes had dismissed feelings and intuitions as untrustworthy,[4] defining humanity through our *thinking* powers, La Mettrie was suggesting the view of 'man as a machine';[5] and the notion that the world itself could be understood – and controlled – scientifically was rapidly gathering pace, setting the scene for the current subordination of the natural world through the production and trade of commodities. In contrast, the conception of nature as inherently organised and intrinsically valuable was enthusiastically advocated by the Romantics. But whereas much post-Kantian philosophy – including that of the German romantic philosopher-scientists of the eighteenth and nineteenth centuries – reacted to the scientifically-informed commercial takeover of nature by retreating into a rarified idealist realm, green theory has typically chosen to confront this takeover more directly by arguing that acquiescence to existing political and economic power implies the abandonment of a world that is wild, intrinsically valuable, often beautiful and structured in ways that are beyond our cognitive comprehension.

Green critical theory has developed somewhat apart from mainstream critical theory, which, even if it is critical of 'rationality', nevertheless tends to be more heavily invested in thought and more human centred ('anthropocentric'). Green theorists are generally critical realists, meaning that they view the natural world as existing independently of how we think about it, so that we do not *construct* it so much as *discover* it by using the senses. Much post-Kantian idealist philosophy views the world essentially as an outgrowth of the mind – a viewpoint that has enjoyed a fashionable makeover in contemporary social constructionist theory. Green theorists tend to see language and theory as inadequate but necessary tools for expressing the much greater sophistication and diversity of the natural world. For example, green theorists do not generally agree with the current fashion for describing sex as 'culturally constructed' or wilderness as 'a product of civilisation', viewing both 'internal' and 'external' nature as prior to their expression within culture or language. Deeply suspicious of the anthropocentric realm of language, discourse and the whole technologically realised fantasy of industrial society, green theorists prefer the untidy realities of the natural world, sharing D. H. Lawrence's view that 'the human race is dying. It is like a great uprooted tree, with its roots in the air. We must plant ourselves again in the universe.'[6] Likewise, Edward Abbey rejects the Platonic preference for a conceptual 'underlying reality of existence', preferring the physical immediacy of such things as

> the grasp of a child's hand in your own, the flavour of an apple, the embrace of friend or lover, the silk of a girl's thigh, the sunlight on rock and leaves, the feel of music, the bark of a tree, the abrasion of granite and sand, the plunge of clear water into a pool, the face of the wind – what else is there? What else do we need?[7]

Those of constructionist inclination often inhabit the urbanised landscapes of Europe or the portion of North America that is east of the Rockies, where it is easier to see the largely domesticated landscape as 'socially constructed'. In contrast, if one lives in the still awesome country to the west, then, as Holmes Rolston suggests, cultural influences on the scenery fade:

> put five miles in good hiking boots between yourself and the trailhead . . . and stop for lunch at a craggy overlook or beside a spring, watch the ravens soar, hear their call, turn an eye on the gathering afternoon thunderstorm; and you are not much inclined to believe that your environment is nothing but a social construction.[8]

This realist preference is a common thread which suffuses the work of each of the green theorists I discuss below.

Peter Singer and Animal Liberation

As a graduate student, Peter Singer was struck by the inconsistencies between the moral philosophies that were applied to humans and non-humans. 'Animal lovers', he relates, were happy to express their affection towards pets – but were equally happy to enjoy a ham sandwich while doing so. Humans had developed moral frameworks for the treatment of other humans; but moral considerability seemed to have reached a limit at the juncture between humans and nonhumans. In his book *Animal Liberation*, Singer exposed the hypocrisy and inconsistency of prevailing morality, arguing that the same arguments which had led to women's voting rights and the abolition of slavery also applied to nonhuman creatures. At the end of the eighteenth century, Jeremy Bentham had suggested that if a creature can suffer, then it should be treated with moral consideration, and that this applied equally to humans and non-humans.[9] Following Bentham, Singer argues that *sentience* – that is, possessing a sensory system which allows a creature to experience pain and pleasure – is the criterion which demands that we accord them the same moral consideration that we would accord another person.

Viewed from this perspective, industrial society – indeed, most societies – is built on a foundation of exploitation, moral inconsistency and denial. We unthinkingly eat our pork chops, buy toiletries that have been tested on animals and buy shoes made from animal skins, ignoring the suffering this entails and denying the continuity between our own capacities for pleasure and pain and those of other creatures. In his later work, Singer argues that during the evolution of humanity there has developed a greater capacity for altruism and empathy, and that speciesism therefore rests on the repression of these evolved characteristics.

John Rodman and the Argument for Wildness

Singer's work has been enormously influential in challenging conventional attitudes towards animals; but other types of green theory have deviated sharply from it. John Rodman's unjustly neglected paper 'The Liberation of Nature?' is of seminal importance in the critique of animal liberation and the development of alternative approaches. Rodman's first problem with Singer's approach is the latter's focus on sentient creatures and his subsequent backgrounding of other participants in the landscape such as plants, rivers or insects:

> I only need to stand in the midst of a clearcut forest, a strip-mined hillside, a defoliated jungle, or a dammed canyon to feel uneasy with . . . the conclusion that no human action can make any difference to the welfare of anything but sentient animals.[10]

An ecologist might add that, in any case, the sentient creatures are dependent on the forest, the hillside, the jungle, or the canyon, and that focusing on the welfare of isolated components of an ecosystem is unlikely to be effective. The essential context of any consideration of animal welfare, therefore, has to be the health of whole ecosystems or even of the entire biosphere. Enlarging the 'circle of moral responsibility' to include a few sentient creatures will not really address the welfare even of these creatures, and even less will it be an adequate response to the fundamental problems of the relationship between humanity – especially industrial humanity – and the rest of the natural world. As Rodman puts it, the animal liberation approach 'is not a revolution in ethics but something analogous to the Reform Bill of 1832, when the British aristocracy extended selected rights to the upper middle class'.[11] By enlarging the 'circle of moral considerability', we are not so much recognising the uniqueness of other species – and the diversity of life as a whole – as inviting a few selected species to be associate members of the human club. A danger in this approach is that the new members will necessarily appear as deficient and inferior compared to human beings, and that we fail to respect them 'for having their own existence, their own character and potentialities, their own forms of excellence, their own integrity, their own grandeur'.[12]

According to Rodman, then, the animal liberation project is based not so much on opening our eyes to the marvellous diversity of life which exists outside human societies as on a limited extension of current human ethical sensibilities towards those creatures most like ourselves – an extension which 'subtly fulfils and legitimises the basic project of modernity – the total conquest of nature by man'.[13] So the issue, according to Rodman,

> is whether contemporary philosophers accompany the advance of technological society the way missionaries once accompanied the march of conquistadors, assimilating the conquered to the culture of the conquerors and ameliorating (making more 'humane') the harshness of the yoke, or whether they criticise the process of conquest in the interest of liberation.[14]

Importantly, this points towards the conflict between our own embodied nature and the industrial system we have been colonised by; and Rodman comments that our

> domestication of nonhuman animals and our division of ourselves into a 'human' part that rules or ought to rule and a 'bestial' part that is ruled or ought to be ruled are by now so hopelessly intertwined that

it seems doubtful that we could significantly change the one without changing the other.[15]

Thus the domestication of nature, for Rodman, goes hand in hand with self-domestication and the generation of a particular sort of personality structure – and both these processes have been progressing for so many generations that 'undoing' them is not possible through any straightforward revolutionary change. Rodman agrees with Marcuse that 'revolutions fail when led by people who perpetuate in their character the authority structure of the old regime';[16] and similar problems arise in the 'liberation' of external nature:

> The buffalo herd in Stanley Kramer's film 'Bless the Beasts and Children' thunders out of the pen, released by the daring efforts of a group of heroic boys, only to stop and graze peacefully on a nearby hill, allowing themselves to be rounded up and imprisoned again. Elsa, the Adamsons' pet lioness, 'born free' and then tamed, must be laboriously trained [*sic*] to become a wild predator before she can be safely released. Of such ambiguous stories is the mythology of the human condition in the 'post-industrial' age composed.[17]

While the superficiality of such liberations are often fairly obvious, deeper and more lasting resolutions require a more profound interrogation of the ideologies that permeate industrial society, and so are more elusive. Part of the problem is the idealist 'notion that objectivity is projected upon the nonhuman world by humans',[18] so that the only *subjective* beings in the universe appear to be humans. Consequently, every nonhuman entity or creature in the natural world appears as a 'thing' or a 'natural resource', ready and waiting to be transformed by 'human intelligence' into a commodity with 'added value'. Just as cultural theorists may see meaning as given by social structures, so the industrialist sees value as *commercial* value rather than 'intrinsic value' – the value an entity has in itself regardless of its usefulness to humans.

Many social theorists, through their exclusive focus on social and cultural structures and their denial of ecological structures, as well as their focus on human subjects and their denial of the subject-ness of nonhuman creatures, collude in forms of oppression that are widespread in industrial society. In this context, perhaps the most important thing we can do is to recognise that theory that is not clearly engaged with the natural world is part of the problem rather than part of the solution, following the example of J. S. Mill, not so much the encyclopaedic philosopher whose *Logic* and *Political Economy* became standard Victorian textbooks, or even the Utilitarian who remained true to Bentham's inclusion of sentient animals within the sphere of morals and legislation, but the lesser-known mountain climber, 'botaniser', and 'lover of Nature' who indignantly protested the Royal Horticultural Society's contest for the two best herbaria collected in each county in England as an event that would make 1864 the last year that many already-rare species would exist. It was this same Mill who . . . as autobiographer, recorded for posterity the classic case study of a sensitive person trained to operate as an analytic thinking-machine who 'died' and was then 'reborn' through rediscovering the capacity for feeling, intuition, imagination, the enjoyment of poetry and natural beauty, the ability to cry and to contemplate – without losing the capacity for rational analysis or practical action.[19]

Much green writing would implicitly approve of such a 'rebirth' – one which launches us out of an intoxication with language and, especially, theory into a fully embodied participation in the world outside ourselves.

Arne Naess and 'Deep Ecology'

Much of what Rodman wrote resonates with the views of 'deep ecologists'. Deep ecology originated with Arne Naess's 1973 paper 'The Shallow and the Deep, Long-Range Ecology Movement',[20] in which he distinguishes between two types of response to ecological problems. The first, 'shallow' response deals with environmental problems such as pollution and resource depletion as isolated issues which have no wider significance, and has as its objective 'the health and affluence of people in the developed countries'.[21] It is therefore anthropocentric and is concerned with the health of the natural world only insofar as it affects our own well-being.

In contrast, the 'deep' approach advocated by Naess sees 'environmental problems' as symptoms of something much more profound – a disturbance in the entire 'biospherical net' of relations of which humans are a part. Nature is not something that can be bracketed off from human life as a separate realm with its own problems. As Alan Drengson notes, 'For Naess, free nature is critical to cultural flourishing, community health, and personal Self-realization'.[22] Like Rodman, Naess rejects the Cartesian – and today widely accepted – view of the person as a largely autonomous being defined mainly by the ability to think, and suggests that we go beyond such assumptions, asking deep questions about ourselves, the character of society and the natural world. In Naess's own words:

> The essence of deep ecology – as compared with the science of ecology, and with what I call the shallow ecological movement – is to ask deeper questions. The adjective 'deep' stresses that we ask why and how, where others do not. For instance, ecology as a science does not ask what kind of society would be the best for maintaining a particular ecosystem – that is considered a question for value theory, for politics, for ethics. As long as ecologists keep narrowly to their science, they do not ask such questions. What we need today is a tremendous expansion of ecological thinking . . . deep ecology, then, involves a shift from science to wisdom.[23]

Naess's own life was a testament to his belief that we are part of a wider 'biospherical net'. An accomplished mountain climber, even in childhood he felt a strong connection to the Norwegian landscape; and until his death at the age of 96, he still enjoyed spending time in the stone hut he built in the mountains. He was also strongly engaged in social issues and actions, once chaining himself together with other protesters to prevent the construction of a hydroelectric dam on the Alta River. There was a marked continuity and coherence between his philosophical views and the way he lived; and, in keeping with this emphasis on the relation between philosophy and lived experience, Naess was critical of the direction taken by academic philosophy and cultural theory, suggesting that 'the turn of philosophy in this century towards language rather than cosmos, towards logic rather than experience . . . is a turn into a vast blind alley'.[24] He was equally critical of postmodernism, which he regarded simply as 'the latest philosophical fad'.[25] In contrast to such approaches, which often seem to have only the most tenuous relationship with lived realities, the questions that Naess addresses are quite down to earth, although not always easy to answer:

> We need to ask question like 'Why do we think that economic growth and high levels of consumption are so important?' The conventional answer would be to point to the economic consequences of not having economic growth. But in deep ecology, we ask whether the present society fulfils basic human needs like love and security and access to nature, and in so doing, we question our society's underlying assumptions.[26]

Just as Rodman saw the destructive domestication of wild nature as inseparable from the taming of human life, so Naess rejected the commonly accepted assumptions that the 'environment' is more or less separate from each of us, and that we are autonomous, egoic individuals dominated by self-concern. Instead, Naess embraces 'Self-realisation!' – that is, a broadening and deepening of the self as we identify with other life-forms and with other features of the natural world. Naess believes that if we realise our own nature as fully as possible, we will quite naturally be concerned with the welfare of the 'biospherical net' of which we are part, recognising other creatures' right to flourish and develop in their own way – a recognition that involves both empathy and intelligence, as the title of his book *Life's Philosophy: Reason and Feeling in a Deeper World* implies.[27] Following on from this, if we achieve a degree of Self-realisation, we will naturally engage in 'beautiful actions', rather than performing these out of a sense of duty or obligation ('dutiful' actions). Unlike 'shallow' approaches, then, deep ecology does not simply take for granted the sort of self that happens to exist but identifies industrialist forms of selfhood as part of the problem, suggesting that we need to reawaken ourselves to extended forms of subjectivity which can reach out to include the ecosphere.

In keeping with his respect for diversity, as exemplified by the attitudes of his intellectual forebears Gandhi and Spinoza, Naess is remarkably undogmatic, believing that each person will develop their own understandings. While he was widely recognised as a leading philosopher, and was clear about his own philosophy (which he refers to as 'Ecosophy T'), he does not regard this as everybody's truth, preferring to recommend some general principles which can be accepted widely. Naess's approach is therefore more *inclusive* than most critical theories, drawing on points of commonality with others rather than finding reasons to reject them, and embracing thinking *and* feeling rather than leaning on one or the other in a dualistic fashion. In keeping with this, the 'deep ecology movement' is not a direct reflection of Naess's personal philosophy but has been developed by him and others such as George Sessions and Bill Devall to include generally compatible views. The basic principles of deep ecology have been summarised most recently in Naess's book *Life's Philosophy* as follows:

1. All living beings have intrinsic value.
2. The richness and diversity of life has intrinsic value.
3. Except to satisfy vital needs, humankind does not have the right to reduce this diversity and this richness.

4. It would be better for human beings if there were fewer of them, and much better for other living creatures.
5. Today the extent and nature of human interference in the various ecosystems is not sustainable, and the lack of sustainability is rising.
6. Decisive improvement requires considerable change: social, economic, technological and ideological.
7. An ideological change would essentially entail seeking a better quality of life rather than a raised standard of living.
8. Those who accept the aforementioned points are responsible for trying to contribute directly or indirectly to the realisation of the necessary changes.[28]

These basic principles, which constitute the 'deep ecology platform', aim to incorporate the wisdom Naess found in a broad range of sources, including Buddhism, Taoism, ecological science, Ghandi's teachings on nonviolence, and the philosophy of Spinoza. The platform is not intended as a set of environmental commandments which are unchallengeable, but rather as a vehicle for bringing together people from different backgrounds, nationalities and religious preferences so that they can jointly work towards a healthier and less destructive way of living. For example, what constitutes a 'vital' need (number 3) will vary from culture to culture, so that hunting might be essential to survival in one society, but not in the industrialised world. Similarly, there will also be a good deal of diversity in the particular contributions to change that each of us are able to make, depending on our circumstances. Generally, then, the deep ecology platform is not intended prescriptively but rather as a guide and an invitation to enhance the welfare of all members of the biosphere, including humans.

Ecofeminism

Ecofeminists see links between the patriarchal domination of women and the patriarchal domination of the natural world, and so explore the common cultural factors in these forms of domination. This general insight has given rise to a large variety of ecofeminisms, of which I will outline some of the more prominent ones. Evidence for linkages between male exploitation of women and nature is not difficult to find. In the sixteenth century, Francis Bacon, who was both a leading populariser of the new scientific approach and Lord

Chancellor of England, saw parallels between the interrogation of 'witches' and the scientific investigation of nature:

> For you have but to follow and as it were hound nature in her wanderings, and you will be able when you like to lead and drive her afterward to the same place again. Neither am I of the opinion that . . . sorceries, witchcrafts, charms, dreams, divinations, and the like should be altogether excluded . . . a useful light may be gained, not only for a true judgement of the offenses of persons charged with such practices, but likewise for the further disclosing of the secrets of nature. Neither ought a man to make scruple of entering and penetrating into those holes and corners, when the inquisition of truth is his whole object.[29]

As Carolyn Merchant notes, Bacon's 'new man of science' must not think that the 'inquisition of nature is in any part interdicted or forbidden'. Nature must be 'bound into service' and made a 'slave', put 'in constraint' and 'moulded' by mechanical arts. Bacon also suggests that 'there are still laid up in the womb of nature many secrets of excellent use'.[30] These statements express with the utmost clarity attitudes towards both women and nature – attitudes which, ecofeminists argue, now permeate science, technology and indeed the entire structure of industrial society, albeit sometimes in more subtle forms.

A scientific perspective on nature, with some exceptions such as conservation biology, leans towards being dominant, controlling and *reductionist*. Reductionism refers to knowledge production by means of dismantling nature into its component 'bits' – for example, chemical analysis or the measurement of species' populations. Science is also largely based on *objectivity*, which eliminates personal feelings and empathy with other creatures in favour of a rational, intellectual approach. Neil Evernden gives an example from the work of the famous nineteenth-century French physiologist and vivisectionist Claude Bernard, who stated that a 'physiologist is not a man [*sic*] of fashion, he is a man of science, absorbed by the scientific idea which he pursues: he no longer hears the cry of animals, he no longer sees the blood that flows, he sees only his idea and perceives only organisms concealing problems which he intends to solve'.[31] Such 'objectivity', ecofeminists have suggested, reflects a quintessentially *masculine* understanding.[32] Whereas deep ecology sees *anthropocentrism* as the key to environmental problems, ecofeminism focuses on *androcentrism*.

These ideas provide a general background to ecofeminist

understandings; but today there is a diversity of feminist approaches, and as much disagreement between ecofeminists as there is between ecofeminists and deep ecologists. One of the main bones of contention among ecofeminists, for example, is the question of whether women have a greater degree of *embodied connection* to the earth than men – a claim that has been justified on the basis of women's capacity for menstruation, childbirth and nursing. Any such gender-based affinity for nature is something of a two-edged sword, since it could be used to justify *either* women's 'inferior' place in the home raising babies *or* their 'superior' status as privileged, ecologically-attuned 'earth mothers'.

Many ecofeminists have moved away from this notion, viewing it as reflecting 'biological essentialism' – the currently unfashionable belief that our behaviour and experience are partly determined by our innate physiology. The emphasis has shifted towards culture as 'constructing' maleness and femaleness and the relation of each of these to the natural world. For example, Val Plumwood – who was also well known for fighting off a crocodile attack in Kakadu National Park – developed the critique of dualistic cultural structures as determining attitudes towards nature and gender roles. Among the more important dualisms she identifies are:

Culture	Nature
Male	Female
Mind	Body
Reason	Matter
Rationality	Emotion
Human	Nonhuman

Such dualisms are imposed so as to exaggerate or manufacture distinctions which allow the exercise of power over the natural world. For example, as we have seen above, the sometimes slight differences in, say, sentience between humans and other creatures are exaggerated so as to allow us to view nonhuman animals as expendable experimental subjects rather than as creatures akin to ourselves. Likewise, rationality's role is to 'control' the emotions; and the female's role is associated with subservience to the 'leadership' of the male. In each case, the first member of each dualism is assumed to be superior and so fit to control the second member, forming a web of instrumental and ethical imperatives which determine attitudes, behaviour and identity. Just as women are brought up to be caring and subservient, so the argument goes, men are brought up to dominate and lead – and both men and women learn that nature is essentially mindless raw material for human requirements.

Criticisms of Green Theory

There is, of course, a great deal of debate, criticism and counter-criticism within and between the various types of green theory; but here I will focus on criticism that comes from outside green writings. As the reader will have gathered, green theory challenges some of the most sacred assumptions of industrial society – that the economy can grow indefinitely, that the natural world is an inexhaustible cornucopia of 'raw materials', that humans have a right to do what we want with the rest of the natural world. It is therefore unsurprising that green theory has drawn vituperative responses from those who have a vested interest in 'business as usual'. But putting aside those responses that are clearly ill-informed, in denial and/or funded by corporate interests, I will focus on two currents of criticism that have more substance.

First, the accusation of 'romanticism' is a well-founded one, as the reader will have gathered from my introduction. Green theorists generally believe that there is more to the world than either 'common sense' or traditional scientific explanations can accommodate, whether this 'something more' involves properties which emerge from the complexity of the natural world, or empathy with nonhuman aspects of nature, or simply an embodied intuition that cannot be ignored. But all these qualities are difficult to express scientifically, or even to express at all; and critics such as Stephen Budiansky suggest that if ecosystems have properties that are more than the sum of their parts, then 'the study of these systems should be carried out by theologians rather than scientists'.[33] Increasingly, however, science is expanding its boundaries to include exactly the sort of emergent properties dismissed by Budiansky – for example, in the work of Stuart Kauffman[34] and in the recognition of previously unrecognised forms of natural order.[35]

Greens would argue that reality is larger than either science or words – or even experience. When Aldo Leopold watched the death of a wolf he had just shot, he thought so too:

We reached the old wolf in time to watch a fierce green fire dying in her eyes. I realised then, and have known ever since, that there was something new to me in those eyes – something known only to her and to the mountain. I was young then, and full of trigger-itch; I thought that because fewer wolves meant more deer, that no wolves would mean a hunters' paradise. But after seeing the green fire die, I sensed that neither the wolf nor the mountain agreed with such a view.[36]

Related to the accusation of 'romanticism' is the claim that green theory is 'regressive', looking back over the shoulder of contemporary society towards a 'golden past' of simple, natural living.[37] Greens reply, however, that almost any challenge to industrial growth and technological advancement is defined as 'regressive', and argue that the spreading colonisation and industrialisation of the past several centuries has been enormously damaging to the natural world and to the cultures of the native peoples who inhabit it, and that we therefore need to rethink some rather basic assumptions about what we and other species require in order to flourish, or even to survive. Given the connections, recognised by all the theorists I have discussed, between ecological and social issues, it may well be that we have lost not only species, but also certain ways of thinking and experiencing – and academia all too often seems intent on colluding with these processes of loss rather than critiquing them. As Alf Hornborg sardonically remarks, the 'closely knit kinship group, locally contextualised ecological knowledge, attachment to place, reciprocity, animism: all of it is suddenly dismissed as myth . . . there emerges the new but implicit message that we have always been capitalists'.[38]

The challenge embraced by the majority of green theorists, then, is to avoid both the 'technological optimism' of assuming that scientific progress will solve all the environmental and social problems of industrial society, and the opposite impulse to reject all post-Enlightenment knowledge as irredeemably tainted. Both these extremes lie on a single, dualistic continuum marked 'progress – regression', whereas green theorists would argue that we need another *kind* of progress – one which acknowledges that we are embodied, ecologically located creatures, not simply disembodied minds. We can, in other words, be *both* thinking *and* feeling creatures who are not only intelligent enough to think rationally but also wise enough to know *when* to think rationally.

Notes

1. Steven Kellert and Edward O. Wilson (eds), *The Biophilia Hypothesis* (Washington, DC: Island Press, 1993).
2. John Livingston, quoted by Peter Hay, *A Companion to Environmental Thought*, p. 3.
3. Edward Abbey, *Desert Solitaire*, pp. 189–90.
4. René Descartes, *Meditations on First Philosophy*, trans. John Cottingham (Cambridge: Cambridge University Press, 1986 [1641]).
5. Julien de la Mettrie, *Man a Machine*, trans. Richard A. Watson (Cambridge, MA: Hackett Publishing, 1994 [1748]).
6. D. H. Lawrence, 'Apropos of Lady Chatterley's Lover', Preface to *Lady Chatterley's Lover* (London: Heinemann, 1961), p. 37.
7. Abbey, *Desert Solitaire*, p. xi.
8. Holmes Rolston III, 'Mountain Majesties above Fruited Plains: Culture, Nature, and Rocky Mountain Aesthetics', *Environmental Ethics*, 30, 1, 2008, pp. 14–15.
9. Jeremy Bentham, *Introduction to the Principles of Morals and Legislation* (Oxford: Clarendon Press, 1789).
10. John Rodman, 'The liberation of nature?', p. 89.
11. Ibid. p. 91.
12. Ibid. p. 94.
13. Ibid. p. 97.
14. Ibid. p. 98.
15. Ibid. p. 104.
16. Ibid. p. 104.
17. Ibid. p. 105.
18. Ibid. p. 108.
19. Ibid. p. 115.
20. Arne Naess, 'The Shallow and the Deep, Long-range Ecology Movements: A Summary', *Inquiry*, 16, 1973, pp. 95–100.
21. Arne Naess, 'Shallow and the Deep', p. 95.
22. Alan Drengson, 'The Life and Work of Arne Naess: An Appreciative Overview', *The Trumpeter*, 21, 1, 2005, pp. 5–43 (6).
23. Stephan Bodian, 'Simple in Means, Rich in Ends: An Interview with Arne Naess', in George Sessions (ed.), *Deep Ecology for the 21ˢᵗ Century* (Boston: Shambhala, 1995), pp. 26–36 (27).
24. Quoted by George Sessions, 'On Being Fair and Accurate towards Arne Naess', *International Society for Environmental Ethics Newsletter*, 17, 4, 2006–7, p. 20.
25. Sessions, 'On Being Fair and Accurate', p. 20.
26. Bodian, 'Simple in Means, Rich in Ends', p. 27.
27. Arne Naess, *Life's Philosophy: Reason and Feeling in a Deeper World* (Athens, GA: University of Georgia Press, 2008).

28. Ibid. pp. 108–9.
29. Merchant, *Death of Nature*, p. 168.
30. Ibid. p. 169.
31. Claude Bernard, quoted by Neil Evernden, *The Natural Alien* (Toronto: University of Toronto Press, 1985), p. 16.
32. See, for example, Vandana Shiva, *Staying Alive: Women, Ecology, and Development* (Atlantic Highlands, NJ: Zed Books, 1989); Evelyn Fox Keller, *Reflections on Gender and Science* (New Haven: Yale University Press, 1985).
33. Stephen Budiansky, *Nature's Keepers: The New Science of Nature Management* (New York: Free Press, 1995), p. 17.
34. Stuart Kauffman, *At Home in the Universe: The Search for Laws of Self-Organisation and Complexity* (New York: Oxford University Press, 1995).
35. William M. Schaffer and Mark Kot, 'Do Strange Attractors Govern Ecological Systems?' *BioScience*, 35, 6, 1985, pp. 342–50.
36. Aldo Leopold, *A Sand County Almanac*, pp. 138–9.
37. Martin W. Lewis, *Green Delusions* (Durham, NC: Duke University Press, 1994).
38. Alf Hornborg, 'Ecological Embeddedness and Personhood: Have We Always Been Capitalists?', *Anthropology Today*, 14.2, April 1998, pp. 3–5.

Major Works by Green Theorists

Leopold, Aldo, *A Sand County Almanac* (New York: Oxford University Press, 1968).
Merchant, Carolyn, *The Death of Nature: Women, Ecology, and the Scientific Revolution* (San Francisco: Harper, 1990).
Plumwood, Val, *Feminism and the Mastery of Nature* (London: Routledge, 1993).
Ponting, Clive, *A Green History of the World: The Environment and the Collapse of Great Civilisations* (New York: Vintage, 2007).
Rodman, John, 'The Liberation of Nature?', *Inquiry*, 20, 1977, pp. 83–145.
Singer, Peter, *Animal Liberation: A New Ethics for Our Treatment of Animals*, 2nd edn (London: Jonathan Cape, 1990).

Suggestions for Further Reading

Abbey, Edward, *Desert Solitaire: A Season in the Wilderness* (New York: Ballantine, 1968).
Adams, Carole, *The Sexual Politics of Meat: A Feminist-Vegetarian Critical Theory*, 2nd edn (London: Continuum, 2000).
Hay, Peter, *A Companion to Environmental Thought* (Edinburgh: Edinburgh University Press, 2002).

Nabhan, Gary P., *Cultures of Habitat: On Nature, Culture, and Story* (Washington, DC: Counterpoint, 1997).

Sessions, George (ed.), *Deep Ecology for the Twenty-First Century* (Boston: Shambhala, 1995).

Turner, Frederick, *Beyond Geography: The Western Spirit against the Wilderness* (Piscataway, NJ: Rutgers University Press, 1992).

Turner, Jack, *The Abstract Wild* (Tucson: University of Arizona Press, 1996).

8

Donna J. Haraway (1944–)

Joan Faber McAlister

Situating Knowledges in Natureculture and Technoscience

Few American scholars can match the breadth and depth of Donna Haraway's contributions to diverse branches of the humanities and social sciences over the last twenty-five years. As noted in the introduction to her Robert and Maurine Rothschild Lecture in the History of Science at Harvard University in 2002, Donna Haraway has become 'about as famous as an academic can be' by authoring key works in cultural studies, feminist theory and science studies.[1] A leading figure in posthumanism and cyberculture studies, Donna Haraway's fame is attributable to the startling originality of the theoretical concepts and critical insights her scholarship brings to important conversations about feminism, environmentalism, science and technology. These concepts and insights have enriched the work of sociologists, literary critics, anthropologists, geographers, primatologists, biologists and scholars in many other disciplines. That Haraway's writing performs a careful engagement with recent philosophy, theory and method and evidences a deep commitment to addressing asymmetrical power relations has added to her substantial appeal.

Donna Jeanne Haraway was born in Denver, Colorado, in 1944 and studied zoology, English and philosophy as an undergraduate before earning her PhD in biology at Yale University in 1972. Although Haraway taught at the University of Hawaii, worked at Johns Hopkins University and currently holds an appointment at the European Graduate School in Saas-Fee, Switzerland, most of her career has been conducted from the University of California, Santa Cruz, where she is Professor of the History of Consciousness and Feminist Studies. In her writing, Haraway often explicitly addresses key elements of her biography that have shaped her scholarship, crediting the Cold War-era Space Race with her access to (co)-education, tracing her love of wordplay to her journalist father and linking her affinity with queer politics to her own intimate networks of kinship and affection. In addition, Haraway carefully considers how social categories pertaining to race, gender, class, age, religion, citizenship and sexuality position her as a subject in the twentieth and early twenty-first centuries in the United States, a time and place immersed in discourses of war and of global capital.

Indeed, situating knowledge production in cultural and histori-cal contexts is a central principle guiding Haraway's writing, which gives the lie to claims of scientific detachment and challenges pre-tences of philosophical abstraction by identifying the ideological and political investments inherent in scholarship. In other words, Haraway exposes how knowledge is produced from particular positions that are always embodied, never 'innocent', and must be seen as part of a complex web of power relations. By pointing out how categorical truths depend on the categories that generate them, Haraway consistently challenges basic assumptions guiding research and cultural practice. Moreover, Haraway locates research *as* cultural practice by illustrating how such factors as perspective, narrative and metaphor shape the observations and arguments of the scientist, philosopher or other arbiter of contemporary knowl-edge. That Haraway's own work is never exempted from such scru-tiny is apparent in the way she consistently marks her own position within intersecting discourses of race, gender, religion, sexuality, nationality and class, even as she confronts and seeks to rewrite the rhetorics and politics of these cultural texts.

Haraway's commitment to locating and critically examining where and how authoritative knowledges are produced makes her scholarship particularly relevant to the discipline of science studies and to debates concerning epistemology. The position Haraway takes up in science studies is a cautious one that would be better described as a careful encounter than a frontal assault. Committed to marking what might be called the rhetorical character of sci-entific discourse – that it is produced through 'negotiation, stra-tegic moves, inscription, translation' – Haraway still views science as a set of real practices and affective experiences that produce 'world-changing' truths.[2] For this reason, she resists adopting social constructionism as the sole basis for critiques of science. For Haraway, identifying scientific knowledges as socially constructed might be the opening of a very specific critique of the implications and investments of a particular set of texts and practices, but it is certainly not enough. Simply pointing to the cultural and historical character of science leaves important questions unanswered, and this introductory move should never operate to exempt critics from locating *themselves* as subjects with ideological and political interests. In Haraway's estimation, the label 'socially constructed' can function as an *ad hominem* attack rather than a careful and critical engagement with scientific discourse, and when terms like 'constructionism' become too established they are no longer 'doing the work' of substantive inquiry.[3]

So, although Haraway wants to complicate the discourse of science by scrutinising how it is produced and shaped, she does so with an eye toward improving the (necessarily partial and certainly cultural) stories that researchers tell. For Haraway, science's facts and fictions, when carefully crafted, are worth knowing. Approaching scientific research as simultaneously material and semiotic, a 'mode of interacting with the world that is relentlessly historically specific', can help avoid tendencies to either enshrine or to discard the knowledge science offers.[4] Such an approach always foregrounds the embodied and linguistic practices of researchers, as limited and inflected and valuable nonetheless. Science studies in her view, then, should concern 'the behavioral ecology and optimal foraging strategies of scientists and their subjects'.[5]

Haraway's own work closely examines how researchers bring their cultural practices into contact with the natural objects they observe (and produce as such) in 'naturecultures', defined as the 'implosions of the discursive realms of nature and culture'.[6] Thus, in viewing science as a set of socially constructed and nature-constructing practices, Haraway complicates (rather than rejects) scientific knowledge, calling for 'politics and epistemologies of location, positioning, and situating, where partiality and not universality is the condition of being heard to make rational knowledge claims' and scientific observation is produced through a 'view from a body, always a complex, contradictory, structuring and structured body, versus the view from above, from nowhere, from simplicity'.[7]

It is from within this political and epistemological orientation that Haraway seeks to forward a 'deeper, broader, and more open scientific literacy' by investigating the dangers and gifts of the interfaces between technology and science in the literal and virtual (hyper)reality of life at the turn of the twenty-first century.[8] Haraway's work illustrates how technoscientific knowledges are linked to new forms of war-making, global capitalism, environmental destruction and worldwide media saturation, and calls attention to the national, racial, gender and class violences inherent in these operations. However, she also considers the capacity of 'technoscientific democracy' to draw attention to inequalities and forward social justice, and finds encouraging signs that this mode of politics can be/is being built.[9]

Refiguring Kinships

In many ways, Haraway is a theorist of relations, examining the interplay between concepts and categories previously treated as distinct. She has an uncanny ability to blur established boundaries (between object and subject, animal and human, nature and culture, body and mind, flesh and machine), always attending to the co-constitutive relationships obtaining between each conceptual category and its 'other'. In Haraway's analysis, the exclusions constituting (post)modern Western Man, 'gods, machines, animals, monsters, creepy crawlies, women, servants and slaves, and noncitizens in general', may be kept 'outside the security checkpoint of bright reason' but they nevertheless have the capacity to inspire terror in 'centers of power and self-certainty'.[10] It is fair to say that much of Haraway's scholarship works to amplify these fears in the interest of eroding the certainties undergirding patterns of social privilege.

In addition to a penchant for making use of new composite words (such as 'natureculture', 'technoscience' and 'material-semiotic') to capture the complex relations between oppositional terms, Haraway has a talent for illustrating particular historical and cultural junctures wherein dualisms dissolve into emergent figures that trouble established subjectivities: machine and woman become 'cyborg' in Cold War America, biotechnology and scientist become 'vampire' in the racialised discourses surrounding the genome project, and dog and human become 'companion species' in twenty-first-century agility sports. Each new figure points to hazards while also opening up new possibilities. Although cyborgs are plugged into military-industrial capital, they offer an escape from traditional markers of gender. If vampires are narrative characters appealing to deeply racist, sexist and homophobic anxieties, they also awaken unnatural impulses latent in naturalised culture. And, despite the history of violent and exploitative practices that burdens dog–human relations, they can bring bodily pleasures that unsettle humanist hierarchies as well as heteronormative conceptions of intimacy.

Haraway's tendency to rethink binaries as relations places her in the company of deconstructionists, and her later work does engage the writing of Jacques Derrida. Haraway's gestures to Derrida are measured and critical, however, as is the case with Michel Foucault and Karl Marx, who figure much more prominently in her writing and clearly inform her thought. Haraway shares Derrida's focus on textual complexity and irreducible difference, Foucault's careful attention to historical archives in tracing the emergence of new terms, subjects and institutions, and Marx's concern with material relations, commodity forms and political allegiances. However, the unique character of Haraway's own analysis, as well as her close affinities with feminist, postcolonial and anti-racist studies, mediates her use of concepts or methods drawn from any of these theorists. Such departures lead Haraway to charge Derrida with failing to theorise (or even fulfil) the duties of companion species,[11] to declare that 'Foucault's biopolitics is a flaccid premonition of cyborg politics',[12] and to reject key ontological, rational and teleological elements of Marx's thought, introducing the terms gender (and race) into the Marxist lexicon and calling attention to the 'commingled histories of Marxism and of imperialism'.[13]

Haraway's careful and copious reading practices are evident in the way that she draws on a wide array of scientific research, cultural studies, philosophical treatises, psychoanalytic feminism, literary criticism, critical race theory, feminist scholarship and post-colonial analyses in her own writing. In addition to conversing with key theorists and researchers, Haraway also generously cites the work of her former students, other junior scholars and even community activists (both published and unpublished), explicitly crediting all of these writers with shaping her thought as her work intersects with theirs. In so doing, Haraway performs both her political commitment to breaking down established status systems and her theoretical commitment to 'becoming with' – thinking subjectivity and agency through companions that merge to become new figures together.

The figure is a central concept in Haraway's writing, and figuration is her signature method. For Haraway, figures are both semiotic and material: they are narrative embellishments as well as lived embodiments. As Haraway explains, figures, or tropes, 'turn' away from the literal/factual/normative script, offering a 'way of swerving around a death-defying and death-worshipping culture bent on total war, in order to re-member – in material-semiotic reality – the fragile, mortal, and juicy beings we really are'.[14] Haraway argues that the tropological character of many words is lost when they become linguistically (and ideologically) sedimented. However, 'the tropic quality of any word can erupt to enliven things for even the most literal minded . . . words trip us, make us swerve, turn us around'.[15]

Each new figure Haraway offers (cyborg, coyote, vampire, companion species) works to theorise complex relations in ways that capture both the problems and possibilities inherent in them. By inhabiting the tensions between concepts or terms, Haraway's work opens up new spaces for critique and imagination. For example, the cyborg figure rethinks the organism–machine opposition as an intimate relation, one that becomes the basis for a (subtle) critique of Cold War defence policies and a (direct) condemnation of the kind of feminism that relies on a 'natural' and 'essential' concept of Woman or 'women's experience'. The cyborg, then, also becomes a way to re-imagine a socialist and feminist politics that can exploit new technology and move beyond essentialist conceptions of gender, embracing the messy complexity of diverse, impure and shifting subjectivities. Such a politics is consistent with Haraway's 'gender-in-the-making', which rejects the notion that gender can be 'a performed category of beings or a possession that one can have', and redefines it as 'the relation between variously constituted categories of men and women (and variously arrayed tropes), differentiated by nation, generation, class, lineage, color and much else'.[16] In passages that are widely cited, she claims that the hybridity of the cyborg 'is our ontology; it gives us our politics' and declares she 'would rather be a cyborg than a goddess'.[17]

Although Haraway's cyborg is her best-known figure, it is only one in a 'whole kinship system of figurations' for critical thinking.[18] The coyote is another, one that she employs to assist in 'revisioning the world as coding trickster with whom we must learn to converse' rather than becoming cynical or hopeless in the face of postmodern technology. The coyote as trickster also illustrates Haraway's effort to think of bodies as realist fictions that are simultaneously natural and ideological, material and semiotic.[19] Her coyote figuration is particularly important for the type of 'feminist objectivity' she wants to promote as an alternative to the either/or dichotomy in which both realist defenders and relativist critics of science seem caught. By refiguring the world as 'witty agent', Haraway encourages an approach that 'makes room for surprises and ironies at the heart of all knowledge production', acknowledging that, instead of controlling the world, researchers 'just live here and try to strike up non-innocent conversations by means of our prosthetic devices', hopefully producing better stories about their objects/subjects of study in the process.[20]

In characterising her particular use of the coyote figuration, Haraway performs her commitment to situate herself in discourses of class, race and gender without becoming fixed or defined by such locations in ways that would block the critical work she is doing. Noting that her own effort to apply the coyote is in keeping with a 'middle-class, white feminist appropriation', that exhibits a 'rather colonial' attitude toward Native American religions,[21] Haraway maintains that figures can exceed their origins to operate in unexpected and unplanned ways. Figures exert their own agency, escaping efforts to fix their meaning, and it is this refiguration that Haraway finds useful. Positing the coyote as a trickster suggests that the world may operate in ways that humans cannot predict or control and requires rethinking it as a figure between subject and object, culture and nature, something *other* than a romanticised Gaia or raw resource for global capitalism.[22]

If Haraway's coyote figuration hints at her attention to issues of race in her feminist critique of technoscience, her use of the vampire makes such concerns explicit. By using a figure that both contaminates and feeds off humanity to examine the 'vectors of infection that trouble racial categories in twentieth century bio-scientific constructions of universal humanity', Haraway is able to point to both the obsession with racial purity and the history of racial violence that studies of genealogy and blood inherit.[23] Vampires, those fascinating villains that walk between death and life, both killing and reanimating those they touch, provide a means for thinking about the perverse appeal of racial (im)purity.

The newcomer to Haraway's kinship of figures is companion species, although it is also a larger category under which cyborgs, coyotes and vampires might fall. Like all of her other figures, companion species merge previously distinct and oppositional categories, such as 'human and non-human' and 'nature and culture', while carefully attending to the particular historical conditions in and through which such unions take place.[24] Companionate figures are formed through an active engagement, an interrelation to which both species make distinct contributions and are transformed in the process. As Haraway explains through her examination of dog–human relations, companion species involve 'human and nonhuman animals' intermingling and 'becoming with' each other, as they are 'messmates at table, eating together, whether we know how to eat well or not'.[25] Such relations are complex, challenging, and both life and world changing.

As a method, figuration operates at a conceptual level through cultural analysis that generates new figures for re-envisioning the corporeal and symbolic relations at work in embodied subjectivity, but it is also performed in language practices that tend toward the tropological. Shot through with metaphors, oxymoronic neologisms and ironies, Haraway texts productively turn cultural narratives in ways that destabilise dualisms and then refuse to resolve the resulting tensions with a coherent unified synthesis. As scholars note, her writing style evidences a 'strong feminist commitment to the ethics and material consequences of playing with metaphor to reimagine life itself'.[26] Many of Haraway's metaphors are drawn from biology and, conversely, she illustrates how biology draws on metaphor in her analysis of the linguistic formations biologists use in their research.[27] In addition, aesthetic features of her writing subtly probe at sacred cultural taboos (examples include analogies of infection and defilement in genetic science and erotic imagery in human–dog relations), keeping readers off-balance in ways that facilitate uncertainty and promote critical inquiry.

Kinship is another important concept in Haraway's thought, one that operates in at least three important ways: (1) as a tool for analysing patterns of cultural logic; (2) as a means of theorising relations without dissolving differences; and (3) as a vehicle for imagining new networks of affinity and affection. In *Modest_ Witness@Second_Millennium*, Haraway employs the notion of kinship to create a chart elaborating on how three 'key objects of knowledge: race, population, and genome' have shaped 'biological discourse about human unity and diversity' in American cultures of affluence during specific historical periods.[28] That the eleven-page chart includes artifacts ranging from genetic databases to clothing advertisements and includes drug testing as well as ecotourism gives some sense of the breadth and detail characterising her cultural analysis. Overall, Haraway illustrates how kin and kinship have been constituted through blood ties that have a bloody history, including such practices as slavery, eugenics and reproductive technology, in order to show how 'race is a fracturing trauma in the body politic of the nation – and in the mortal bodies of its people'.[29]

When using kinship as a way of conceptualising non-identical relations, Haraway applies it to depict linkages that do not absorb their constituents into a unified whole. Indeed, the prospect that 'human beings might encounter difference in ways that do not seek to incorporate, tame, resource, or annihilate it' has been called a persistent concern in her scholarship.[30] The figuration of companion species helps to capture the view of kinship Haraway is after. When analysing the 'webbed bio-social-technical apparatuses of humans, animals, artifacts, and institutions' caught up in the companion species relation between dogs and humans, Haraway attends to the 'thick and dynamic particularities of relationships-in-progress'.[31] While her affective investment in how dog-and-human are becoming-subject together is evident, she resists the temptation to imagine either component as capable of outrunning the very different (and violently unequal) histories attached to each. Despite her own intimate (and loving) relation to the dog Cayenne Pepper as they 'make each other up, in the flesh', she recognises that a radical alterity makes them 'significantly other to each other'.[32] Theorising kinship offers her a way to dispel a fantasy played out in both 'science fiction and fictions of science', as exemplified by 'evolutionary biology's bottom line on difference': that it impedes collaboration and can hasten extinction.[33] For Haraway, difference is the lifeblood and challenge of companionate relations.

Establishing new patterns of kinship is also an important political principle for Haraway, not only because she prefers coalition-building to identity as a basis for action but also because she is invested in interrupting conventional narratives structuring familial relations along the familiar paths of gender- and heteronormativity. Her own networks of kin extend to queer intimacies that locate love and commitment outside the boundaries of reproduction, in places wherein sexual (and species) identity are less relevant than the obligations that cohabiting companions have to one another.

Affinities and Differences

In her scholarship, Haraway inhabits a series of paradoxical positions, embracing their internal tensions to establish new perspectives that avoid problematic assumptions and open up new possibilities. As a scientist who exposes particular fantasies of (pure) rationality and (disembodied) objectivity and articulates a political agenda for research, an environmentalist who finds radical potential in new technology, and a feminist who rejects the essentialist and racist strands underwriting a politics of 'sisterhood', Haraway's approach to conventional topics is anything but conventional. A brief overview of her critiques of primatology, feminism, capitalism, humanism and environmentalism helps to sketch some of the unique stances she assumes.

Haraway's critique of primatology brings to light how researchers project cultural narratives (starring white Western male heroes) onto their subjects to produce particular conclusions about what is 'natural' in reproduction and survival strategies. Arguing that such an approach (re)produces hierarchies of gender, race and sexuality, she also points out how primatologist's preoccupation with acts of sex and violence causes them to overlook less dramatic (but more efficient) practices that may not fit the narrative logic at work in the literature of the field, but do help populations to flourish.[34] That Haraway wants to recover and highlight important research by feminist primatologists that runs counter to traditional narratives, rather than to dismiss all scientific knowledge as ideological, indicates that her critiques are precise interventions rather than indiscriminate attacks on entire branches of science. It is also worth noting that the feminist contributions to primatology that she admires do not simply replace masculine accounts of reproduction and survival with feminine versions relying on broad assumptions about inherently female characteristics and experiences. Eschewing such gynocentric correctives is consistent with her critique of (white, affluent US) feminism.

Both a famous feminist scholar and the author of texts that are sharply critical of some central tenets of feminist theory and politics, Haraway has made some important contributions to conversations about sex and gender. Deeply informed by feminist scholarship and animated by feminist political aims, she argues that both have often made investments in essentialism and identity politics that undermine hopes for radical change. For example, her appraisal of the approach that popular US feminist and legal scholar Catharine McKinnon takes to activism is that it produces 'a theory of experience, of woman's identity, that is a kind of apocalypse for all revolutionary standpoints' in that it 'does not so much marginalize as obliterate the authority of any other woman's political speech and action'.[35] Regarding the price of unity in the women's movement (a universal figure of Woman with essential and natural defining characteristics) to be too high, Haraway declares that any 'adequate feminist theory of gender must *simultaneously* be a theory of racial and sexual difference in specific historical conditions of production and reproduction'.[36]

Heavily influenced by (and in conversation with) Marxian thought, Haraway's analysis of late capitalism is inflected through her attention to its role in forwarding 'neo-imperialism and the technocratic actualization of masculinist nuclear fantasies'.[37] Owing to her commitment to address multiple vectors of difference and her appreciation for post-structuralist theory and postmodern cultural studies, her work tends to confront the modernist subject at the centre of Marx's historical narrative. Calling cyborgs the 'illegitimate offspring of militarism and patriarchal capitalism' (as well as 'state socialism'), Haraway asserts that 'illegitimate offspring are often exceedingly unfaithful to their origins' since 'their fathers are, after all, inessential'.[38] Such an analysis can point to both the problems and possibilities within late capitalist formations, while reworking Marxist thought through the thematic of difference to expose the 'pre-eminently Western self' at the heart of 'Marxian humanism'.[39]

The challenges that difference poses to unifying theories of subjectivity also factor into Haraway's critique of humanism. Although uncomfortable with the transcendence implied in the term 'posthumanism', she is committed to decentring the modernist liberal subject that stars in humanist narratives by attacking the Eurocentric and masculinist biases woven throughout these texts. Resisting the temptation to dream of a unifying human condition between (or even *within*) subjects, she instead insists on the radical difference of the 'I and we that is/are never identical to itself, and so has hope of connection to others'.[40] Hence, connections are not enabled through stable identity categories of being but through ongoing and shared practices of becoming. Condensing the 'spiritual and political meaning of poststructuralism and postmodernism' into the insight that 'nobody is self-made, least of all man', she explores new ways of thinking humans in relation to organisms, technologies and environments.[41] In so doing, she refuses to reconstruct humanism's inviolable boundaries between subject and object, culture and nature. In her recent work on companion species, Haraway depicts 'human exceptionalism' and the 'humanist doctrine that holds only humans to be true subjects with real histories',[42] in a light that renders humanism akin to other forms of bigotry, such as sexism and racism.

Haraway's rejection of the species bias implied in humanism suggests an affinity with some strains in environmentalism, yet she is also a critic of that movement's technophobic tendencies and fondness for romantic (humanist and sexist) narratives of nature, the organic body and Mother Earth. In the essay entitled 'Otherworldly Conversations; Terran Topics; Local Terms', she objects to common views of nature:

> [N]ature is not just a physical place to which one can go, nor a treasure to fence in or bank, nor an essence to be saved or violated. Nature is not hidden and so does not need to be unveiled. Nature is not a text to be read in the codes of mathematics and biomedicine. It is not the Other who offers origin, replenishment, and service. Neither mother, nurse, lover, nor slave, nature is not matrix, resource, mirror, nor tool for the reproduction of that odd, ethnocentric, phallogocentric, putatively universal being called Man. Nor for his euphemistically named surrogate, the 'human'.[43]

Counter to such views, Haraway reminds us that nature is both *topos* and *tropos*, a common topic that performs important rhetorical functions in public discourse, as well as a figure for altering the human environmental relations that discourse constructs by re-envisioning them as co-constitutive operations within naturecultures.

Critics and Allies

It is not surprising that controversy follows on the heels of Haraway's scholarship, as the unique critical positions she creates make for only partial and uneasy alliances. Cultural critics willing to abandon terms such as science, objectivity, rationality and truth as hopelessly polluted by modernist (and masculinist) ideology may be dismayed by her commitment to rescue such principles by demanding 'accountability and responsibility' from researchers and locating their practices of knowledge production in specific times and places.[44] Her work has even been the occasion for vicious attacks on her politics and on her person. Haraway herself acknowledges that some feminist scholars have read her Cyborg Manifesto as the 'ramblings of a blissed-out, technobunny, fembot',[45] and recounts how environmental activists who objected to the 'organic-technological hybrids' she describes symbolically 'raped' her in literature they distributed at one of her lectures.[46] Animal-rights advocates, whom Haraway charges with depicting animals as 'permanent dependents ("lesser humans"), utterly natural ("nonhuman"), or exactly the same ("humans in fur suits")',[47] have called her work 'extremely disturbing' and 'dismissive' in its treatment of the principles guiding feminist vegetarianism.[48]

Haraway cites her use of subtle irony when making observations about features of late capitalism, imperialism and patriarchal culture as one possible reason that some see her as a foe rather than an ally. A more generous reading of her work, one that takes into account both stylistic elements and nuanced political views, can appreciate how her texts appeal to audiences that may be quite familiar with critiques of conservative ideologies but less so with critiques of (white American) feminism, (masculine Western) environmentalism and other politically liberal schools of thought.

Although she has collected her share of critics, a wide array of scholars who appreciate the concepts and positions in Haraway's writing have productively applied them in varied branches of the humanities and sciences. A handful of examples illustrates the diverse ways in which her work has influenced scholarship. In feminist theory, Rosi Braidotti adapts Haraway's account of figuration as 'a style of thought that evokes or expresses ways out of the phallocentric vision of the subject'.[49] Treating Haraway as both a political and theoretical resource, Braidotti reads her work as advancing a new ethics of affinity across difference and a revolutionary theory of embodied female subjectivity. This reading is the basis for the new figure Braidotti herself offers (the nomad) for reorienting contemporary feminist philosophy and ethics. In literary theory, N. Katherine Hayles borrows Haraway's concept of 'informatics' to analyse dramatic changes in how information technology relates 'human and textual bodies' through virtual reading practices.[50] In anthropology, Arturo Escobar calls on Haraway's identification of 'the postmodern reinvention of nature' and her analysis of the often-obscured connections between scientific knowledge and social practice to consider the formation of the Third and First Worlds (as such) in late capitalist geo-political relations.[51] And in cultural geography, Suzanne H. Steinmann uses Haraway's complex reading of located identities to examine 'often-hidden gendered environmental knowledges, resource management responsibilities, and power relations that affect the creation or destruction of cultural and ecological spaces' in Moroccan villages.[52] The theoretical and methodological paths that Haraway has taken in her scholarship, travelling through evolutionary biology, primatology, women's studies and other territories, continue to lead the way for scholars with critical impulses and interdisciplinary interests. Given the character of her most recent writing, she is likely to continue to prompt readers to re-examine and re-imagine themselves and the social worlds they inhabit.

Notes

1. Donna J. Haraway. 'From Cyborgs to Companion Species: Kinship in Technoscience', Robert and Maurine Rothschild Lecture in the History of Science, Introductory remarks by Charis Thompson, Harvard University, 2002.
2. Haraway, *Primate Visions*, p. 6.
3. Schneider, *Donna Haraway*, p. 155.
4. Haraway, *How like a Leaf*, p. 133.
5. Haraway, *The Haraway Reader* (New York: Routledge, 2004), p. 200.
6. Haraway, *How like a Leaf*, p. 105.
7. Haraway, *Simians, Cyborgs, and Women*, p. 195.
8. Haraway, *Modest_Witness*, p. 11.
9. Ibid. p. 95.
10. Haraway, *When Species Meet*, p. 10.
11. Ibid. pp. 22–3.
12. Haraway, *Haraway Reader*, p. 8.
13. Haraway, *Simians, Cyborgs, and Women*, pp. 127–8.
14. Haraway, *Haraway Reader*, p. 2.
15. Ibid. p. 201.
16. Haraway, *Modest_Witness*, p. 28.
17. Haraway, *Haraway Reader*, pp. 8 and 39.
18. Ibid. p. 327.
19. Haraway, *Simians, Cyborgs, and Women*, p. 209.
20. Ibid. p. 199.
21. Haraway, *Haraway Reader*, p. 327.
22. Ibid. p. 328.
23. Haraway, *Modest_Witness*, p. 214.
24. Haraway, *The Companion Species Manifesto*, p. 4.
25. Haraway, *When Species Meet*, p. 301.
26. Bartsch, DiPalma, and Sells, 'Witnessing the postmodern jeremiad', *Configurations*, 9, 2001, pp. 127–8.

27. Haraway, *How like a Leaf*, p. 50.
28. Haraway, *Modest_Witness*, pp. 218–30.
29. Ibid. p. 213.
30. Schneider, *Donna Haraway*, p. 75.
31. Haraway, *When Species Meet*, p. 134.
32. Ibid. p. 16.
33. Haraway, *Primate Visions*, p. 369.
34. Ibid. especially pp. 307–11.
35. Haraway, *Haraway Reader*, p. 18.
36. Ibid. p. 57.
37. Haraway, *Primate Visions*, p. 373.
38. Haraway, *Haraway Reader*, p. 11.
39. Ibid. p. 17.
40. Ibid. p. 48.
41. Ibid. p. 49.
42. Haraway, *When Species Meet*, pp. 32, 66–7.
43. Haraway, *Haraway Reader*, p. 126.
44. Haraway, *Simians, Cyborgs, and Women*, p. 196.
45. Haraway, *Companion Species Manifesto*, p. 3.
46. Haraway, *When Species Meet*, p. 10.
47. Ibid. p. 67.
48. Tom Tyler, 'An Animal Manifesto: Gender, Identity, and Vegan-Feminism in the Twenty-First Century, an interview with Carol J. Adams', *Parallax*, 38, January–March 2006, pp. 120–8 (124–5).
49. Rosi Braidotti, *Nomadic Subjects: Embodiment and Difference in Contemporary Feminist Theory* (New York: Columbia University Press, 1994), p. 1.
50. N. Katherine Hayles, *How We Became Posthuman: Virtual Bodies in Cybernetics, Literature, and Informatics* (Chicago: University of Chicago Press, 1999), p. 29.
51. Arturo Escobar, *Encountering Development: The Making and Unmaking of the Third World* (Princeton, NJ: Princeton University Press, 1995), p. 204.
52. Suzanne H. Steinmann, 'Changing Identities and Changing Spaces in Village Landscapes of Settled Pastoralists in Eastern Morocco', in Ghazi-Walid Falah and Caroline R. Nagel (eds), *Geographies of Muslim Women: Gender, Religion, and Space* (New York: Guilford Press, 2005), pp. 91–125 (96).

Major Works by Haraway

The Companion Species Manifesto: Dogs, People, and Significant Otherness (Chicago: Prickly Paradigm Press, 2003).
Crystals, Fabrics, and Fields: Metaphors That Shape Embryos (Berkeley: North Atlantic Press, 1976).

'Ecce Homo, Ain't (ar'n't) I a Woman, and Inappropriate/d Others: The Human in a Posthumanist Landscape', in J. Butler and J. W. Scott (eds), *Feminists Theorize the Political* (New York: Routledge, 1992), pp. 295–337.

The Haraway Reader (New York: Routledge, 2004). A good place for initiates to start, as it contains a selection of key essays and book excerpts in a single volume that opens with an introduction by their author.

How like a Leaf: An Interview with Thyrza Nichols Goodeve (New York: Routledge, 2000). The explanations Haraway offers in this volume of the personal motives, ethics and sentiments that have driven her scholarly development provide a helpful overview of her thought.

'Manifesto for Cyborgs: Science, Technology, and Socialist Feminism in the 1980s', *Socialist Review*, 80, 1985, pp. 65–108.

Modest_Witness@Second_Millennium: FemaleMan_Meets_Oncomouse™: *Feminism and Technoscience* (New York: Routledge, 1997).

'Otherworldly Conversations; Terran Topics, Local Terms', *Science as Culture*, 3, 1, 1992, pp. 59–92.

Primate Visions: Gender, Race, and Nature in the World of Modern Science (New York: Routledge, 1989).

'The Promise of Monsters: A Regenerative Politics for Inappropriate/d Others', in L. Grossberg, C. Nelson and P. Treichler (eds), *Cultural Studies* (New York: Routledge, 1992), pp. 295–337.

Simians, Cyborgs, and Women: The Reinvention of Nature (New York: Routledge, 1991). Her essay 'Gender for a Marxist Dictionary: The Sexual Politics of a Word', succinctly addresses the complex ways in which her work intersects with Marxist and feminist thought, illustrating how and why the former needs to be radically retooled to address the problematic of difference.

'Situated Knowledges: The Science Question in Feminism as a Site of Discourse on the Privilege of Partial Perspective', *Feminist Studies*, 14, 1988, pp. 575–99.

'Teddy Bear Patriarchy: Taxidermy in the Garden of Eden, New York City, 1908–1936', *Social Text*, 11, 1984/85, pp. 19–64.

When Species Meet (Minneapolis: University of Minnesota Press, 2008).

Suggestions for Further Reading

Bartsch, Ingrid, Carolyn DiPalma and Laura Sells, 'Witnessing the Postmodern Jeremiad: (Mis)understanding Donna Haraway's Method of Inquiry', *Configurations*, 9, 2001, pp. 127–64. This article devotes attention to Haraway's method as a performance of her feminist politics. Particularly useful for those interested in the unique rhetorical character of Haraway's writing.

Bell, David, *Cyberculture Theorists: Manuel Castells and Donna Haraway* (New

York: Routledge, 2007). Focuses on Haraway's contributions to cyber-theory and relates her work to that of other pioneering scholars in the field of cyberculture studies.

Schneider, Joseph, *Donna Haraway: Live Theory* (New York: Continuum, 2005). An excellent secondary source on her theories, methods and contributions that provides a good introduction and helps to place her work in scholarly contexts.

9

Ernesto Laclau (1935–) and Chantal Mouffe (1943–)

Simon Tormey

Ernesto Laclau and Chantal Mouffe are the principal figures associated with the emergence of 'discourse analysis', 'post-Marxism'
and 'radical democracy' as key theoretical interventions in contemporary critical theory. Their best-known joint work, *Hegemony and
Socialist Strategy* published in 1985, became emblematic of a certain
brand of left progressive thought that sought to reconceptualise
radical politics 'after' Marx.[1] Since writing *Hegemony and Socialist
Strategy*, Laclau and Mouffe have published widely under their
own names. Laclau's works such as *Emancipations* and *On Populist
Reason* continue the exploration of the theoretical and conceptual
basis of radical democracy. Mouffe's works such as *The Return of the
Political* and *The Democratic Paradox* engage directly with debates in
contemporary political thought, and in particular with democratic
theory in which she has articulated a distinct position, 'agonistic
democracy'.

Both Laclau and Mouffe have strong connections to social
movements and political campaigns. Laclau was born in Argentina
and maintains a deep interest in the politics of Latin America
and with populism as a political form and strategy. He has held a
variety of posts over the past three decades, most notably at Essex
University where he has been the leading figure in the 'Ideology
and Discourse Analysis' programme which forms an important institutional locus for work in this area. Mouffe was born in Belgium and
was a student of Laclau's at Essex before herself assuming a number
of academic affiliations, including most recently at the Centre for
Democracy at the University of Westminster. She is also active in

various movements, including the Social Forum process and the international global justice network, Association pour la taxation des transactions pour l'aide aux citoyens (ATTAC).

Laclau and Mouffe's intellectual legacy can be usefully captured in terms of a couple of key problematics. How does one remain a radical after the basic tenets that informed Marxist radical politics became an irrelevance over the course of the latter half of the twentieth century? How in particular can the 'anti-essentialist' insights of those working at the cutting edge of human enquiry such as Lacan, Derrida, Wittgenstein and Foucault come to inform a politics that escapes the narrow sectarianism of Leninism, the party form and 'democratic centralism'?

Marxism in Question

The animating problematic of Laclau and Mouffe's work is situated in the specific context of the crisis of Marxism and the collapse of communism as the locus for radical theory and politics after 1968. The inability of communist parties in western Europe to develop a politics consonant with 'new times' led to the collapse of support for communism in previous strongholds such as France and Italy and thus the need to re-examine the expectations that had informed Marxist radical politics since the late nineteenth century.[2] These expectations concerned the relationship between the economic base and the ideological and political superstructure. To Marx it was developments in the base that determined to greater or lesser extent the extant political forms, whether considered as the values, morals, laws or institutions of a given society. Changes in these forms were precipitated by changes in the material base, so that as new forms of technology emerged and became part of the reproduction of society so new classes, forces and ideas emerged to facilitate the passage from one form of society to another. Revolutions are in this sense the product of an 'exogenous' imperative that creates the conditions in which social change becomes not merely desirable but necessary. Radical politics is in this sense propelled by forces that lie outside the domain of politics itself.

To be Marxist was on these terms to be committed to a teleological conception of social change. Given the inevitable lag between the development of the base and the development of the requisite class consciousness needed to overthrow an anachronistic social order, Marx posited the need for a party that would represent the interests of the exploited mass. The party would be composed of 'leading' elements of the working class and intellectuals such as himself who understood the unfolding historical narrative and who could guide the class to the desired outcome: revolution and thence communism. This sets up a 'Jacobin' dynamic familiar to students of radical politics in the early twentieth century in which the capture of the state and the transition to a state-governed form of socialism becomes imperative. However, as Laclau and Mouffe argue:

> What is now in crisis is a whole conception of socialism which rests upon the ontological centrality of the working class, upon the role of Revolution, with a capital 'r', as the founding moment of a transition from one type of society to another, and upon the illusory prospect of a perfectly unitary and homogenous collective will that will render pointless the moment of politics.[3]

In particular Laclau and Mouffe contest the idea that capitalism contains irresolvable 'contradictions' which necessitate a final crisis and overthrow of the system. Capitalism may be antagonistic in the sense that, as a class system, there are clashes of interest and ideology to contend with; but capitalism is not doomed to collapse as orthodox Marxists insist. Capitalism demonstrates a resilience and adaptability that means that it could stave off crisis, and which means that radicals had to enter the arena of the political to make progress. More than this, capitalism had given witness to the unfolding 'democratic revolution' that it was the task of radicals to promote and nurture rather than to contest and overthrow.

Finally, contemporary political mobilisation gave the lie to the notions of agency preferred by Marxists. The radicalism of the late twentieth century was not necessarily 'class' in character, but rather one propelled by specific injustices, oppressions and exclusions that pointed towards an amelioration of the system, rather than its overthrow. It was the 'new social movements' who provided political energy and impetus to change, not the working class, which was merely one among a number of political actors who had to be addressed by radical theorists. Progressive thought could not turn its back on these challenges or deny their existence (as they thought many more orthodox Marxists were prone to do), but needed to rethink radical politics under conditions that made old orthodoxies irrelevant. How?

146

Ernesto Laclau (1935–) and Chantal Mouffe (1943–)

Rethinking Hegemony

In their own terminology Laclau and Mouffe are 'post-marxist', insisting that they work within the broader expectations that Marx had himself articulated: the insufficiency of liberalism; the persistence of deep inequality and exclusion; and thus the necessity to further radicalise the 'democratic revolution'. Two figures were of particular importance in this rethinking: Antonio Gramsci and Louis Althusser. From Gramsci they take the idea of 'hegemony' and the necessity for thinking social change as a consequence of forming political alliances as a 'historical bloc', as opposed to waiting for social change to be generated from without in the form of economic crisis. From Althusser they take the idea of society as a complex totality that is 'overdetermined', meaning that it has to be reproduced ideologically to make up for an absent 'fullness'. There is always an insufficiency or lack that requires the operation of the state and other agencies to cover over the antagonisms and fissures that complex entities manifest.

Gramsci was a thinking person's revolutionary – a hero of the Italian communist party who wrote much of his best-known work in the 1920s while a prisoner of the Italian state. Following the disastrous experiment of the Bolshevik Revolution, Gramsci sought to reconstruct Marxism by paying attention to the different modalities of political struggle and contestation. Famously, Gramsci contrasted the approach of the Bolsheviks, which he characterised as an embrace of a 'war of manoeuvre', with the more subtle radicalism needed under contemporary capitalist conditions, which he characterised as 'war of position'.[4] The point emphasised a minor refrain in Marx's own thinking: that culture and historical tradition were important determinants of political structure and action; that small movements needed to join up with larger movements in order to challenge dominant forces; and that progressive politics needed an alternative vision in order to succeed. Sometimes challenging the stock of norms, values and assumptions that permitted the ruling class to maintain legitimacy as consent, which Gramsci refers to as the 'common sense' nostrums that underpin social orders, was more sensible than confronting it head on. The inference was clear: if radicals wanted to bring about lasting change (as opposed to mere political upheaval), then they needed to critique, undermine and supplant the common-sense ideas that maintained the present in being.

Gramsci's approach, however, still privileged the working class as a primary identity, not seeing that 'unfixity becomes the condition for every social identity'.[5] The emergence of new social movements showed that identity could be constructed in many ways with many different effects and demands attached to them. The missing link in Gramsci's approach was the idea of the 'equivalence' of contrasting, even conflicting, political demands, and thus the necessity to find ways in which the different goals attached to different subject identities (race, class and so on) could be knitted together ('sutured') so that both the particularity and universality of these demands could be respected and built upon. 'Working-class' identity was increasingly weak as far as the populations of advanced industrial societies were concerned, so a notion of hegemony could not privilege it.

Hegemony after Gramsci

To reformulate hegemony in new times, Laclau and Mouffe revisited the orthodox Marxist notion that an external cause (the base) acts upon an interior superstructure. They conjoined Althusser's ruminations on the 'relative autonomy' of the ideological superstructures with insights from post-structuralism and the psychoanalytic approach associated with Lacan and his followers. These approaches share an 'anti-essentialism' or a hostility towards the idea of an 'outside' of an extra-discursive kind that determines who we are and how we think about the world. Laclau and Mouffe insist that this world is constructed in and through 'discourse' that is never complete or self-present. Language, as Saussure showed, is composed of signifiers whose sense is determined through the play of difference with other signifiers. Discourse is constituted not in relation to 'reality', posited as an 'exteriority' which it is language's function to reveal, but in relation to an evolving system of meaning that searches constantly for anchors or *point de capiton* to fix itself. Discourse is based on a lack of access to an underpinning reality, to the world, to meaning – or, as Lacan puts it, to the Real. It is this 'unfixity' that must govern our thinking about how to construct a new hegemonic project – or to put the same matter differently, 'plurality' must be 'the starting point of the analysis'.[6]

Laclau and Mouffe do not merely invert Marx's materialism in favour of neo-idealism. Their point is that the social is a discontinuous terrain in which concepts are fixed and unfixed, and in which there is a permanent struggle of interpretation and meaning. There is nothing that determines the social from the outside, and no teleology that guarantees an overall evolutionary path that society must follow. There are no extra-historical or extra-social 'essences', but rather only the *appearance* of essence, fixity, truth, which reflect the hegemonic understandings that happen to be in a position of temporary or contingent power. Recognition of the social construction of narratives and the interplay of myth, symbolism and imagery in support of normative or political schemas implies that bourgeois liberal myths should be displaced not by the Truth, but by more *progressive* myths that serve the need for something to fill the void.[7]

Essential to Laclau and Mouffe's approach is the dispelling of the story of the left's inevitable or necessary coming to power. The left cannot rely on capitalist crisis, which at best only evinces an antagonism and thus a political opening in which hegemony can be contested. It cannot rely on the development of class consciousness because identity is not formed in and through the extra-social operation of economic antagonism, but through the ceaseless shifting of the social terrain in response to all manner of contingencies and events, some of which have their origin in economic causality – but many of them not.

The success or failure of progressive movements thus depends on their ability to articulate a counter-hegemonic vision that resonates sufficiently to effect a mobilisation, which may in turn lead to a challenge to the dominant value system. 'Articulation' is thus a key concept for Laclau and Mouffe, helping to provide the link between social groups, social structures and change. Discourse analysis shows how these articulations come about, how they evolve and engage the wider public.[8] It shows how successful movements link generally discrete demands that would otherwise founder for lack of popular support, creating a political dynamic leading to change. For Laclau and Mouffe, change can only be understood as a *function* of articulation, rather than the other way round. This is a crucial gesture for cultural theorists who seek to valorise the role of art, the media and politics – considered as a broad field of contestation – in thinking about the dynamics of social change. Ideas matter, so do many other kinds of cultural products, in the on-going struggle to produce a critique of the dominant norms and values that will in turn mobilise people behind progressive projects.[9]

Towards a Radical and Plural Democracy

Laclau and Mouffe's analysis is informed by attachment to a normative project: 'radical democracy'.[10] The novelty of their approach is that it proceeds not by stating what the essential constituents of such a democracy might be (the traditional 'leftist' approach) but by telling us what democracy must not be or become: totalising, utopian, ahistorical, acontextual. 'Democracy' is a free-floating signifier and thus needs to be defined and redefined by progressive movements in contradistinction to elite-driven understandings. 'Radical democracy' is in this sense the collective enactment of the ontological and epistemological contingency embraced in discourse analysis. It is democracy freed from the limited understandings of the use and legitimacy of power deployed by dominant social groups. Discourse analysis renders visible the 'hegemonic' claims of distinct interests and identities. It shows how these claims are historically and contextually situated and thus emphasises how matters might otherwise be constructed or established on the basis of different, yet equivalent claims. Democracy is a specially privileged term, at the heart of which are the animating principles of contingency and uncertainty.

Radical democracy embraces the contingent nature of power in modern society, seeing the task of the radical as the creation and perpetuation of a progressive alliance of forces able continually to enlarge the realm of representation and the sphere of democratisation. In this sense Laclau and Mouffe reject the 'Jacobin' legacy that posits the need for a 'break' before the reconstruction of society according to a utopian blueprint. Such an understanding is in their view implicitly totalitarian. It fails to see that the condition of possibility of a democratic politics is the recognition of the contingency of subject positions, overlooking the necessity to reaffirm progressive positions through alliance and the contest of power. As they put it, 'The task of the Left therefore cannot be to renounce liberal-democratic ideology, but on the contrary, to deepen and expand it in the direction of a radical and plural democracy.'[11]

Notwithstanding the rejection of teleology and indeed of normative politics per se, Laclau and Mouffe's own position is thus itself quite strongly teleological. Their hostility towards redemptive schemas is owing partly to their explicit anti-utopianism, partly to their belief that the democratic form enacts an institutionalised 'anti-essentialism' of a kind that makes more radical transformation of the basis of contemporary society unnecessary. Utopias, whether of the left or the right, represent the end of politics, antagonism and conflict. They cannot cope with pluralism, and with the necessity for the active construction of an identity in opposition to other identities, forces and positions. 'Radical democracy' is thus an avowedly *anti-utopian* project that seeks to build on the forms of contestation to which modernity gives rise. In this sense their politics follows in the footsteps of other critical theorists such as Jean-François Lyotard, Jacques Derrida and Agnes Heller.[12] These figures reject the traditional leftist insistence on pursuing a certain image of human rationality and thus rejecting the inevitably *political* dimension of processes of social change.

Trajectories of Radical Democracy: Laclau

Hegemony and Socialist Strategy was a bold, demanding marker for debates concerning the future of progressive politics at a point in time when conservatism was very much in the ascendency and neo-liberalism the 'hegemonic' articulation of choice. The realist 'mood', pessimistic overview and pragmatic conclusions matched the times and provided a handy theoretical backdrop to the unfolding drama of the collapse of communism in Europe, and the emergence of new, and sometimes unsightly, identities in ex-Yugoslavia, the Middle East, Africa and elsewhere. The world of the late 1980s and early 1990s seemed at one level to confirm Laclau and Mouffe's analysis more fully than they could conceivably manage themselves.

Laclau's ensuing work unpacks the theoretical basis outlined earlier, particularly by attending to the tension intrinsic to the 'post-Marxist' venture between universalism and particularism. This is otherwise expressed in terms of the opposition between the modernist ambition to comprehend the totality as a prelude to changing or transforming it and the postmodernist imperative to abandon 'metanarratives' and with it the alleged totalitarian impulse to recreate society according to a redemptive blueprint. In a series of essays published as *Emancipations*, in the exchanges with Slavoj Žižek and Judith Butler in *Contingency, Hegemony, Universality*, and latterly in *On Populist Reason*, Laclau offers an analysis that mediates between these poles, or which keeps in play the universalist dimension with a recognition of the inevitable plurality and difference that attends modern existence, in turn informing the proliferation of identities, subject positions and political causes. How in short to maintain a progressive 'political logic' among the kaleidoscopic character of modern society which seems to make something as singular as *a* logic meaningful and politically effective?

The key to unlocking the point of mediation is the notion of equivalence touched on above. In Laclau's view, even the most 'particularist' of demands contain a universalist dimension, whether it be in terms of the assertion of the need for a 'right' to something, or for recognition of a specific entitlement or injustice. Thus the feminist demand for the same rights and privileges as men not only pertains to women; it is also *universalist* in the sense that it uses the language of equality to further the particular demands. In this sense feminism, even while built on the premise of a fundamental 'difference' between women and men, is nonetheless 'equivalent' to the demands of myriad other groups seeking to be included in extant definitions of equality.[13] They all exceed current definitions, and their success in bringing about change equates to an enlarging of equality in society and thus a broadening of the democratic revolution. Difference is not itself a barrier to the development of a universalist political project. On the contrary, difference can only be promoted and protected as *part of* a universalist project whose function is to preserve and enhance different identities and subject positions. The problem in contemporary settings is identifying the vehicle that can mediate between these different facets of political life. For Laclau the mass party is an anachronism standing for universalism at the cost of particularity. What vehicle might be used then to ensure that *both* the universalist and particularist elements of contemporary demands are translated into an *effective* politics?

Interestingly, Laclau reaches back into his own Argentinian past for the solution: populism. Populism, Laclau argues, is incorrectly understood if by the term we mean a politics that only operates at the level of the emotions or symbolism. Equally, it misses the point to reduce populism to a particular kind of movement – often of course right wing or nationalist. The success of populism is as a political logic that recognises the necessity to evoke the universal as a means of securing support or, more technically, hegemony. Particularistic demands are by definition advanced by a section of the population; universal demands constructed as demands of 'the people' have as their ambition a wide base of support and thus give hope that discrete demands are met. In this sense populist movements embrace the notion of mediation articulated by Laclau. The self-conscious appeal to 'the People' as the subject of political change is a recognition of the need to forge that sense of greater purpose and identity without which any movement will founder. This would be by contrast to universalist movements such as communism which, as Žižek reminds us, transcend particularity altogether through grasping an essential Truth or Universality that is exterior to the process of political struggle itself.[14] As Laclau explains: '"Peoples" are real social formations, but they resist inscription into any kind of Hegelian teleology.'[15] 'The People' is not a passive pre-existing identity, but rather the object and subject of the political battle otherwise known as the war of position – or hegemony.

For Žižek, Laclau's politics panders to the preciousness of particularistic identities (race, sexuality and so on) thereby guaranteeing that liberal-capitalism is never identified as the enemy and the proper subject of a transformative politics. Populism is, on this reading, just a political logic – and does not describe an end goal to be realised as constitutive of a properly populist politics. To Laclau, however, the privileging of the universal as working class effectively ignores the transformation of capitalism over the course of the twentieth century, and the supplanting of the working class as the primary agent in contemporary social struggles. The message is clear enough: if progressives want to be effective then they need to ensure that they do not ghettoise themselves through alienating or antagonising groups who might not otherwise be attracted to their message. They need to see that populism is the political form of the struggle for hegemony, and a necessary component of progressive struggles that seek to change or transform existing conditions in a socialist direction.

Trajectories of Radical Democracy: Mouffe

The nature of politics as an aspect of democratic contestation preoccupies Mouffe in her recent work. As we noted, one prong in the criticism of orthodox Marxism was the idea of the goal of progressive politics as the realisation of 'transparency' or 'self-presence' ('the sutured society'). Another way of putting this would be that Laclau and Mouffe are critical of the idea that the goal of transformative politics should be a world without conflict, divisions or antagonisms. As Mouffe puts it: 'Instead of shying away from the component of violence and hostility inherent in social relations, the task is to think how to create the conditions under which those aggressive forces can be defused and diverted and a pluralist democratic order made possible.'[16]

Fundamental to Laclau and Mouffe's ontology is the idea of individual and collective existence as marked by 'lack' – lack of 'fixity', 'essence' or any other exteriority that can anchor identity and meaning. It follows that we are forever searching for meaning, for life's prime wants, for collective cohesion. The problem, as Mouffe sees it, is that political theorists are in denial about the primordial nature of lack and thus dismissive of the need to generate normative and conceptual schema that embrace 'lack' and reject the siren call of redemptive schemas. This goes even for contemporary liberalism which embraces plurality as intrinsic to human flourishing. The problem is that liberals have seen their task as setting out the normative basis for a just society, which in turn negates the 'political' as a distinct site or activity, and democracy as a necessary component of a properly plural society. The influential liberal theorist John Rawls – with whom this approach is most readily associated – is determined to delineate the universal determinants of the just society allowing, paradoxically, liberalism to withdraw from thinking about the constituents of a properly political life. Justice has become a theoretical holy grail to the exclusion of thinking about how power and the state are to be configured so as to preserve and enhance pluralism. As Mouffe intones:

> Every pretension to occupy the place of the universal, to fix its final meaning through rationality, must be rejected. The content of the universal must remain indeterminate since it is this indeterminacy that is the condition of existence of democratic politics.[17]

It is not only liberals who have a problem coping with the political, however, but much of the contemporary left as well. Figures such as Jürgen Habermas are, in Mouffe's view, still in thrall to enlightenment universalism as reconciliation and the end of the political. The idea of, for example, democratic deliberation as a process of consensus formation (arriving at a decision that is acceptable to all participants in a discussion) misses the point of contestation, namely, that it expresses the 'agonal' quality of fully functioning plural societies. The task of a properly radical agonistic politics is not to deny the necessity for contestation but to promote and nurture it in institutional forms that are productive of community and collectivity even while they enshrine difference. What has to be avoided is the *antagonism* that emerges from a fractious politics of particularism, fundamentalism and dogmatism of the kind so prevalent in the twentieth century, and which is equally complicit in the emptying out of politics as communal-collective process. Particularism induces private certainty, not public deliberation. It renders politics a sub-set of morality, and reduces political dilemmas to questions of right and wrong. This moralising of the realm of the political, very characteristic of politics in the United States (and increasingly so in Europe), is just as damaging to on-going public discourse as the pursuit of larger ideological projects that claim the mantle of universalism for themselves.

Mouffe's project is less orientated towards a counter-hegemonic or transformative project than Laclau's, as indicated by her extensive deployment of figures such as Carl Schmitt and Thomas Hobbes in her recent work.[18] The use of Schmitt in particular is controversial given his associations with the Nazi regime. Yet, Mouffe's resort to these figures underlines the point that mainstream political theory has been much more ready to embrace the dimension of the utopian, the reciprocal and redemptive, than admit the need to make space for contestation, plurality and difference. She resorts to figures such as Schmitt in order to recover what she feels to have been lost in the contemporary obsession with consensus and unity, whether deliberative or intuitive, as in the Rawlsian design. Political theories that do not signal the need for a space of contestation lose touch with what democrats should in her view embrace: a willingness to celebrate the indeterminacy and contingency of politics and thus of collective life.

By contrast with Laclau, Mouffe's vision of the good life emphasises the cut and thrust of politics and its ability to create and maintain divisions. Mouffe leaves us with the impression that we need to reach back to civic-republican themes in order to reinvigorate democracy, in common with liberal-conservative figures such as Michael Oakeshott and Hannah Arendt. Mouffe's would be a robustly 'agonistic' democracy in which difference and plurality are considered virtues in themselves, and where the absence of consensus and harmony are taken to be signs of the health or vigour of the community, as opposed to perhaps a 'lack' indicating the failure of institutional design or stunted deliberation. It is a classical model of competitiveness and individualist striving, one that in evoking Schmitt as intellectual precursor valorises the idea that politics is about decision-making and the necessity for winners and losers.

Laclau's project remains within a more recognisably Marxist or post-Marxist frame, seeing the task of progressive politics as incipiently 'counter-hegemonic', if not anti-capitalist. Like Mouffe, it is a politics of us-and-them, but it is one in which the 'us' is always framed collectively. It is the 'us' conceived as the mass, the non-elite or, in populist guise, 'the people' – and less 'us' qua individuals pursuing our distinctive agendas in a pluralist atmosphere. As the embrace of populism is intended to maintain, Laclau's politics is still a politics of large-scale movements, mobilisations and 'historical blocs' competing for power to pursue universalist agendas.

Conclusion: Difference/Identity?

Whether the differences between Laclau and Mouffe are seen to outweigh the similarities is very much a question of the position from which one is observing the unfolding of these intellectual trajectories. To classical Marxists such as Norman Geras, Laclau and Mouffe appear as two manifestations of the same species: post- or non-Marxist radicals who have abandoned the basic ontological and epistemological coordinates that inform a critical, socialist perspective.[19] On his reading, the abandonment of the idea of the primacy of production in structuring social life equates to the embrace of a liberal or bourgeois perspective in which the muscularity of class struggle recedes into the background to be displaced by an effete postmodern concern with pluralism, diverse subject positions and rainbow alliances. In the meantime, as other left critics such as Žižek and Townshend argue, capitalism becomes a vanishing referent that cannot be approached or criticised in the abandonment of the terrain from which such a critique would be mounted.[20]

It is certainly true as these critics point out that it is difficult to find the resources to generate a transformative politics in Laclau and Mouffe's ruminations on the fate of universalism and particularism. Mouffe has avowedly embraced liberal presuppositions regarding the structure of political contestation, which is a short step to embracing liberal presuppositions *tout court*. Laclau, while maintaining a recognisably Marxian language of counter-hegemonic struggles and historical blocs, is arguably more interested in the formal properties of 'radical' politics than in the substantive or normative conclusions that such a language traditionally generated. Laclau's concern is essentially Machiavellian, if not Leninist, in orientation. His interest is in the question of power: how it is captured, maintained, reproduced. What substantively this power is to be used for is it seems a 'contingent' question – a question of the particular form that 'universalist' demands manifest under the particular hegemonic-populist struggle that is being pursued. 'Universalism' is curiously unexamined in the sense that we seem to lack the coordinates needed to judge between competing images *of* the universal.

Even to non-Marxists, the similarities between these positions are more marked than the differences. Andrew Robinson for example, offers a pungent critique of Laclau and Mouffe's common ontological presuppositions, informed by what he terms a 'lackist' framework.[21] For Robinson and others, this amounts to the consecration of a new essentialism – albeit in 'anti-essentialist' garb. Far from doing away with foundations, Laclau and Mouffe merely exchange Marxian foundations for post-structuralist (non)foundations, losing in the process the reservoir of humanist values that insist on the availability of non-alienated, non-exploited forms of life based on reciprocity and solidarity. 'Lack' here becomes the ideological underpinning for a politics that is expressly anti-utopian, anti-idealistic and anti-humanist, one that in turn consecrates struggle, competition, winners and losers – and the liberal-capitalist status quo.

If we judge a theoretical intervention on the basis of its ability to generate a group of self-identifying followers and practitioners, it is undeniable that Laclau and Mouffe have had a very significant impact. The Essex programme has produced a generation of younger scholars wedded to the framework and analysis associated with their work – so much so that it is now common to read about the 'Essex School' of theory. Moreover, as a cursory glance at textbooks on 'methods' reveals, discourse analysis has become a standard approach in social science research and critical theory more broadly.[22] Whether the political baggage that Laclau and Mouffe think comes with the method is acknowledged or not, there are a great many academics and students who deploy a theoretical arsenal informed by if not actually dependent upon the claims Laclau and Mouffe articulate in *Hegemony and Socialist Strategy* and elsewhere.

More substantively, there is a sense in which Laclau and Mouffe reshaped the terrain for debates on the left concerning in particular the appropriate response to the triumph of liberal-capitalism and the fall of the Berlin Wall. Even those who disagreed with them have had to acknowledge the importance of the intervention, even if it is in terms of trying to disarm the analysis it offers. Laclau and Mouffe offered a concrete alternative to classical Marxism from a position they characterised as radical, in turn forcing Marxists to re-examine the terms and conditions of their own attachments. At the same time, they provoked post-structuralist theorists into a reassessment of their own 'radicalism' in the realm of politics. Theorists such as Judith Butler had to address the possibility that their own 'particularist' concerns, whether driven by issues of gender, sexuality or ethnicity, left the world around them intact, or whether there was a universalist dimension and broader political relevance to their work.[23] Whether one agrees with them Laclau and Mouffe individually and jointly have provoked debate across otherwise ghettoised communities and between academia and the wider activist community.

Notes

1. See Tormey and Townshend, *Key Thinkers from Critical Theory to Post-Marxism*.
2. See Laclau, *New Reflections*, Chapter 2.
3. Laclau and Mouffe, *Hegemony and Socialist Strategy*, p. 2.
4. Ibid. Chapter 2.
5. Ibid. p. 85.
6. Ibid. p. 140.
7. Ibid. Chapter 1.
8. See D. R. Howarth, J. Torfing et al., *Discourse Theory in European Politics: Identity, Policy, and Governance* (Basingstoke, Hampshire; New York: Palgrave Macmillan, 2005).
9. See J. Gilbert, *Anticapitalism and Culture: Radical Theory and Popular Politics* (Oxford; New York: Berg, 2008).
10. Laclau and Mouffe, *Hegemony and Socialist Strategy*, Chapter 4.
11. Ibid. p. 176.
12. See J. Derrida, *Specters of Marx: The State of the Debt, the Work of Mourning, and the New International* (London: Routledge, 1994); F. Feher and A. Heller, *Eastern Left, Western Left: Totalitarianism, Freedom, and Democracy* (Cambridge: Polity Press, 1987); J. F. Lyotard, *The Postmodern Condition: A Report on Knowledge* (Manchester: Manchester University Press, 1984).
13. Laclau, *Emancipation(s)*, pp. 28–30.
14. S. Žižek, 'Have Michael Hardt and Antonio Negri Rewritten the Communist Manifesto for the Twenty-First Century?', *Rethinking Marxism* 13, 3/4, 2001, pp. 190–8.

15. Laclau, *Populist Reason*, p. 226.
16. Mouffe, *Return of the Political*, p. 153.
17. Ibid. pp. 146–7.
18. See Mouffe, *The Challenge of Carl Schmitt* and *Democratic Paradox*.
19. See N. Geras, 'Post-Marxism', *New Left Review*, 163, 1987, pp. 40–82.
20. See Butler, Laclau and Žižek, *Contingency, Hegemony, Universality*; T. Brockelman, 'The Failure of the Radical Democratic Imaginary: Žižek Versus Laclau and Mouffe on Vestigial Utopia', *Philosophy and Social Criticism*, 29, 2, 2003, pp. 187–212; J. Townshend, 'Laclau and Mouffe's Hegemonic Project: The Story So Far', *Political Studies*, 52, 2, 2004, pp. 269–88.
21. A. Robinson, 'The Political Theory of Constitutive Lack: A Critique', *Theory & Event*, 8, 1, 2005.
22. J. Townshend, 'Discourse Theory and Political Analysis: A New Paradigm from the Essex School?', *British Journal of Politics and International Relations*, 5, 1, 2003, pp. 129–42.
23. See Butler, Laclau and Žižek, *Contingency, Hegemony, Universality*.

Major Work by Laclau and Mouffe

Hegemony and Socialist Strategy: Towards a Radical Democratic Politics (London: Verso, 1985).

Major Works by Laclau

Butler, J., E. Laclau and S. Žižek, *Contingency, Hegemony, Universality: Contemporary Dialogues on the Left* (London: Verso, 2000).
Emancipation(s) (London: Verso, 1996).
New Reflections on the Revolution of Our Time (London: Verso, 1990).
On Populist Reason (London: Verso, 2005).

Major Works by Mouffe

The Challenge of Carl Schmitt (London: Verso, 1999).
The Democratic Paradox (London: Verso, 2000).
The Return of the Political (London: Verso, 1993).

Suggestions for Further Reading

Geras, Norman, *Discourse of Extremity, Radical Ethics and Post-Marxist Extravagance* (London: Verso, 1990). Critique of Laclau and Mouffe's intervention from a classical Marxian perspective.
Howarth, David, *Discourse* (Buckingham: Open University Press, 2000).

Useful account of the nature and applications of discourse theory in contemporary political analysis.

Smith, Ann-Marie, *Laclau and Mouffe: The Radical Democratic Imaginary* (London: Routledge, 1998). Sympathetic advanced overview of the trajectory of Laclau and Mouffe's work.

Tormey, Simon, and Jules Townshend, *Key Thinkers from Critical Theory to Post-Marxism* (London: Sage, 2006). Situates Laclau and Mouffe's work in relation to Post-Marxism and contemporary political theory.

10

Bruno Latour (1947–)

Ilana Gershon

Introduction

Bruno Latour is one of the leading figures in an approach ambivalently called Actor-Network Theory (ANT).[1] Actor-Network Theory originally was developed by sociologists of science in response to methodological and theoretical dilemmas these scholars encountered as they explored how scientists produced and circulated scientific facts. ANT has transcended its science and technology studies' origins and is now deployed by scholars in anthropology, geography, economics, organisational studies, history, literature, media studies and other disciplines. Other theorists who have played a significant role in the development of ANT are Madeleine Akrich, Michel Callon, Donna Haraway, John Law, Anne Marie Mol, Michel Serres and Susan Leigh Star.

In Latour's words: 'I am from the typical French provincial bourgeoisie, from Burgundy where my family has produced wine for generations, and my only ambition is that people would say 'I read a Latour 1992', with the same pleasure as they would say, 'I drank a Latour 1992!''[2] He was trained as a philosopher at the University of Tours, but began to be interested in science studies during his military service in Cote d'Ivoire. There, he was encouraged to pursue a sociological project on how the French export their industrial education to their former colony, Cote d'Ivoire, by ORSTOM (Institut français de recherche scientifique pour le développement en coopération). He was asked to focus on why African executives appeared to have such difficulties adapting to modern industrial

161

life. The only form of explanation available at that time in the sociological and anthropological literature would have compelled Latour to argue that Africans simply had a different mentality, that their mental capacities were fundamentally different from that of Europeans. Latour rejected this style of explanation, especially when he turned to the education system in place in Cote d'Ivoire. He noticed that the French teachers often required African students to diagram engines before they were ever shown an actual engine. They were, understandably, not terribly adept at imagining engines based only on these black-and-white diagrams, which led French educators to suspect that African students lacked the capacity to visualise objects in three dimensions.[3] Latour argued that it was the schools' techniques for circulating knowledge, not the African students' mental capacities, that were causing the problems. Even in his first post-doctoral research, Latour focused on how one creates and relates to an elite form of knowledge, a concern that he has pursued since.

Early Ethnographies of Science Studies

While Latour was strongly influenced by anthropology during his time in Cote d'Ivoire, and in particular his conversations with anthropologist Marc Augé (then director of ORSTOM), when he returned to France he did not continue studying non-Western cultures. Instead, in 1973, he met Roger Guillemin, a neuroendocrinologist working at the Jonas Salk Institute for Biological Studies in San Diego, who granted Latour complete access to his laboratory. Latour spent two years at the Salk Institute, participating in and observing the daily routines of Guillemin's laboratory. At the time, he thought he might be observing what is often described as 'normal' science, the day-to-day operations of a scientific laboratory. Yet what he was in fact observing was Guillemin and Schally's competition to isolate the peptide TRF(H), which occurred during his stay. They jointly received the Nobel Prize in medicine two years later, in 1977, for this discovery. Latour wrote an account of this discovery with Steve Woolgar, a sociologist of science, in *Laboratory Life*, which was the first ethnographic study of a laboratory. In this account, Latour and Woolgar focus on how TRF(H) is produced as a scientific fact, focusing on citation practices, and, in particular, how experimental actions are transformed into various forms of inscriptions that circulate in patterned ways.

This study was Latour's first venture into science studies. Upon returning to France, Latour began to carve out a space for science and technology studies, which had no institutional backing in the French academic system at the time. Along with Michel Callon and John Law, he began to develop the methodological and philosophical armature of ANT, summarised below. In addition to various theoretical books on the contours of ANT,[4] he has written *The Pasteurization of France,* a historical exploration of how Pasteur's success was fashioned by refiguring various networks. He has also authored *Aramis,* an account of the failure of a personal rapid transit system in Paris, and *Politics of Nature,* a treatise on how environmental movements could, but are not, transforming assumptions about the connections between nature and society.

Actor-Network Theory

When Latour gives an account of his theoretical perspective he often starts by explaining the dichotomies he rejects, in part because of his unease about his work being turned into a theoretical movement. To clear an analytical space, he rejects dichotomies between self/other, material/semiotic, nature/culture, agency/structure, knowledge/power, active/passive, human/non-human and truth/ falsehood. By rejecting these dualisms, Latour presumes that everything and everyone is profoundly relational – that entities only have qualities, attributes or form as a result of their relationships with other entities. This is a familiar claim for people who analyse how words acquire meanings. One cannot attribute meaning to the word 'hat' without presuming distinctions in sound ('hat' versus 'cat', 'sat' and 'mat'), as well as distinctions in reference ('hat' versus 'cap', 'shirt;' 'hair' and 'wool'). 'Hat' exists as a word with meaning because it exists in a web of oppositional relationships to other words and other referents. Latour takes this a couple of steps further, and suggests that a hat condenses historical relationships of manufacture (How was the material made? How did someone learn the necessary skills to operate the tools to make the hat? From when did the tools for hat-making come?), relationships of exchange (what money, trucks, roads, stores, traders had to exist to move the hat from hat-maker to hat-purchaser?), relationships of use (What other hats are possible? When does one wear this particular hat? What signs of wear will this hat have over time because of how the shape of the head and this hat interact?) and so on.

Hats, people, trains, everything in the world condenses a specific set of heterogeneous relationships, and then interacts with other condensations of different sets of heterogeneous relationships. Actors are condensed bits of a network; networks are fashioned through the interactions of actors. The hyphen in Actor-Network Theory is a trickster placeholder, separating what really can only be spoken in the same breath, representing the constant flow between these two nouns. Actor-Network Theory is fundamentally a theory of relationality, with the analytical task of figuring how these relationships condense in various people and objects. This radical commitment to relationality has four major conceptual consequences.

First, everyone and everything contributes to how interactions take place – in this sense, microbes are participants, or actants, as much as people. Latour coined the term *actant* to describe anything that has agency (and for Latour, everything does). ANT scholars are unwilling to attribute agency only to humans. Rather, every node in the network, or web of relationships, shapes the ways in which interactions in the network will occur, be the node a microbe, a sheep, a test tube or a biologist. In *Pasteurization of France,* Latour describes how Louis Pasteur's success hinged on his ability to turn microbes into a very particular type of ally. Microbes were invisible until Pasteur's techniques of isolating and growing bacteria made them visible. Outside the laboratory, microbes mixed with other beings willy-nilly, not only invisible to the human eye but so intricately entangled with other life that they were difficult to isolate. Pasteur, however, removed them from their concealing context. He took them into isolated spaces – petri dishes – where he provided them with a feast that encouraged them to multiply until they betrayed their existence and became visible to the human eye (and hence potentially destructible). For Pasteur to turn microbes into allies that helped build his reputation, he had to have some knowledge of how the microbes act on the world. He had to find some way to isolate them as agents, and doing so required complicity with what is peculiar to the microbes' appetites and ways of navigating the world.

Because Latour wants to distribute agency as broadly as possible as an initial premise, he must then address the question: what labour goes in to allocating responsibility and agency only to some actants and not to others? Part of the work of being an Actor-Network theorist is to figure out why people in a particular context will attribute responsibility and agency to certain actants in a context and not others. When do mobile phones actively seem to thwart what one attempts to do, and when do these mobile phones appear to be seamless extensions of one's body? When are the microbes understood to act, and when Pasteur? The analyst uses variants of this question to map out the power relationships enacted in a given context. In practice, this means that the ANT analyst refuses to determine who the relevant actors are before beginning analysis. Instead, one pays careful attention to how people and objects interact, and how their interactions unfold. By doing so, Latour is able to explore what social practices contribute to the labours of division that produce the aforementioned dualisms, dualisms that often seem to dominate scientific and other contexts.

The second consequence is that not all actants are the same, and it is important to pay attention to the historical and material bases for these differences. In part, the differences are a result of the unique social and historical trajectories that shape the people and objects that comprise a network. Yet as importantly, the differences lie in the forms that the actants have – the microbe is a different actant than the sheep because of the differences in each actant's physicality. The form in which someone or something exists in the world matters – that is, matter really matters. One's material form helps determine connections to others in a network: the physical simultaneously shapes and limits the ways in which interactions can occur and unfold. Latour describes how European hotel keys are designed to affect how their customers will store them. Hotel managers want their customers to leave room keys at the hotel lobby to prevent their hotel keys from wandering through the city in neglectful and forgetful hotel guests' pockets. Simply posting a sign encouraging guests to leave their keys turns out not to be effective. So an innovator encouraged hotel managers to tie a heavy weight to the key. 'Customers suddenly become only too happy to rid themselves of this annoying object which makes their pockets bulge and weighs down their handbags: they go to the front desk on their own accord to get rid of it. Where the sign, the inscription, the imperative, discipline, or moral obligation all failed, the hotel manager, the innovator, and the metal weight succeeded.'[5] Where a hotel key should be placed is a social assumption; hotels in other countries have taken to creating disposable and recodable keys as those hotel managers anticipate careless and forgetful hotel guests. Matter condenses social assumptions, and thus the material limitations shaping how networks form are also always social. It is in this sense that Latour rejects the dualisms of the material/semiotic or technology/society.

Third, Actor-Network Theory insists that performance creates the relations and the objects/people/actants constituted by these relationships. Networks and actors do not exist prior to performance but are constituted by performance. Sometimes particular actants become visible only when others can observe them clearly contributing to a network. As I mentioned, Latour talks about how important it became for Pasteur to be able to isolate microbes. He removed them from one network filled with farmers, soil and animals. He then put the microbes into sterilised dishes, into contexts that Pasteur could control to a relatively high degree. When Pasteur isolated microbes, making them visible to the human eye, he also made visible that microbes were in a relationship with other objects. Only when the agency of the microbe became visible could one say that the microbe exists. After Pasteur made the microbes visible, they existed in a form that people could interpret in retrospect as timeless; only after 1864 did the microbe always exist.

If all relationships fundamentally emerge out of performance, then for Latour everything and everyone is uncertain. Relations and qualities are in principle reversible. In this sense, performance is key to Actor-Network Theory, in that durability only exists because something is repeatedly performed in familiar, patterned ways. In science, this takes on a peculiar form, since what scientists seek to do is create stable referents to objects that can be moved from context to context (from test tube to graph) and back again. No matter the medium in which something is represented, it is always supposed to be traceable; one is always supposed to be able to trace precisely the labour that went into producing a graph.

In *Pandora's Hope*, Latour describes how scientists collect and circulate soil samples from the Brazilian rainforest. Latour is interested in how the meaning of soil samples is made stable. He explores how certain signs keep their referents the same as they move from context to context. To understand this process, Latour follows a team of scientists as they take soil samples in the Brazilian forest. He explores in great detail how they remove bits of soil, recording each location with enough markers so that ideally anyone could return to that site and locate from where the soil was removed. The information on the soil is then transformed into numerical data, again through techniques that should allow anyone to 'read' the information back into the soil samples. As the scientists bring the soil and its descriptions into each new context, they attempt to ensure that the referents can be traced through each context back to the original location in the Brazilian forest. In analysing this example, Latour argues that scientists construct reversible indexicalities, defining indexicalities as Peircean signs that point to aspects of a context or state of affairs. According to Latour, for signs to be able to represent truth in a scientific network, the referents must exist as a stable chain that point in both directions as the referents move between contexts. He argues: 'For this network to begin to lie – for it to cease to refer – it is sufficient to *interrupt* its expansion at either end, to stop providing for it, to suspend its funding, or to break it at any other point.'[6] To keep a scientific network from producing scientific facts, all one must do is find a way to keep the scientific inscriptions from referring backwards through all the previous contexts, or pointing forwards to other recontextualised referents. In short, what is important for Latour is recognising the labour that goes into constructing reversible indexicalities.

If instability is the given condition, one must labour to create consistency and coherence. For Latour, durability is always an achievement and needs to be analysed as such. One of his primary analytical questions is: how are actants performed and how do they perform themselves into relations that are relatively stable? This focus on durability shapes his theoretical lens for understanding power relationships, which from this perspective become indistinguishable from sustaining relations that last.

Fourth, not all actants are equal. Every actant is heterogeneous, condensing disparate relationships. As a result, not all heterogeneous actants have the same abilities to navigate networks or to move between different networks. In his study of Pasteur, Latour points out that Pasteur was able to use the laboratory to cross many networks. Farmers and sheep were not so privileged. Pasteur affected the network between farmers, sheep and microbes to such a degree that if farmers wanted to change the ways the anthrax microbe was affecting their sheep they had to interact with Pasteur and his laboratory. Farmers were restricted to their network in a way that Pasteur, as a scientist interacting with politicians, public hygienists and military physicians, was not. Some actants are privileged in particular networks, and able to cross networks, others are not. This is another way in which ANT can make power relations visible, by addressing the costs of particular networks for the actants navigating them.

Ilana Gershon

Towards a Typology of Actants

Focusing on how actants circulate within a network draws attention to the ways certain actants move within and between networks. In the course of his work, Latour has called attention to three ways actants can engage with networks that reveal how they circulate: as intermediaries or mediators, immutable mobiles and black boxes. In *Re-Assembling the Social,* Latour discusses the distinction between intermediaries and mediators in terms of how actants can have a network circulate through them. Intermediaries are actants who do not reconfigure the network at all as it flows through them. They are transparent, able to transmit without leaving traces of their presence. While Latour suggests that many people in different networks believe intermediaries exist, Latour himself is sceptical. Instead, he argues that every node in a network is a mediator, contributing and shaping the networks as networks flow through each node. Mediators always affect whatever flows through them or whatever network to which they contribute. For Latour, networks are chains of mediators, in which knowledge and networks alter a little through every node through which they flow.

As Latour began to specify precisely how mediators circulate and affect circulation, he came up with two other types of actants: immutable mobiles and black boxes. Immutable mobiles are, for Latour, actants that remain stable enough to retain their shape or configuration as they circulate through and across networks. Or, put another way, these are actants that can be reproduced throughout a network without being altered (examples include maps, photographs and graphs). Many actants as they circulate seem unstable. Farmers saw anthrax as a dangerous disease with unpredictable causes. Pasteur saw anthrax as a puzzle, potentially but not necessarily isolatable. Sheep experienced anthrax as death, swift and painful. It was not until Pasteur's successful laboratory trials that anthrax could be described through various techniques of inscription. Only after Pasteur found ways to inscribe anthrax's form and circulate these inscriptions did anthrax become an immutable mobile as a deadly bacteria. Through depictions which were reproducible, anthrax stabilised, not only in the context of the lab. Its form stabilised initially throughout Pasteur's network, then across other networks as well. Immutable mobiles circulate with a high degree of stability, being resistant to many (not all) of the transformations with which networks refigure the actants that condense them.

168

A different type of actant, a black box stands for and condenses an actively engaged and complex network. This is a particularly useful concept for analysing how scientific practices move through a network. I turn to how proofs circulate in mathematics as an example. First, a relatively famous mathematician, a geometer, suggests a conjecture – something that the geometer thinks is likely to be true and may lead to further interesting mathematics. Because this mathematician is relatively well known, other geometers pay attention to this conjecture, which has perhaps been introduced to a group of her closest mathematical colleagues at a conference's problem session (a session where people propose mathematical problems for others to solve) funded by the US National Science Foundation. Several mathematicians try on and off to prove this conjecture to no avail. Seventeen years go by, proving that this conjecture is widely understood to be difficult – skilled people have tried and failed. Certain mathematics could be done, if only this conjecture were proven. This conjecture is very much an active part of a lively network. Then a young geometer, with a penchant for talking to scholars in many branches of mathematics, notices in conversation that a technique some topologists have known about for years could be used to prove this conjecture. After the illuminating chat, he goes to a nearby coffee shop and outlines the proof, vindicating yet again the saying that mathematicians are machines for turning caffeine into theorems. He spends the next six months writing the proof and giving talks about it in conferences and at various mathematics departments – his theorems have begun to circulate. He posts the paper on the ArXiv, a website for distributing pre-reviewed scientific articles, then submits the paper to a journal. Once the paper is reviewed by a fellow geometer and accepted by the journal, the most significant theorem in the paper gains the author's name, in part because it solved a seventeen-year-old conjecture – Fisher's theorem. People stop reading the paper with the theorem, and Fisher stops speaking about the proof at conferences. Fisher's theorem has become black boxed. The name 'Fisher's theorem' is now a dense node and a shorthand that stands for and conceals all the complex networks that contributed to the theorem's existence and circulation.

Latour's initial theoretical intervention was to provide the armature for thinking about how truths and facts are constructed, both through scientific practice and elsewhere. The ANT perspective turns to knowledge circulation as the process through which the social construction of truths takes place. Information becomes facts by travelling through networks in patterned ways that imbue the piece of knowledge with authority and relevance. Latour and other ANT scholars discuss how scientists have used public demonstrations, citations, styles of publication, among other strategies, to circulate information as facts.[7] The methodological question is to determine how a particular network circulates information as fact or truth, which requires analysing the structures of a network as well as how a network allocates authority and certainty. The ANT perspective insists that circulation is at the heart of how the network functions. As a consequence, to understand how information comes to be interpreted as facts entails understanding the processes of circulation underpinning how facts are made. Latour argues that all beings and objects, whether constructed as volitional or not, are actants that actively contribute to the network. This involves refusing to take people, animals and objects as simply standing for particular symbolic meanings or information, but rather viewing all as structuring engagements in their own right.

The Usefulness of Rejecting Dualisms

While rejecting dualisms such as subject/object opens the door to new perspectives on how actants influence flows of knowledge, Latour has also explored what other analytical possibilities are enabled, by refusing to adopt dualisms. Latour's accounts of how to analyse the ways people produce dualisms from a theoretical standpoint that rejects dualisms has proven especially influential in other fields. In this section, as an example, I discuss Latour's take on a particular dualism – the local/global divide – and then turn to Latour's approach to interpreting people who are prone to incorporating dualisms in their visions of the world.

Latour points out that accepting the local/global dichotomy involves taking rather too seriously the effects of an actor-network, especially when the local is taken to be a specific bounded place often filled with face-to-face interactions and the global is the unlocatable sum of all these bounded contexts. From an ANT's perspective, it is perhaps easier to dismiss quickly the illusion of the global. After all, the global evokes precisely the type of generalisation that Latour argues against, a generality devoid of materiality and specific actants producing the global. The minute one begins to turn to those actants who produce the global – all that goes into the World Bank or the United Nations – the particularities of the ways that specific actor-networks create the effect of globality undercuts any claims to truly being global. It is precisely these particularities to which Latour recommends ANT scholars pay attention. Thus ANT's methodology is useful for revealing that the global is always already the effect of how a specific and locatable actor-network functions.

Yet Latour points out that the local too vanishes when examined through an ANT lens. When one begins to investigate those scenes labelled local, all of a sudden other places, other times and other actants become crucial for this 'local' moment to exist. As Latour points out about a lecture hall, which may seem like a quotidian local site:

> If we wanted to project on a standard geographical map the connections established between a lecture hall and all the places that are acting in it at the same time, we would have to draw bushy arrows in order to include, for instance, the forest out of which the desk is coming, the management office in charge of classroom planning, the workshop that printed the schedule that helped us find the room, the janitor that tends the place, and so on. And this would not be some idle exercise, since each of these faraway sites has, in some indispensable way, anticipated and preformatted this hall by transporting, through many different sorts of media, the mass of templates that have made it a suitable local – and that are still propping it up.[8]

Latour continues by discussing how diachronic the local is in fact – composed by materials and designs fashioned not only in other places but also at other times. The local is always composed of the results of actions that took place elsewhere and elsewhen, undercutting it as 'local'. Latour explains:

> In most situations, actions will already be interfered with by heterogeneous entities that don't have the same local presence, don't come from the same time, are not visible at once, and don't press upon them with the same weight . . . Stretch any given inter-action and, sure enough, it becomes an actor-network.[9]

For Latour, the local is as much an effect of an actor-network as the global, both sides of the dualisms being misrepresentations or misrecognitions of the historical trajectories that lead to the 'local' or 'global' interactions.

While dualisms may distort, many people still invoke them with conviction and dedication when interpreting the world. This raises an interesting question for ANT scholars – how best to engage with all these actants whose interactions in various networks depend upon assuming precisely the dualisms that Actor-Network Theory rejects. Latour tackles this issue in *We Have Never Been Modern,* where he explores the effects of certain dualisms on how those in the West carve up the world. He argues that people in the West often invoke dualisms to create an analytical tension that they find particularly compelling. Westerners will distinguish terms from each other – traditional/modern, nature/culture, terms that point to actants that have artificially been purified and separated from each other. Once this dichotomy has been successfully imposed, Westerners' analysis entails the surprise of uncovering this dualism, followed by the additional surprise of its inadequacy. Western thinkers will then try to combine precisely what they themselves distinguished in the first place.[10] A good example of this is Latour's slightly ironic use of the term 'hybrid' in *We Have Never Been Modern.* For Latour, hybridity points to an illusion of combination. The term hybrid as a referent claims to combine two already pure entities, as though there were actants who were not hybrid, precisely the illusion that Latour writes against. In rejecting these analytical moves, Latour advocates that one should embrace every actants' mixtures instead of trying continually to purify and recombine.

Criticism

While some critics of Latour will take on board ANT characterisations that all actors are condensed networks, they still have much to say about how Latour depicts networks. For example, Donna Haraway points out that Latour invokes only a few narrow and suspiciously agonistic narratives to account for how networks emerge. She explains:

> The action in science-in-the-making is all trials and feats of strength, amassing of allies, forging of worlds in the strength and numbers of forced allies. All action is agonistic; the creative abstraction is both breathtaking and numbingly conventional. Trials of strength decide whether a representation holds or not. Period. To compete, one must either have a counter laboratory capable of winning in this high-stakes trials of force or give up dreams of making worlds.[11]

As Haraway argues, this is an impoverished set of narratives to draw upon for understanding alliances and their persuasiveness. Latour does not offer multiple ways of understanding how networks interact; in his accounts it all revolves around competing shows of strength, with clear-cut and (for Latour) easily discernible successes and failures.

Latour's simplified set of narratives opens the door to another critique by Susan Leigh Star. In her article, 'Power, Technology and the Phenomenology of Conventions', Star delineates how much one's perspective as an advantaged or disadvantaged actant in a network shapes one's understandings of how networks function. She begins by using her own allergy to onions as a point of departure for revealing the exclusion and inequities in some standardised networks. Different networks emerge out of these varied patterned sets of interactions. Some networks privileged actants who were actively excluded or isolated in other networks. Star encourages people to move beyond Latour's centre-of-the-network perspective and ask about the exclusions and their prices.

Marilyn Strathern, in her article 'Cutting the Network' suggests that Latour's focus on how networks expand does not take into account an equally important aspect of networks – how they are cut. She argues that networks are often cut or stopped for reasons that have little to do with the intrinsic techniques the network deploys to incorporate others and expand. Instead, networks are often curtailed for external reasons that reveal how power is distributed and enacted by forces such as law or putative property rights. She discusses how culturally specific concepts of ownership cut networks differently. She suggests that to understand more fully how actants are linked or disconnected from each other, one has to pay attention to two issues. First, one should take into account the epistemological assumptions embedded in network exchanges about how relationships are formed. Second, one must pay attention to the techniques for cutting networks as much as the techniques for expanding networks, especially since disconnections often reveal the relationships of power shaping the network.

Lastly, Donna Haraway also criticises Latour's focus on those the networks favour. She argues that identity categories are all network-effects, that class, race, gender are not a priori to but created by networks.[12] In Latour's analysis, these categories appear as given, as qualities that actants appear to bring to their interactions, rather than emerging from these encounters. Haraway urges Latour and other ANT scholars to be sensitive to how the networks they study have social effects beyond those effects most apparent when one focuses on the production of scientific facts.

Conclusion

Latour and Actor-Network Theory in general have become popular outside of the original disciplinary confines of science and technology studies as scholars are increasingly committed to moving beyond the dichotomies of the material versus the social, or agency versus structure. Actor-Network Theory offers a new methodological and theoretical approach to studying how ideas and objects travel, which scholars of democracy, organisations, markets and media have found helpful. In addition, it provides techniques for analyzing the social construction of facts and truth which go beyond studying the discourses shaping what counts as truth. Latour has cleared a space so that scholars can begin asking new questions of topics that have become perhaps a little too familiar.

Notes

1. Latour renounced Actor-Network Theory in his article, 'On Recalling Actor-Network Theory'. He has since retracted his rejection in *Re-Assembling the Social*, p. 9.
2. T. Hugh Crawford, 'An Interview with Bruno Latour', *Configurations*, 1, 1990, p. 248.
3. *Laboratory Life*.
4. *Science in Action*; *We Have Never Been Modern*; *Pandora's Hope*; *Re-Assembling the Social*.
5. Bruno Latour, 'Technology Is Society Made Durable', in John Law (ed.), *A Sociology of Monsters* (London: Routledge, 1991), p. 104.
6. *Pandora's Hope*, p. 76.
7. *Laboratory Life*; Steven Shapin, *A Social History of Truth* (Chicago: University of Chicago Press, 1995), pp. 355–407.
8. *Re-Assembling the Social*, p. 200.
9. Ibid. p. 202.
10. *We Have Never Been Modern*, p. 78.
11. Haraway, *Modest_Witness*, p. 34.
12. Ibid. pp. 23–48.

Major Works by Latour

Aramis, or, The Love of Technology, trans. Catherine Porter (Cambridge, MA: Harvard University Press, 1996).

Laboratory Life: The Construction of Scientific Facts, with Steve Woolgar (Princeton: Princeton University Press, 1986 [1979]).

Pandora's Hope: Essays on the Reality of Science Studies (Cambridge, MA: Harvard University Press, 1999).

The Pasteurization of France, trans. Alan Sheridan and John Law (Cambridge, MA: Harvard University Press, 1988).

Politics of Nature: How to Bring the Sciences into Democracy, trans. Catherine Porter (Cambridge, MA: Harvard University Press, 2004).

Re-Assembling the Social: An Introduction to Actor-Network Theory (Oxford: Oxford University Press, 2005).

Science in Action: How to Follow Scientists and Engineers through Society (Cambridge, MA: Harvard University Press, 1987).

We Have Never Been Modern, trans. Catherine Porter (Cambridge, MA: Harvard University Press, 1993).

Suggestions for Further Reading

Akrich, Madeline, 'The De-scription of a Technical Object', in W. A. J. L. Bijker (ed.), *Shaping Technology/Building Society: Studies in Sociotechnical Change* (Cambridge, MA: The MIT Press, 1991), pp. 205–24. This article discusses the tension between the implied user and actual user in a designed object, which becomes most visible when the object travels across cultural contexts.

Callon, Michel, 'Some Elements of a Sociology of Translation: Domestication of Scallops and the Fishermen of St. Brieuc Bay', in John Law (ed.), *Power, Action and Belief: A New Sociology of Knowledge?* (London: Routledge, 1986), pp. 196-229. An early ANT discussion of how even scallops have agency.

Haraway, Donna, *Modest_Witness@Second_Millennium.FemaleMan©_Meets_OncoMouse™* (London: Routledge 1997). Chapter 1 offers a good summary of critiques of Latour.

Latour, Bruno, 'On Recalling Actor-Network Theory', in J. Law and J. Hassard (eds), *Actor Network and After* (Oxford: Blackwell, 1999), pp. 15–25. In this article Latour renounces ANT, claiming that all elements of the name, from actor, network to hyphen, are nonsensical.

Law, John, and John Hassard (eds), *Actor Network Theory and After* (Oxford: Blackwell, 1999). A collection of articles by ANT scholars. The introduction is a cogent overview of Actor-Network Theory.

Leigh Star, Susan, 'Power, Technology and the Phenomenology of Conventions: On Being Allergic to Onions', in John Law (ed.), *A Sociology of Monsters: Power, Technology and the Modern World* (London: Routledge, 1991), pp. 26–56. Star points out that networks privilege some actants and disadvantage others, even along unlikely lines such as allergies to onions.

Leigh Star, Susan Griesemer and James Griesemer, 'Institutional Ecology, Translations, and Boundary Objects: Amateurs and Professionals in

Berkeley's Museum of Vertebrate Zoology, 1907–1939', *Social Studies of Science*, 19, 1989, pp. 387–420. This article adds to Bruno Latour's various discussions of different kinds of actants, such as the immutable mobile or black boxes. This article suggests that actants can also be boundary objects, which are objects that are underdetermined enough to move easily across networks.

Strathern, Marilyn, 'Cutting the Network', *Journal of the Royal Anthropological Institute*, 2, 1996, pp. 517–35. This article offers an engaging critique of Latour's focus on network expansion and recruitment using ethnographic examples from the Solomon Islands and US patent history.

11

Antonio Negri (1933–)

Arianna Bove

Antonio Negri's work ranges from philosophical exegesis and Marxian political economy to political pamphleteering and play-writing, spanning a period of fifty years. If anything connects this vast differentiated body of work, it would be the search for the logic of social ontology. This chapter focuses on Negri's political and historical reworking of the notions of class, the economy, power relations and conflict; his critique of dialectics and transcendental philosophy; and the location of an affirmative subjectivity in the creative power of historical subjects, while also charting his own involvement in practices of resistance and liberation.

Born in Padua, Northern Italy, in 1933, Negri was a child during the Second World War. In the early 1950s, as a student of philosophy, Negri travelled to Paris where he was taught by Jean Hyppolite, the French translator of Hegel's *Phenomenology*, and witnessed the debate on Hegel that was to influence a whole generation of critical thinkers.[1] Later, in Germany he read Franz Rosenzweig and the Frankfurt School. Immersed in the traditions of postwar radical humanism, the critique of alienation, reinterpretations of dialectics and historical materialism, Negri returned to Italy determined to bring this new theory to bear on political practice. He joined the mass working-class movement of the North and the new wave of resistance that spread from Turin in 1962, where thousands of workers protested against the trade unions' compromises with the car manufacturer FIAT. This was the first of a number of the conflicts, retaliations and betrayals that would come to characterise the turbulent relationship between the left and its representative bodies and eventually give rise to autonomous Marxism. The years between 1960 and 1977 saw a long series of different anti-capitalist uprisings against trade unions, the communist party and industry that met with violent police repression. In the absence of postwar de-fascistisation, society had remained sharply divided along political lines; the permanent class conflict that marked these two decades saw Italy in a state of simmering civil war.[2]

A New Mode of Marxist Inquiry

Fully engaged in these struggles of the 1960s and 1970s, Negri wrote numerous essays and pamphlets on state theory, the juridical history of constitutionalism, state administration in times of crisis, as well as Karl Marx and capitalism, where he developed the notions of class composition and the state form. Many of these appeared in journals and were distributed outside factories before being unceremoniously pulped by the police.[3] Negri argued for a form of Marxism conceived of as an open materialist theory with a changing real referent and no internal continuity: a philosophy of praxis for a changing subject. In the midst of widespread social antagonism, debates on workers' forms of organisation and the failure of successive workers' revolutions, from the Spring of Nations in 1848 to the Council communism of the early twentieth century, were generally framed by two alternatives: phenomenological critiques of the commodity form and materialist analyses of productive cycles and crises from the standpoint of capital. The former resulted in more or less optimistic prescriptions about the level of class consciousness and the need for ideology critique; the latter described the objective tendencies of capitalism to subsume and overcome its internal contradictions. Dissatisfied with both approaches, Negri championed a political perspectivism that moves from the standpoint of workers' subjectivity and from the assumption (against Hegelian forms of dialectical recuperation of negativity) of an irreconcilable asymmetry in the relationship between labour and capital.

As part of what became known as the current of *operaismo*, which used sociological inquiry as an ethical and political research device to organise social antagonism, Negri began to investigate class composition, the political, economic and social characters of this changing subject and the expressions of its insurgent practices. 'The concept of asymmetry (of proletarian power versus capitalist development) means that the autonomy of class is not

178

recognisable if one looks for it through the categories of capital.'[4] By class autonomy Negri refers to all moments of auto-valorisation that characterise 'living labour' in its struggle against exploitation and subsumption under capital, as opposed to the dead labour embodied in the commodity form. Negri sees auto-valorisation as a continuation of Marx's method of the critique of political economy with an emphasis on subjectivity and the critique of labour. The latter, he claims, 'is always an analysis of the mode of production of a society (its base and substance) against the value-form it uses (its mystification)'.[5] Against objectivist interpretations of Marx that emphasised continuity and synthesis, Negri speaks of ruptures and metamorphosis.

Class Struggle, Class Composition and the State

Negri charts a genealogy of the productive forces and relations of production in three main ruptures of capitalist development, corresponding to metamorphoses in the forms of political sovereignty. In his genealogies, the insurgent subjectivity of the side of labour in the capital–labour relation is the main driving force of social change: for Negri, 'every innovation is a failed revolution'.[6] During the nineteenth and the early twentieth century, the working class emerged as a strong political subject, headed by the figure of the skilled worker whose privileged position in relation to the means of production afforded the worker a prominent role in struggles against exploitation and for control over the productive process. The existence and resistance of this particular section of the working class affected a metamorphosis of the mode of capitalist production as a whole. After the Russian Revolution, the threat presented by this new political subject – the self-styled vanguard – demanded that class antagonism be taken seriously and accounted for in the process of capitalist accumulation. Frederick Taylor's methods of scientific management and Henry Ford's introduction of the moving assembly line, standardisation and mass production responded to this threat by forcibly severing the link between the political and the economic, the vanguard and the masses. These methods restructured the productive forces and their technical composition through deskilling and, by the discipline imposed by assembly lines, broke down the energy and vitality of the workers, creating a docile labouring class.

At the level of state theory, Negri's critique of labour extends to the direct involvement of the state in production not only as the guarantor of the smooth workings of capital but also as the organising force of the exploitation of labour. In his writings on John Maynard Keynes and the New Deal, Negri traces the state's response to the communist threat in western capitalist countries in its introduction of welfare services and the use of public spending. For Negri, Fordism in production was matched by the governmental form of the planner state. The state is the representative of what Engels called the 'ideal collective capitalist', striving towards stability through the creation of social surplus value and the overcoming of 'frictions between individual capitalists'.[7] Laissez-faire and unregulated markets were remnants of the ideology of the early bourgeoisie: the planner state recognises the dangers presented by the working class and so it 'continuously recreates the sources of its legitimacy in a process of permanent adjustment of the conditions of equilibrium'.[8]

Though speaking in the interests of capitalists, Keynes had registered the need for balancing social forces and in so doing recognised the autonomy of the working class as an 'independent variable'. In contrast, those who claimed to adopt the standpoint of labour either made socialist demands for self-management as an alternative to unregulated markets or plotted to seize the power of the state. Negri insists that the left have wrongly underestimated the role of the state, because they think it can be merely ignored or that by seizing its power they can end capitalist contradictions. Rather, the state form changes in response to developments in class subjectivity, developments that need to be charted in a work of inquiry that recognises the subversive position of the working class, its agency and forms of expression.

Refusal

Negri investigated class subjectivity in the hidden spontaneous forms of antagonism in factories during the 1960s and 1970s while adopting the subjective standpoint of labour. He found that beyond wage demands, class struggles were taking place in the form of refusal, wild cat strikes, sabotage, absenteeism and moving from one employer to another, all of which occurred autonomously from the political exigencies and programmes of the representative structures of trade unions, the communist party and the planner state.[9]

> The refusal of labour is the immediate synthesis of struggle and innovation, life and productivity. It is the potency of the negative, obviously, what the bosses call the negative in so far as it negates *their* rationality. But their rationality is the expropriation of the power of innovation, of workers' productive power; it is the command over the working day; whereas workers' rationality is the augmentation of labour productivity for the benefit of all, from the factory, to society.[10]

According to Negri, with Fordist production, rather than following a logic of appropriation (of means of production and government structures), the insurgent forces of labour adopt refusal, or the expenditure of social energies and surplus outside the factory walls, as the practice of alternatives to capitalism. Importantly, this is not always a self-conscious operation of those who struggle; it is also present as an unconscious social power, a desire with its own irreducible logic. Consequently capitalist economics 'defines its production no longer in a determinate relationship to individual labour but with the whole of the social productive forces'.[11]

In this period, termed the 'real subsumption of society under capital', the distinctions between the particular and the general, the economic and the political, the private and the public, no longer apply.[12] Negri distinguishes between the function of the planner state and that of the state as enterprise: while the former reforms itself and the make-up of the working class, restructuring social relations to control productive cycles and maintain economic equilibrium in the context of a general social belief in the progressive potential of the realm of production, the latter also imposes new class divisions and a new regime of command. Negri argues that restructuring in times of crisis is not only an effort to reform capitalism internally but also, and more importantly, to present productive power as belonging to capital rather than labour.[13]

In this context, Negri draws on Marx's *Grundrisse* to argue that crisis is determined and affected by class struggle. However, when capital begins to organise society as a whole rather than discipline a section of the working class, it directly contributes to the production of subjectivity, one that it strives to control. As the professional worker's demands were absorbed by Keynesian schemes, antagonism shifted towards demands of liberation of work and a separation of income from labour. A new class combination emerged when workers engaged in new practices of auto-valorisation outside and despite the negotiation of socialist and communist political

181

parties and trade unions with the state and industry. This new composition included the figure of the 'socialised worker' or the 'affective labourer', whose struggles took place outside the factory at the level of the production of subjectivity and alternative forms of life. We shall return to this genealogy in the last section, after a discussion of the philosophical foundations of Negri's materialist ontology.

The Critique of Dialectics: Modernity and Anti-modernity

As antagonism spread outside the factory walls, the Italian government tried to bring it to a close in 1977 with a large clampdown on social movements and the arrest of over 10,000 people from the extra-parliamentary left. Negri was one of them. He spent four and a half years in various special prisons awaiting trial for a string of charges that kept changing, during which time he wrote his most dense philosophical essays. In the face of escalating levels and changing forms of social antagonism, Negri declared the theoretical and political inadequacy of radical humanist interpretations of dialectics as a philosophy of praxis. As a method, dialectics were trapped in a particular historical development and could no longer describe the basic characteristics of the relationship between labour and capital: not only had working-class conflict been subsumed and profitably utilised in capitalist restructuration but also it continued to change the places and terms of its engagement with it. Negri exposes Hegelian dialectics as self-defeating in practice: 'The Hegelian working class movement recognises itself as slave and as slave it organises itself in front of the master. Organisation emerges as substitutive will, as compensation, as tension on the negative, of the negative.'[14] Dialectics sees negation as a moment to be overcome to achieve the fullness of being, whereas for Negri resistance is immediately productive. In his view, dialectics describes the capture of the dynamism of social relations of production from the standpoint of capital and portrays the workers' movements for the liberation of labour as the moment of negativity in progress. But for Negri, far from negation, antagonism is self-affirmation and valorisation: the real motor of innovation and progress. In so far as the relation between capital and labour is asymmetrical and heteronomous, it cannot be resolved or overcome; it can only be replaced by a social revolution. 'Dialectics, in as much as it forms transcendental thinking, denies the decision the power to generate *ex nihilo* and to produce plenitude, fullness of being in the void, against the void'.[15]

Negri paints the theoretical landscape as an involution of modernity and its values. Modernity's promise of progress, freedom and democracy was a mask for bourgeois sovereignty and transcendent power. From prison, he traced the emergence of another modernity, found not in the apologetics of René Descartes, Jean-Jacques Rousseau and Georg W. Friedrich Hegel, but in immanent materialism, a legacy left by Nicolo Machiavelli, Baruch Spinoza, Giacomo Leopardi and Karl Marx. This opposition between immanent materialism and a transcendental view of sovereignty (both ontological and epistemological) has informed all of Negri's philosophical writings, which often take the form of deep, close political readings and intellectual histories. The tracing of the emergence of this other modernity is also an application of the immanent materialist method, one that does not formalise the workings of reason in order to impose them on reality, but intervenes critically in the real to identify its potential. Much as Negri's treatment of class composition sought to reveal the dynamics of actual conflicts, he explores theoretical tendencies to uncover their emancipatory logic.

In *Political Descartes,* Negri situates the thought of the father of modern rationalism in the first historical crisis of the bourgeois project.[16] Living in the aftermath of the Reformation and Counter-Reformation movements, involved as a soldier in the Thirty Years War (1618–48), Descartes supported the political development of absolutism and divine right theories of sovereignty. Negri interprets Descartes's rationalism and dualism politically to show how philosophies of transcendence emerge as a reactionary response to crisis; in this case, to the failure of the humanist project of the Renaissance to free humankind from religious dogma and authority and assert its power to make history and give meaning to its own affairs. Descartes's ambiguous adherence to anti-libertine polemics and his critique of epistemological scepticism are seen by Negri as a protest against the cynicism ensuing from this crisis. Libertinism signalled an involution of the humanist civic and political hopes, where 'the ideal is freed from the temptation of becoming collective . . . In the words of the libertine motto: within as you please, without according to custom'.[17] On the one hand, the libertine rebellion registered the separation of civil society from the state and the retreat from utopias of collective freedom into the inner self and private life; on the other hand, the sceptics' response to the impossibility of matching reality with reason in the pursuit of science epitomised the epistemological crisis of the Renaissance. These two questions of politics and epistemology were attempts to confront the historical separation of the bourgeois ideal of universal progress of science from the experience of diversity and multiplicity. Descartes resolved both of these problems through mediation: the former, by accepting absolutism as the only guarantor of peace; the latter, with a retreat into metaphysics, mathematical formalisation and the mistrust of the senses. In doing so, he neutralised the immediacy of experience and the contradictory nature of the relation between the individual and the world into the pacified and controlled de-realised world of a solitary thinking subject that avoids collision with it. The mind takes precedence over experience in the search for a fictitious unity; there, and only there, can Descartes discover the bourgeois subject.

In Negri's view the dynamics of appropriation of the world of things, nature and history characterised the utopianism of the Renaissance but were not resolved in a philosophy of praxis: this was the failure of the first liberal bourgeois project to give itself a political form. Descartes, the ideologue of the bourgeoisie *par excellence*, resorted to rational theology and transposed the relation between the world and the individual onto his or her relation to God. Finding no correspondence to ontological individualism in reality, Descartes fictionalises it in an abstraction. A factor that is outside, over and above reality, is called upon to mediate the exigencies of the real and provide the justification for fictitious dualisms such as the juxtaposition of productive forces and relations of production. For Negri, the betrayal of the bourgeoisie consists in this politics of mediation, falsification and transcendence, in hiding the violence of mechanisms of appropriation and presenting the realm of circulation and the market as a universal, and undivided, second nature.

> The utopia of productive force, which is the indestructible legacy of the humanistic revolution, is shattered and reproduced: shattered in the illusion of a social and collective continuity of a process of appropriation of nature and wealth; reproduced, at first, as the idea of command and, subsequently, as the hypothesis of an abundant and progressive appropriation in the form of profit. This is the idea of the market: a (mysterious and sublime) duplication of labour and value. Progressive optimism, rational direction and faith in the results of optimisation all extend across the relationship exploitation-profit.[18]

184

Negri finds a critical alternative to the bourgeois project of transcendence in Baruch Spinoza's materialist philosophy of immanence.[19] For Spinoza, the elucidation of connections in logic does not merely serve the purpose of clarity of thought. Spinoza believes that the order and connections of ideas can be treated as the order and connections of things. For a philosophy of immanence, there is no external cause to the world. The world contains its own explanation. From the dark margins of seventeenth-century philosophy, Spinoza renewed the Renaissance humanist project and found a way to integrate a theory of political power into the development of social forces and refuse their mediation in a separate and transcendental function of command.[20] Negri's intellectual history unravels the concrete practices and determinations of society in relation to and often in conflict with the ideological alternatives of the historical period, showing that in Spinoza's immanent materialism the antinomies of bourgeois thought implode. In Spinoza's metaphysics, liberation is a necessity. Science does not irremediably command; on the contrary, science can be a machine of liberation. Science is not subordinated to development and domination; it is the expression of consecutive moments of cumulated acts of collective liberation. In this and other respects, Spinoza is an anomaly of the seventeenth century. The prevailing philosophies of the time reproduced the antinomies of bourgeois thought in metaphysics and politics, limited to 'the discovery of the antagonistic character of capitalist accumulation with respect to the unitary utopia that had been set in motion'.[21] But for Spinoza productive power is only subordinated to itself.

Following this ontology, in so far as production is the constitution of being, for Negri the critique of labour goes beyond the immanent critique of the contradictions of capital; the negative aspect of critique is not isolated but only one movement of the desire for emancipation and self-expression on the part of social subjects. Yet this movement is incommensurable, unstoppable and non-teleological: '*the desire for liberation has an irreducible ontological logic of its own*'.[22] Throughout his philosophical work, Negri's materialism is characterised by an unrelenting attack on the dialectics and dynamics of resolution and pacification of political resistance. The tension of the negative is rejected and an ontology of potentiality asserted against all tendencies of critical thought to dwell on negation as a stage of progress.

From his earlier Marxian analysis of the changes in the

capital–labour relation, Negri develops a political theory of constituent and constituted power based on the distinction between *potentia* and *potestas* as found in Spinoza. Power is never presented solely from the perspective of limitation; power is equally possibility and capacity. The form of domination of constituted power, or *potestas,* is always contextualised in the possibilities of resistance that are open and never reduced to the mask that power itself wears. The formal exercise of power as *potestas* is only ever set in motion in response to the creative energy it tries to contain. In Spinoza's political theory, Negri finds the tools to describe the subject of a radical, direct and immanent democratic form of government, the embodiment of this desire for liberation.

Continuing in this trajectory of alter-modernity, Negri dedicates a book to the Italian poet and essayist Giacomo Leopardi, who was steeped in the turbulent years of the early nineteenth century.[23] Negri reinterprets Leopardi as a thinker of the crisis of formal subsumption of society under capital, as capitalism establishes its hegemony over the social order in the name of progress and positivism. Working in the tradition of the Enlightenment sensualism of Condillac, a particular variant of empiricism and materialism, and living in the aftermath of the French Revolution, Leopardi was witness to a radical change and its suppression, a revolution and the restoration of order, to which he responded with his own version of open materialism that is 'as powerful as it is disenchanted'.[24]

Comparing it with the Renaissance, Negri sees the Enlightenment as a social revolution that was betrayed. Leopardi showed the collective side of European Romanticism that embraced a cosmic view of the world instead of retreating to variants of aesthetic individualism in search of the absolute. Here Negri returns to a problem that recurs in his intellectual histories of this period: the inability of society to give itself forms of organisation that remain true to its political ideals and the spirit in which social revolutionary subjects are formed, the transitions from constituent to constituted power. Throughout these writings, Negri bears witness to the social and political aspirations of generations repressed or betrayed yet unable to constitute themselves into long-lasting political organisational forms. The difference between constituent and constitutive power is crucial not only to an analysis of dynamics of appropriation and reappropriation but also to the realisation of the political power of revolutionary subjects.

In 1983, elected to the Italian government as a member of the

Radical Party, Negri was released from prison on grounds of parliamentary immunity, but the Parliament rescinded his immunity. Rather than be returned to prison, Negri fled to Paris where he remained in exile for fourteen years. There he deepened his analysis of the 'socialised worker' and immaterial labourer in various studies on the sociology of work in collaboration with Maurizio Lazzarato. In this period he came closer to the thought of Michel Foucault, Gilles Deleuze and Felix Guattari. With the latter, he published *Communists like us*,[25] a strong intervention in the debate about the new social subjects of the 1980s, referred to as the age of defeatism, cynicism, opportunism and fear. Negri also developed his critique of the labour theory of value and corresponding forms of sovereignty that would culminate in the thesis of *Empire*. In 1997 Negri returned to Italy to argue for an amnesty for all the political prisoners and exiles of the 1970s, but after Parliament rejected the proposal he served the last six years of his sentence until his release in 2003.

New Class Composition, Immaterial Labour and *Empire*

Empire was published in 2000, bringing together much of the work by Negri in previous years in an introductory form and accessible prose. Negri and his co-author Michael Hardt updated the analysis of class composition and the 'socialised worker' by introducing the notion of immaterial labour, which they identify as an emerging figure of labour that becomes increasingly dominant with the informatisation and globalisation of the economy. The quality of labour and class composition had changed in the shift from Fordist mass production to Toyotist lean production, a model in which, prior to being manufactured, a product must be sold. Lean production required the establishment of a system of communication between production and consumption, factories and markets. Here the social factory is made profitable and an increasing proportion of capital must be invested to develop the possibilities of communicative techniques, corresponding to the increasingly cerebral nature of labour. The refusal of labour of the mass worker had initiated the development of labour saving technologies. Negri talks about the tertiarisation of industry and the spread of the service sector where knowledge, affects and subjectivity itself is made productive.

Robert Reich calls the kind of immaterial labour involved in computer and communication work 'symbolic-analytical services'- tasks that

187

involve problem-solving, problem-identifying, and strategic brokering activities. This type of labour claims the highest value, and thus Reich identifies it as the key to competition in the new global economy.[26]

The idea that immaterial labour directly produces the capital–labour relation changes the configuration of power and the possibility of refusal and auto-valorisation. Immaterial workers are primarily producers of subjectivity. This aspect of immaterial labour constitutes its 'affective' character. Affective labour is 'embedded in moments of human interaction and communication'. It acts wherever human contact is required and is essentially involved in the production of 'social networks, forms of community and biopower. What is created in the networks of affective labour is a form-of-life'.[27]

In Negri's view, with the emergence of affective and immaterial labour, it is no longer possible to measure value according to the time necessary to produce a commodity and to reproduce the worker. The 'labour theory of value' was only appropriate to the time when labour was outside capital and needed to be reduced to labour power. But when production is directly involved with the production of social relations, it becomes coextensive with social reproduction. Negri and Hardt adopt Foucault's notion of biopower to describe this new mode of production. 'Empire' is the process representing the corresponding command over this form of labour: since actual work is different in Empire, mechanisms of social control directly affect subjectivities. The biopolitical notions of life and body are determined in the political constitution and in the real daily affirmations of social subjectivity.

The emergence of Empire as a global mode of governance responds to the crisis of disciplinary modes of control that erupted in the refusal of the mass worker. The traditional centres in which discipline is deployed (class, party, school, nuclear family, factory) undergo a crisis, as a result of which disciplinary rationality is substituted by more efficient, economic, discrete and implicit procedures aimed at governing people. Biopower takes life as its object. For Hardt and Negri real subsumption of society under capital operates at the level of biopolitical production because production tries to subsume life itself. The mode of governance of Empire takes the form of preventive control: from a predictive medicine where society is treated as a reserve of diseases and individuals as carriers of pathologies; to an education that is transformed into life-long learning where everyone is compelled to remain productive throughout their life; and a surveillance that is used not to discover crime but as a preventive tool for recognising, inserting into databases and scanning human bodies and behaviour. Individuals are carriers of calculable risks.

Negri and Hardt endorse much of Foucault's analysis of biopower, regarding biopolitical production under Post-Fordism as the apex of a process of struggles to dominate the social body. In Post-Fordism, the body is fixed capital and the instruments of labour are the brain-machines of social cooperation.[28] As the institutions of disciplinary power break down so does the function of representation, negotiation and delegation. Insisting on the difference between constituent and constitutive power, Negri is able to highlight the role of social movements and dynamics as arising from the grassroots and affecting responses. The irreducible and heterogeneous antagonist of Empire is the multitude.

Multitude

The concept of multitude is derived from Spinoza's political theory. Negri and Hardt see it as the constituent subject in the age of Empire that forces a shift in power relations. As a political subject, the multitude refuses the functions of representation and exercises its right to disobedience in the practice of exodus, constantly reconfiguring the places and scope of antagonism. The multitude is the political expression of a new social composition that uses technology, machines and social cooperation as instruments of liberation, thus constantly changing the possibilities of its capture in capitalist valorisation.[29] In Negri's view, government, or governance, becomes a flexible machine of recuperation and disavowal of social value, while capitalism is increasingly dependent on the innovations of the social factory. The value created by subjectivities in social cooperation is beyond measure. Attempts to subsume it under the exploitative mechanisms of capitalist valorisation appear as increasingly parasitical and abusive.

> Today there is no longer any measure, and hence there is no longer any reasonable appropriation either. Today, we are outside measure and that is so because we are in a state of productive surplus. We could easily satisfy all the needs of the populations in the world: this is not a potentiality; this is a calculable, economic possibility.[30]

This productive surplus of subjectivity is the object of the last volume of the trilogy of *Empire, Multitude* and *Commonwealth*. In

Commonwealth, Negri and Hardt conceptualise the common as the realm of constitution of the multitude that lies beyond the distinction of public and private. They develop an analysis of the current composition of capital, and the forms of its accumulation in finance and rent, that responds to new processes of biopolitical production concommitant with the creation of scarcity and the insecurity of labour, to which Negri refers as the 'precarisation of labour'. 'Capitalist accumulation today is increasingly external to the production process, such that exploitation takes the form of *expropriation of the common.*'[31] To the republic of property, they oppose the multitude of the poor in a genealogy that charts the struggles between those who have no part in the management of the common and those who control it, those who produce common wealth and those who de-socialise it.

Negri has come under heavy criticism from both the left and the right. The right portrays him as a 'dark and evil guru'.[32] Most of the left critically engaged with his writings from *Empire* onwards.[33] Some accused him of Euro-centrism: the notion of immaterial labour as a tendency is said to underplay the current role of factory workers in the global economy and a-critically bypass questions of race and gender. Others dismissed *Empire* as an analysis of the 'Clinton era' that can hardly be applied to the new Neo-Con-inspired global order emerging after the fall of the Twin Towers. The concept of multitude has been seen as a weak sociological category that is not fit to replace the category of the working class. These criticisms have largely been addressed in the second and third volume of the trilogy: the authors discuss anti-colonial, anti-racist and feminist struggles in the context of the tradition of alter-modernity, define recent US policy as the last gasp of a waning hegemony, and reassert a definition of the multitude as a class concept, both ontologically and politically. The multitude is also the protagonist of Negri's recent theatre plays, a *Trilogy of Resistance* on the relationship between the production of the common and violence.

Negri's contribution to critical theory cannot be underestimated. His writings on ontology, his lineage of revolutionary thinkers otherwise forgotten, the productive encounter of Marxism and post-structuralism, and his intervention on the politics of theories of modernity bred new life in the otherwise stale and cynical debate on the postmodern. His affirmative politics has been influenced by and has in turn influenced two generations of militants, from worker autonomists to the anti-capitalist movement, and this symbiotic relationship has undoubtedly contributed to a revival of critical theory as a production of knowledge that is also an ethical and political task.

Notes

1. 'Hegel was a funnel: he gathered everything the history of thought had produced after him. Like an Egyptian pyramid, everyone, slaves and masters, had put their own brick on it, it was impossible to move it so everyone was climbing it.' Antonio Negri, *Pipeline. Lettere da Rebibbia* [Pipeline. Letters from Rebibbia – Special Prison] (Turin: Einaudi, 1982), p. 41. Jean Hyppolite was a reader and commentator on Hegel, whose teachings played a crucial role in the philosophy of Gilles Deleuze, Jacques Deridda and Michel Foucault amongst others.
2. See N. Balestrini and P. Moroni (eds), *L'orda d'oro* (Milan: Feltrinelli, 1988), for a rich collection of documents from this period.
3. Some of these are collected in *Books for Burning*.
4. Negri, '20 Theses on Marx: Interpretation of the Class Situation Today', in S. Makdis, C. Casarino and R. E. Karl (eds), *Marxism beyond Marxism* (New York: Routledge, 1996), pp. 149–80.
5. Ibid. p. 165.
6. Negri, *Pipeline*, p. 83.
7. This was informed by the notion of social capital, further analysed by Mario Tronti in 'Social Capital', *Telos*, 17, Autumn 1973, pp. 60–85.
8. Negri, *Revolution Retrieved*, p. 13.
9. Negri, 'Logic and Theory of Inquiry', trans. Arianna Bove and Nate Holdren <http://www.generation-online.org/p/fpnegri20.htm>.
10. Negri, *Pipeline*, p. 83.
11. Negri, *La Fabbrica della Strategia, 33 Lezioni su Lenin* (Padua: Collettivo Editoriale LibriRossi, 1976), p. 162; *The Factory of Strategy. 33 Lessons on Lenin* (New York: Columbia University Press, forthcoming).
12. The term is derived from the unpublished Chapter 6 of volume 1 of Marx's *Capital*: see 'Appendix' to *Capital, vol. 1* (London: Penguin, 1992).
13. Hardt and Negri, *Labor of Dionysus*.
14. Negri, *Pipeline*, p. 121.
15. Negri, *Time for Revolution*, p. 251.
16. Negri, *Political Descartes*, p. 116.
17. Ibid. p. 119.
18. Negri, *The Savage Anomaly*, p. 218.
19. For more on the revival of Spinoza, also influenced by Pierre Macherey, Gilles Deleuze and Louis Althusser, see W. Montag and T. Stolze (eds), *The New Spinoza* (Minneapolis: University of Minnesota Press, 1998).

20. Negri, *The Savage Anomaly*, pp. 136–43.
21. Ibid. p. 18.
22. Negri, *Time for Revolution,* p. 134.
23. Negri, *La Lenta Ginestra* (Milan: Sugarco, 1987).
24. Negri, 'The European Leopardi', trans. Timothy Murphy, *Genre*, 33, 1, Spring 2000, p. 18.
25. Felix Guattari and Antonio Negri, *Communists Like Us: New Spaces of Liberty, New Lines of Alliance* (New York: Semiotext(e), 1990).
26. Hardt and Negri, *Empire*, p. 289.
27. Michael Hardt, 'Affective Labour', *boundary2*, 26, 2, Summer 1999, p. 92.
28. Negri, 'Back to the future', in J. Bosma, P. van Mourik Broekman, T. Byfield, M. Fuller, G. Lovink, D. McCarty, P. Schultz, F. Stalder, M. Wark and F. Wilding (eds), *Read me! Ascii Culture and the Revenge of Knowledge* (New York: Autonomedia, 1999), p. 182.
29. One example of this is how the practice of file sharing online has prompted the introduction and enforcement of intellectual property regimes, affecting the whole of the information economy.
30. Negri and Casarino, *In Praise of the Common*, p. 77.
31. Hardt and Negri, *Commonwealth*, p. 112.
32. Brian C. Anderson, 'Brothers in Marx', *Wall Street Journal*, 7 October 2009.
33. A useful collection of criticisms and reviews can be found in a special issue of *Rethinking Marxism*, 13, 1, 2001. For a comprehensive list, see <http://multitudes.samizdat.net/The-discussion-about-Empire>.

Major Works by Negri

Books for Burning: Between Civil War and Democracy in 1970s Italy, trans. Arianna Bove, Ed Emery, Tim Murphy and Francesca Novello (London: Verso, 2005 [1971–7]).

Commonwealth, with Michael Hardt (Cambridge: Harvard University Press, 2009).

Empire, with Michael Hardt (Cambridge: Harvard University Press, 2000).

In Praise of the Common: A Conversation on Philosophy and Politics, with Cesare Casarino (Minneapolis: University of Minnesota Press, 2008).

Insurgencies. Constituent Power and the Modern State, trans. Maurizia Boscagli (Minneapolis: University of Minnesota Press, 1999 [1992]).

The Labor of Dionysus: A Critique of the State Form, with Michael Hardt (Minneapolis: University of Minnesota Press, 1994).

The Labor of Job: The Biblical Text as a Parable of Human Labor, trans. Matteo Mandarini (Duke University Press, 2009 [2002]).

Marx beyond Marx: Lessons on the Grundrisse, trans. Harry Cleaver, Michael Ryan, and Maurizio Viano (New York: Autonomedia, 1991 [1979]).

Antonio Negri (1933–)

Multitude: War and Democracy in the Age of Empire, with Michael Hardt (New York: Penguin Press, 2004).

Political Descartes: Reason, Ideology and the Bourgeois Project, trans. Matteo Mandarini and Alberto Toscano (London: Verso Books, 2007 [1970]).

Revolution Retrieved: Selected Writings on Marx, Keynes, Capitalist Crisis and New Social Subjects, trans. Ed Emery and John Merrington (London: Red Notes, 1988 [1968–83]).

The Savage Anomaly: The Power of Spinoza's Metaphysics and Politics, trans. Michael Hardt (Minneapolis: University of Minnesota Press, 1991 [1981]).

Time for Revolution, trans. Matteo Mandarini (London: Continuum, 2003 [1982–2000]).

Suggestions for Further Reading

Murphy, Timothy S., and Abdul-Karim Mustapha (eds), *The Philosophy of Antonio Negri: Resistance in Practice* (London: Pluto Press, 2005).

Murphy, Timothy S., and Abdul-Karim Mustapha (eds), *The Philosophy of Antonio Negri: Revolution in Theory* (London: Pluto Press, 2007). Each of these volumes, the first English-language collections of essays about Negri, considers the major themes of his work such as labour, capital, power, the state and revolution.

12

Jacques Rancière (1940–)

Samuel A. Chambers

Jacques Rancière may perhaps *best* be described as a 'contemporary critical theorist' precisely because his work crosses so many areas of inquiry, in the light of its thoroughly interdisciplinary nature, and given that he himself consistently resists any categorisation of his thought. That is, the broad title that brings together the writers in this volume serves to capture much of the flavour of Rancière's thought – which is no doubt thoroughly critical and theoretical – without limiting his project to any particular disciplinary domain. Unlike many of his contemporaries – whose thought was often pigeonholed – Ranciére's work has 'elude[d] classification',[1] probably because his writings span so many domains: stretching from labour and intellectual history to aesthetics, from democracy to literature, from politics to cinema. Rancière's education and early training followed well-worn paths. Like both Althusser and Derrida, Rancière was born in Algeria, in 1940; like both Derrida and Foucault, Rancière went on to study under Althusser at the École Normale Supérieure in Paris. Rancière contributed to Althusser's *Reading Capital*, but his essay was excluded from English translations of the work. The events of May 1968 proved to have a profound and longstanding impact upon his thought but, unlike better-known French critical theorists of his time, Rancière's turn away from Althusser led him to archival work. Rancière's so-called historical work did not receive the same attention in the Anglophone world of critical theory, and these texts were not translated into English until the very end of the 1980s. Despite Rancière having published works over five decades, Gabriel Rockhill, writing in 2004, could still properly describe him as someone whose voice has 'yet to be heard in full force in the English-speaking world'.[2] Nevertheless, his voice is growing louder: over the past decade Rancière's writings have quickly become one of the more important resources for rethinking politics and for extending the project of 'aesthetics' well beyond the domains of 'mere art'.

The Break with Althusser

The events of May and June 1968 are nothing if not nuanced and complex, but we can safely say this: the student protests and general uprising that they sparked neither were predicted by the so-called 'scientific' Marxism of Althusser nor were they led by the PCF (French Communist Party) of which he was a committed member. Indeed, the students whose actions eventually led to a general strike by almost two-thirds of the French workforce[3] were surely *not* the proletariat as described by Althusser's Marx. Rancière conceived of the May 1968 student revolt as necessitating a rejection of Althusser, and in formulating that critique in essays written between 1969 and 1974 Rancière also planted the seeds for much of his future thought. Rancière's turn away from Althusser pivoted on his critique of Althusser's insistence on the *purity* of Marxist thought, particularly on the purity of the category of the proletariat. Althusser criticised the student movement precisely because, in his terms, it was a 'petty bourgeois' movement. The development of Rancière's independent (non-Althusserian) thought emerges out of his insight and his instinct that the category of the political subject (the worker, in this case) cannot and must not be sanitised by the work of the intellectual. Most importantly, Rancière contends that the effort to maintain the unalloyed categories of the worker and the intellectual make Althusserianism into 'a philosophy of order'.[4]

In refusing this approach, Rancière turns away not only from Althusser but also from Marx and Marxism. He looks instead to the archive, in the form of an intellectual history of labour. Rancière attempts not to recover the virtue of the worker or the workers' thought, but rather to refute definitively the distinction upon which Althusser's critique of the student movement rested. Rancière writes: 'history shows us that the workers have never ceased to act like these "petty bourgeois"'.[5] In *The Nights of Labor*, his first major work to be published in English – a work whose homonymic link to the American labour movement, fittingly, only exists in the translation of the title – Rancière gives his readers a glimpse of workers who do not necessarily identify first as workers, who do not necessarily take pride in their work, and who do not necessarily want to be (only) workers. And Rancière shows that workers resist not merely the hardships of work; they resist the very system that confines them to the role of 'workers' in the first place. In his archival work Rancière discovers the 'disorder' of nineteenth-century French workers, their refusal to play only the part they have been given, their insistence on breaking the central Platonic rule, 'one man, one art'.

The Critique of the Platonic Order

It is thus essential to see Rancière's critique of Plato's systematic thought (and all the other later philosophies that Rancière will describe as Platonic in their insistence on philosophical ordering), neither as a departure from his archive work nor as a shift to some other sort of project. It is precisely the *impropriety* of nineteenth-century workers that Rancière wishes to bring to bear against Plato. The uneven and erratic process of translation has helped to obscure the centrality of Rancière's challenge to the Platonic/philosophical order (for Rancière, Plato is, above all, a *philosopher*). While *The Philosopher and His Poor* was published in French only two years after *The Nights of Labor*, the former work did not appear in English until fifteen years after the latter. This may have encouraged the view that Rancière's earlier, ostensibly 'historical' works belong to a different theoretical trajectory than his 'political' works of the 1990s; it surely has led to the relative neglect of those early works within Anglophone critical theory. However, the central argument of *The Philosopher and His Poor* proves to be an essential development of the earlier writings and a fundament of Rancière's later thought.

There is nothing confusing or contentious about Rancière's description of Plato as a philosopher of order, but Rancière sets out the baseline account of the 'ordered city' in Plato's *Republic* so that he can go on to ask *how* Plato establishes and maintains that order. The noble lie provides a key part of this answer, but Rancière argues further, and crucially, that the 'order of the city' can only be maintained through an 'order of discourse'. Thus, Rancière turns to those passages of the *Phaedrus* made famous by Derrida's deconstruction of them.[6] However, Rancière sees here not merely a privileging of speech over writing but rather a preference for the 'living dialectic' to 'fabricated rhetoric'. For Plato, written discourse must be criticised and banished because it does not know when to remain silent; *it fails to play its proper role.*[7] Thus, the threat that the sophist poses to the ordered city is the threat of writing, or what Rancière will later call 'literarity'.

'Literarity' serves to identify that dangerous possibility of an excess of words; it illuminates the possibility that not just the philosopher but *anyone at all* might have access to the contaminating power of these words. In other words, Plato must contain the order of discourse so as to maintain the order of the city. And thus, on Rancière's reading, the greatest threat to the city is the worker who philosophises. All role-mixing is bad, for Plato, because it violates the first rule of the city – 'one man, one art' – but none can be worse than trying to play the highest role (philosophy) when your nature is not the highest.[8] Above all, Plato wants the worker kept in his place; he wants, says Rancière, a 'pure proletarian' as Plato constructs him in the *Meno*.[9] And this means that the order of discourse must be preserved and protected; therefore writing, rhetoric and sophistry must be banished from the city.

Nonetheless, it is precisely the 'problem' with writing – that it can never shut up – that makes it impossible to vanquish. The excess of words means that writing will always return. Rancière calls Plato's critique of rhetoric 'reassuring', since it seems to have put writing back in its proper place, and thereby to have (re)established the order of the city. *But writing has no proper place.* Writing, like those nineteenth-century workers who spent their nights composing and writing poetry, is scandalously improper. And Rancière insists, against Plato, that the impropriety of writing, of literarity, will always undo the philosophical order. Proper order will always be interrupted by impropriety. In this early work Rancière refers metaphorically to writing as an 'uncontrolled democracy';[10] such an account sets the stage for his better-known and thoroughly provocative conception of politics – and for his insistent defence of democracy *as* scandalous.

Politics and 'Police'

With Rancière, we might be tempted to sum up the last ten years or so of the twentieth century as simultaneously the 'end' of politics and the 'return' of political philosophy. Two phenomena appear at roughly the same time: on the one hand, the end of the Cold War, the prominence of 'third way' solutions, the emergence of consensus democracy and the rise of neo-liberalism all seemed to diminish politics to mere bureaucratic engineering; on the other, theorists of a 'pure politics' grew in popularity as interest resurged in the idea of taking up political philosophy as 'a noble pursuit'.[11] Rancière's writings from the 1990s implicitly connect these two threads, as he both depicts and challenges the dominant vision of political philosophy by revealing its commitment to the very elimination of politics. Rancière must therefore struggle against mainstream conceptions of politics, in terms not only of popular understandings of politics but also in relation to formulations of 'politics' and 'the political' by other theorists. Put more bluntly, Rancière redefines politics in a way that cuts significantly against the grain of almost all other approaches.

To rethink politics so radically (conceiving it anew, from the *root*) requires Rancière to throw off a large number of previously-accepted understandings of politics. Thus we must start with negative definitions. First, politics does not refer to any form of regime. While we will see below that democracy for Rancière proves to be the very essence of politics, he repeatedly declares that democracy is not a regime, not a system of governance, and not a type of State.[12] Politics, therefore, does not refer to any set or system of institutions. Rancière thus distances himself from most social science and legal approaches to politics that would take it as an empirical object of study, embodied either in constitutions and laws or in parliaments and presidencies. But Rancière also seeks to separate his approach to politics from methodologies more familiar within contemporary critical theory. Rancière rejects what he sees as a Foucauldian tactic, one that would associate politics with power relations, identify the latter as ubiquitous and thus conclude that politics is everywhere. But, as many others have already noted, if politics is everywhere it is nowhere. 'If everything is political, then nothing is.'[13]

Rancière is not naive; he understands what politics is typically taken to be about and he recognises that he cannot simply ignore such phenomena. This is what makes Rancière's novel definition of politics different in both form and substance from that of Hannah Arendt: Rancière does not wish to reconstitute politics in a sealed space that would be preserved from contamination by other spheres of activity (in Arendt's case, economic and social). In an important passage that highlights his common-sense grasp on the everyday meaning of politics, Rancière writes: 'Politics is generally seen as the set of procedures whereby the aggregation and consent of collectivities is achieved, [it denotes] the organization of powers, the distribution of places and roles, and the systems of legitimizing this distribution.'[14] Rancière's entire politico-theoretical project hinges upon the next move that he makes, when he suggests the following with respect to this distribution system: 'I propose to call it *the police*.'[15]

The word police typically calls to mind what Rancière refers to as 'the petty police': officers on the street, armed with sticks or guns, whose job it is to carry out the *force* of the law. But Rancière argues that the petty police proves to be a particular and concrete manifestation of a larger order that he here names the police. The police order is a regime that distributes proper roles, that allocates the particular parts that make up a society: it is that 'distribution of places and roles' that serves as the fundamental structure at any given time or place. The police order determines the realm of intelligibility: 'it is the order of the visible and the sayable'.[16] Thus, it requires no leaps in logic to see clearly that the Platonic order as built in the *Republic* proves to be a police order *par excellence*, but, for that matter, so does the philosophical order produced by a structural or scientific marxism – one that would insist on a base/superstructure model or one that would not tolerate the adulteration of the primary marxist category, the proletariat. By identifying the police order (and by renaming familiar phenomena in order to do so), Rancière manages with one swift conceptual move to capture the link between the contemporary enervation of politics and the concomitant shift in critical theory toward a 'pure politics'. If most of what we typically take to be politics today is actually a matter of policing – of shoring up the allocation of roles, the distribution of bodies – then theory will be forced to search for a non-contaminated form of politics.

By imaging the police order so starkly, Rancière makes it possible to pursue a completely distinct approach to politics. If the police order determines the distribution of parts, then politics will name that insurrectionary force that disrupts this order and challenges this distribution. Rancière argues that politics occurs, and only occurs, when the logic of domination intrinsic to any police order (since all police orders are hierarchical orders) finds itself confronted with a different logic, the logic of equality. Politics therefore proves to be the *demonstration of the assumption of equality*. In other words, politics happens – and Rancière stresses that it does not happen frequently – when a confrontation is staged between the disparate logics of equality and domination. Politics occurs when these logics come into contact and conflict. This meeting of the heterogeneous occurs because of an assumption of equality, and when it occurs that equality is demonstrated. Equality, then, is neither a substantive good nor an ideal telos. In other words, politics does not occur because of equality, nor does politics achieve equality; instead, politics challenges and thwarts the police order.

The regime of the police determines the distribution of parts; it determines who has a part or who counts. It renders them intelligible just as it renders some other sphere unintelligible. This conception of the police can again throw politics into relief: politics is the taking part of those who have no part; it is the emergence of a party that is not a party. Politics comes about when those who do not count make some claim to be counted; hence, for Rancière, politics names 'a fundamental miscount'.[17] At its root, politics is dissensus. It is the rending of the police order by a subject that does not exist prior to the scene of politics. This explains Rancière's otherwise cryptic claims that democracy is not a regime, and it deepens our understanding of his assertion that we do not live in democracies but rather in regimes of oligarchic law.[18] A claim like this should not be reduced to a cynical comment on the plutocratic elitism of 'actually existing democracies', but taken rather as a sharper reconceptualisation of what the democratic moment must entail – most importantly, that it can only ever be a moment. This argument brings into focus Rancière's account of the relation between democracy and politics: 'there is politics . . . because there is democracy'.[19] Without democracy there would only ever be police. Democracy names the taking part of those who have no part, that is, politics.

Politics can never be pure precisely because politics names a fundamental impurity, an essential impropriety that renders all essentialism futile. This is why Rancière can describe the *logos*, that 'reasoned speech' that Aristotle says distinguishes 'man' as a political animal from all other animals, as *tainted* from the start.[20] Contra Aristotle, politics is not founded upon the difference between *phone* (mere voice, the ability to make sounds) and *logos*; rather politics is that which stages a conflict over the interpretation of *phone* and *logos*. After all, when confronted with a creature that makes sound, only politics can determine whether we hear in that sound *phone* (a decision that would lead us to treat the creature as a 'mere' animal) or *logos* (which would grant that creature a part in the political community). Like Aristotle, Rancière thinks the question of language or speech is a fundamentally political question. But Aristotle makes language a predeterminant for politics: 'man is a political animal'. In important contrast, Rancière subjects the human being to the excess of words: man is 'a literary animal', not in the sense of having an explicit interest in literature but in being exposed to that *literarity* from which Plato – and every other philosopher of order – had hoped to shield us.[21]

Because he conceives of the human animal as a 'literary' animal in this exact sense, Rancière's thinking of politics distinguishes itself from not only Aristotle but also Habermas. Because he rejects the project of philosophical order, he separates his work from not only Plato but also Marx. And because he refuses *any* purity of politics, he tries to detach his project from not only Arendt but also Foucault. In this last case, the difference hinges on Rancière's argument that 'nothing is political in itself'.[22] Nonetheless, anything at all could become political if it staged the confrontation between the logics of domination and equality. Politics then does not have to do with power relations for Rancière. Politics concerns itself instead with *world relations*. To elaborate: what a police regime does is *order* the world; what politics does is break up that ordering. Therefore while he might resist the idea of labelling it as such, Rancière's 'fundamental ontology' deals with the way the world is ordered and reordered. This ontology links those writings of his that seem explicitly concerned with politics to the work that seems more concerned with literature, cinema and art. He calls this, *Le Partage du sensible*.

Le Partage du sensible

Although 'police', for Rancière, specifies a hierarchical distribution of roles, places and bodies, and thereby names a system of domination, Rancière insists that 'police' is not inherently pejorative.[23] This claim becomes more cogent when we notice that the police is but one particular form that *le partage du sensible,* 'the partition of the sensible', can take. As Rancière explains in the seventh of his 'Ten Theses on Politics', police is a partition of the sensible that insists there be neither a *void in* that partition nor a *supplement to* it. That is, 'police' is a partition of the sensible that is complete, totalising, without remainder. But 'partition of the sensible' refers not simply to a given empirical order; it points more generally and more fundamentally to the *intelligibility* of that order. Rancière says that the partition of the

201

sensible is what 'define[s] the modes of perception' that make that order visible and sayable in the first place. Any configuration of the world depends upon an ontologically prior partition. 'The partition of the sensible is the cutting-up of the world and of "world"'.[24] This definition has two distinct elements. First, the 'cutting-up' points to a *partition* (of the world) in that it simultaneously separates and joins; it excludes and, at the same time, it 'allows participation'. Secondly, the 'cutting-up' refers to the *sensible* (the 'world') in that it determines what can be seen and what can be heard.

The idea of *le partage du sensible* appears to capture and rede-scribe a great deal of Rancière's earlier thinking. The relation between world and 'world' in the partition of the sensible can be traced back to Rancière's critique of Plato's attempt to sustain the order of the city through the order of discourse. This argument also helps to frame the deconstructive reading of Aristotle in which the difference between *phone* and *logos* can only be determined by what it was supposed to be based upon: namely, politics. The parti-tion of the sensible is the 'general law' that structures this account in the first place. In other words, one partition of the sensible will make *logos* audible where another will only produce *phone*. And poli-tics occurs only when these distinct partitions come into conflict. Rancière therefore insists that politics has no proper object, since 'its form is that of a clash between two *partitions* of the sensible'.[25] And we can extend this logic further: in their stubborn insistence on trying to philosophise, the artisans in Plato's city disrupt the given partition of the sensible. Hence Plato must banish them as well as the poets and sophists who would let writing circulate freely (thereby tempting anyone and everyone to philosophise). And, in their curious dabbling in the arts, those nineteenth-century workers (like those twentieth-century students who will follow them) chal-lenge the given partition of the sensible just as they undermine the philosophy of order proposed by the structural marxists.

Just as the notion of a 'partition of the sensible' serves to draw together the threads of Rancière's earlier writings, so also it acts as the lynchpin of what some would call his recent 'turn to aesthet-ics'.[26] Yet Rancière has not so much shifted as he has broadened his central philosophical project. Just as politics has no proper object to which it would 'apply', so aesthetics does not name some new field to which Rancière could 'turn'. Instead, Rancière argues that 'aesthetics' proves fundamental to politics. We find 'aesthetics at the core of politics', an aesthetics 'that has nothing to do with' what we typically refer to as the aestheticisation *of* politics.[27] Aesthetics, for Rancière is another name for the partition of the sensible. He defines a 'primary aesthetics' as: 'a delimitation of spaces and times, of the visible and the invisible, of speech and noise'.[28] This logic explains the choice to translate Rancière's book, *Le Partage du sensible* into English as 'The Politics of Aesthetics'. The English title refers to the idea of a 'core' aesthetics within politics as Rancière defines it. But this should not be taken to *reduce* aesthetics to a philosophical concept, as if to suggest that it had nothing to do with art. As Rancière explains, 'artistic practices' are 'forms of visibility' that can themselves serve as interruptions of the given partition of the sensible. And therefore work on aesthetics in this fundamental sense – that is, work on politics, work on the partition of the sensible – must also be taken up in the form of work on 'aesthetics' in the sense of Rancière's specific writings on 'literature', 'the arts' and 'film and television'.

The inverted commas around these terms serve to specify them as objects of Rancière's discourse, but they also call attention to the unique if not eccentric ways in which Rancière reconceptualises them. Rancière's earliest works in this broad area of inquiry deal with the question of literature.[29] Literature must be distinguished from 'literarity'. The latter, as discussed above, always refers to a particular status of impropriety of the written word: its capacity to escape systems of legitimation, its ability to travel where it ought not to travel, to wind up in the hands of those who should not, by all rights, have access to it. Yet literature can itself partake of a certain literarity, since literature 'lives', says Rancière, by its refusal and evasion of incarnation.[30] Nonetheless significant differences remain, and Rancière seeks more often to mark the differences – to highlight the *specificity* of 'literature' – than to draw connections: 'literature' refers to 'an historical system of the art of writing'.[31] However, it does not refer to just any such system, and it does not refer to a certain 'literary quality', as if anything written down would be literature. Instead, Rancière severely circumscribes the realm of literature: it points specifically to a system of writing that emerges both in a particular time and place and in response to that which precedes it. In this particular understanding, literature is marked out as distinct precisely because it 'no longer recognizes "rules of art" or boundaries'.[32] Rancière associates literature in this precise sense with a particular regime of the arts, which he calls 'aesthetic'.

The aesthetic regime arises as a rejection of the poetic regime.

The poetic regime, in turn, emerged in contradistinction to the ethical regime. Rancière thereby argues that there have been three historical 'regimes of the arts'. Starting at the beginning, then, Rancière characterises the *ethical regime* as, properly speaking, a regime of 'images' rather than of art. This regime is the one in which Plato works. It focuses wholly on the origin and use of images in relation to the *ethos* of individuals and communities. Thus, in this regime one asks: how does the image affect ethos? Plato's tirade against the imitative arts, argues Rancière, has nothing to do with 'politicising art' and everything to do with the *ethics* of images. 'Art' as a discrete entity only emerges with the *poetic regime* which 'breaks away' from the ethical regime.[33] This regime identifies the core of art with the mimetic principle, but this principle is not an artistic process or technique but a 'regime of visibility' – yet another *partage du sensible*. The arts, under this regime, are 'ways of doing and making', and the central question here is 'which are the better' ways of making and doing. Finally, then, the *aesthetic regime* separates itself from the poetic regime by marking a much more fundamental partition. This regime first identifies a singular *art* (as opposed to 'the arts'). It frees art from operating under any other ordering principle – frees it of rules. At the same time, the aesthetic regime refuses the distinction between an artistic mode of making and any other. Rancière writes: 'the aesthetic regime asserts the absolute singularity of art and, at the same time, destroys any pragmatic criterion for isolating this singularity'.[34] Literature, in the sense defined above, operates within the paradoxes of this aesthetic regime – the regime that interests Rancière the most. Film operates here as well.

Rancière's most recently translated works centre on 'the image' and on film, topics that have become increasingly popular for critical theory. But when it comes to the question of film, Rancière refuses all the usual academic celebrations of this medium. Rancière argues that the history of cinema, and particularly the history of film criticism, has been both marked and marred by an effort to celebrate cinema only by first splitting cinema into two. 'Pure cinema' has repeatedly been extracted from: (1) everything that would distort it by linking it to previous genres and (2) everything that would debase it by connecting it to popular culture. The effort to make cinema entirely new – a mark of film criticism since the invention of the moving image – has wrested the project of distinguishing the cinematic art of the sensation, the image, the moment, from the old process of storytelling (from narrative and drama and all the rest). Rancière not only, and repeatedly, calls this a bogus move on the part of critics (since cinema constructs and depends upon all those same old techniques of plot and narrative) but also goes on to show that everything critics wish to celebrate about cinema actually *depends upon* that which the critic would reject. This problem plagues not just film criticism; it thwarts the efforts of the most well-known academic theorists of cinema. About Deleuze and Godard, for example, Rancière argues: 'they both extract, after the fact, the original essence of the cinematographic art from the plots the art of cinema shares with the old art of storytelling'.[35] But if this is a post-hoc extraction, then surely there is no 'original essence' of cinema. The drive to find one probably owes something to the effort to maintain a dichotomy between 'principles of art and those of a popular entertainment'.[36]

It almost goes without saying that for Rancière there is no pure plasticity of art, and no pure cinema either. This means that he rejects any effort to distinguish cinema by its particular techniques or technology, and it entails his refusal of the common distinction between film and television. Since there can be no pure cinema that would free us from the banality of popular storytelling, and since there can be no special status to cinema (because, for example, the cinema screen is lighted from a distance while the television screen is lighted internally – all nonsense for Rancière),[37] then *Film Fables*, the title of his most important work on cinema, names both the effort by critics and academics to tell fables about film and also the particular nature of the fables that film tells. Film fables are, for Rancière, foiled fables. Rancière writes: 'the art and thought of images have always been nourished by all that thwarts them'.[38]

Rancière's common refrain, that aesthetics names a partition/ distribution of the sensible, remains central to these arguments. This explains why 'cinema aesthetics' could never be reduced to technique and why Rancière argues that a cinema aesthetics, 'cinema as an artistic idea', emerges well before we have the technical means necessary to make a movie.[39] As with literature and art, what is important about cinema is its aesthetics in this sense – its potential, even if unrealised, to produce a new partition of the sensible.

Rancière and Critical Thinking

Rancière's writings have had an important impact on debates concerning education, particularly in France but now also more broadly. He has attracted the attention of literary theorists and those working in cultural studies. But his rethinking of politics/police, and his linking of politics to aesthetics – thought broadly as the partition of the sensible – has probably been Rancière's most important contribution to date and will likely constitute the signal influence of his work in the future. He offers a critical defence of democracy and a thinking of the relation between 'art' and politics that stands apart from other critical writings in these areas. Rancière makes politics distinct without making it pure; he makes aesthetics 'political' without aestheticising politics. Above all, and aside from any particular disciplinary influences his work might have, Rancière's writings prove profound precisely because they offer an argument for equality that cannot be reduced to *any* philosophy of order. While liberalism and Marxism both give equality a central place within their theory, they make equality into an organising principle, a given or a goal that in either case serves as the spoke out of which they spin their philosophical system. But Rancière turns to equality as only someone who is first and foremost a democrat can, seeing in it the disorder that calls any system of domination into question. Equality manifests itself in such a way as to thwart even those politico-theoretical systems that would make equality fundamental.

The particular form of his turn to equality and the democratic gives Rancière's work a productive promise for critical thinking. By making equality an 'axiom', rather than a starting principle or end goal, Rancière offers the hope of a different kind of politics. But this also makes Rancière's a different kind of critical theory. In a very recent lecture given in English, he describes the fundamental mechanism of a critical 'apparatus' (*dispositif*) as identifying a reality that lies hidden behind mere appearance.[40] Such critical thinking comes coupled with an 'interpretive suspicion': that is, critical thinking is 'guided by the idea that words always hide something profound below'.[41] Critical thinking therefore consists of unmasking the secret, where the secret is usually some form of domination. Rancière goes on to show that those authors who would identify the so-called abandonment of either critical thinking or enlightenment rationality, far from rejecting the critical apparatus, *actually depend upon it* for their very argument. They have not rejected the critical turn, but merely conducted one more twist within it. Yet, for Rancière, in stark contrast with Jürgen Habermas, rather than proving the truth of the appearance/reality dichotomy, the replication of this logic indicates instead the very hollowness of the critical apparatus in the first place.

Whereas critical thinking saw emancipation in the effort to reveal the truth beneath appearances, so-called postmodern thought argues that all is appearance – it disconnects the mechanism of the critical apparatus from the emancipatory perspective.[42]

Rancière does not wish to abandon all insights of critical thinking, but he insists on a radical approach to 'emancipation'. After all, emancipation was supposed to *produce* equality, but Rancière says equality can only ever be assumed and/or demonstrated – it can never be materialised. Rancière's understanding of both equality and of language means that he must maintain a certain essential distance from critical theory as it has typically been understood. He overturns much of the common-sense understanding of 'critical thinking' by refusing to take up a critique of 'appearances' in the name of an underlying 'reality', and by rejecting the hermeneutics of suspicion that accompanies this method. Here we see Rancière's most recent writings circle back to his fundamental critique of Plato, since Platonic metaphysics depends precisely upon discovering the underlying reality beneath mere appearance. Hence we also glimpse the vast gap that separates Rancière's thought from that of Alain Badiou, another well-known French critical theorist who is also today's best-known Platonist.

A critical thinking for today, first, will require a genealogy of critical theory's terms and, second, it will depend upon a different set of starting assumptions. What if we refuse both the assumption that appearance is not reality (that secret domination lies below everything) and the assumption that all is appearance? Rancière argues provocatively that to do so would mean taking up an utterly different assumption: 'that the disabled are able, that there is no hidden secret of the machine'.[43] Rancière himself calls this 'a foolish assumption indeed', but if it seeks to remain vibrant and relevant, this may be an assumption that contemporary critical theory cannot afford *not* to make.

Notes

1. Kristin Ross, 'Translator's Introduction', in Rancière, *The Ignorant Schoolmaster,* pp. vii–xiii (viii).
2. Gabriel Rockhill, 'Translator's Introduction', in Rancière, *The Politics of Aesthetics*, pp. 1–6 (1).
3. Kristin Ross, *May '68 and Its Afterlives* (Chicago: University of Chicago Press, 2002).

207

4. Donald Reid, 'Introduction', in Rancière, *The Nights of Labor*, quoting Rancière, pp. xv–xxvii (xvi).
5. Ibid. p. xxii.
6. Rancière, *The Philosopher and His Poor* and *The Ignorant Schoolmaster*.
7. Rancière, *Philosopher,* p. 39
8. Ibid. p. 31.
9. Ibid. p. 38.
10. Ibid. p. 40.
11. Rancière, 'Ten Theses on Politics', *Theory & Event,* 5, 3, 2001, paras 1–3.
12. Rancière, *Hatred of Democracy,* p. 72.
13. Rancière, *Disagreement,* p. 32.
14. Ibid. p. 28.
15. Ibid. p. 28, emphasis in original.
16. Ibid. p. 29.
17. Ibid. p. 7.
18. Rancière, *Hatred of Democracy,* p. 72.
19. Jacques Rancière, *On the Shores of Politics*, trans. Liz Heron (London: Verso, 2007), p. 94
20. Rancière, *Disagreement,* p. 16.
21. Jacques Rancière, 'Dissenting Words: A Conversation with Jacques Rancière', *Diacritics*, 30, 2, 2000, pp. 113–26 (115).
22. Rancière, *Disagreement,* pp. 32–3.
23. Rancière, *Disagreement,* p. 28.
24. Rancière, 'Ten Theses', par. 20.
25. Ibid. par. 25, emphasis added.
26. See, for example, the 2009 American Comparative Literature Association (ACLA) seminar, <http://www.acla.org/acla2009/?p=256>, accessed 22 October 2008.
27. Rancière, *Politics of Aesthetics,* p. 13.
28. Ibid. p. 13.
29. Jacques Rancière, *The Flesh of Words: The Politics of Writing*, trans. Charlotte Mandell (Stanford: Stanford University Press, 2004); Rancière, *The Names of History*, trans. Hassan Melehy (Minnesota: University of Minnesota Press, 1994).
30. Rancière, *Flesh of Words,* p. 5.
31. Jacques Rancière, 'Literature, Politics, Aesthetics: Approaches to Democratic Disagreement', interview with Solange Guénoun and James Kavanagh, trans. Roxanne Lapidus, *Substance*, 92, 2000, pp. 3–24 (8).
32. Rancière, 'Literature, Politics, Aesthetics', p. 7.
33. Rancière, *Politics of Aesthetics,* p. 21.
34. Ibid. p. 23.
35. Jacques Rancière, *Film Fables*, trans. Emiliano Battista (New York: Berg, 2006), p. 6.
36. Ibid. p. 10.

37. Ibid. pp. 4, 18; Rancière, *Future of the Image*, trans. Gregory Elliott (London: Verso, 2008), pp. 2, 6.
38. Rancière, *Film Fables*, p. 19.
39. Ibid. p. 6.
40. Jacques Rancière, 'Misadventures in Critical Thinking', unpublished manuscript, p. 2.
41. Rancière, 'Dissenting Words', p. 114.
42. Rancière, 'Misadventures', p. 13.
43. Ibid. p. 15.

Major Works by Rancière

Disagreement: Politics and Philosophy, trans. Julie Rose (Minneapolis: University of Minnesota Press, 1998 [1995]).
Hatred of Democracy, trans. Steve Corcoran (London: Verso, 2006 [2005]).
The Ignorant Schoolmaster: Five Lessons in Intellectual Emancipation, trans. Kristin Ross (Stanford: Stanford University Press, 1991 [1987]).
The Nights of Labor: The Workers' Dream in Nineteenth-Century France, trans. John Drury (Philadelphia: Temple University Press, 1989 [1981]).
The Philosopher and His Poor, trans. Andrew Parker (Durham: Duke University Press, 2004 [1983]).
The Politics of Aesthetics: The Distribution of the Sensible, trans. Gabriel Rockhill (London: Continuum, 2004 [2000]).

Suggestions for Further Reading

Chambers, Samuel, 'The Politics of Literarity', *Theory & Event*, 8, 3, 2005. An effort to synthesise Rancière's critical theory by linking his novel conception of politics to his understanding of language and literarity.
May, Todd, *The Political Thought of Jacques Rancière: Creating Equality* (Edinburgh: Edinburgh University Press, 2008). Perhaps a slightly misnamed but nonetheless significant work that mobilises Rancière's thinking about politics in an effort to develop a radical and viable anarchist politics.
Parker, Andrew, 'Mimesis and the Division of Labor', in Rancière, *The Philosopher and His Poor*, pp. ix–xx. An excellent overview of what may be Rancière's central philosophical idea, and a good introduction to the context of Rancière's thinking.
Reid, Donald, 'Introduction', in Rancière, *The Nights of Labor*, pp. xv–xvii. Perhaps the best detailed account available in English of Rancière's critique of Althusser, the post-1968 politics of France and a summary of Rancière's thinking in the 1970s and 1980s.

13

Gayatri Chakravorty Spivak (1942–)

Stephen Morton

Gayatri Chakravorty Spivak is one of the most influential post-colonial intellectuals of the contemporary period. She is best known for her controversial essay 'Can the Subaltern Speak?' and for her English translation of the French philosopher Jacques Derrida's book *De la Grammatologie,* which was one of the first translations of Derrida's work to appear in English. But Spivak's thought is also significant for her deconstructive rereading of Marx's labour theory of value, her critical contribution to feminist thought, and more recently for her reflections on human rights and globalisation. Spivak's work has always challenged the authority of western philosophy, literature and culture by focusing on the histories and voices of those constituencies who are excluded from its purview: women, the colonised, the immigrant and the global proletariat.

Life and Intellectual Context

Gayatri Chakravorty was born in Calcutta on 24 February 1942, the year of the artificial famine in India and five years before India gained independence from British colonial rule. This radical political and cultural context in pre-independence Calcutta shaped Spivak's earliest childhood experience, providing memories of the economic injustices wrought by British colonial policy and shaping Spivak's own engagement with the global economic text. Gayatri Chakravorty came from a middle-class Hindu family and attended a missionary school in Calcutta, where she was taught by tribal Christians, who were 'lower than middle class by origin, neither

Hindus nor Muslims, not even Hindu untouchables, but tribals –
so-called aboriginals – who had been converted by missionaries'.[1]
Such an encounter with women 'who were absolutely underprivi-
leged, but who had dehegemonized Christianity in order to occupy
a social space where they could teach their social superiors' has
continued to mark the trajectory of Spivak's work.[2]

Spivak graduated from Presidency College of the University
of Calcutta in 1959 with a first-class honours degree in English.
The teaching of English literature in Indian universities could be
seen to continue the ideological legacy of British colonial education. Nonetheless, the students attending the college were socially
mixed, and there was also a politically active intellectual Left at
the college, as in West Bengal generally. Such a political influence
can be seen in Spivak's published work from her articles and essays
published in the early 1980s to the present.

After taking a master's degree in English at Cornell University
in the United States, and a year's fellowship at Girton College,
Cambridge, England, Spivak took up an instructor's position at
the University of Iowa. While at Iowa she completed her doctoral
dissertation on the work of William Butler Yeats, which was super-
vised by the literary critic Paul de Man at Cornell University. Spivak
subsequently went on to translate Jacques Derrida's *Of Grammatology*
and taught at a number of academic institutions around the
world before she was made Avalon Foundation Professor in the
Humanities at Columbia University.

Spivak and Deconstruction

One of the distinctive trajectories of Spivak's thought is her political engagement with deconstruction, the first sign of which was
her 'Translator's Preface' to Derrida's *Of Grammatology*. As well
as offering a rigorous and engaging introduction to Derrida's
thought, which situates Derridian concept metaphors such as the
trace, *archécriture* and erasure in relation to the European thought
of Hegel, Nietzsche, Freud, Husserl and Heidegger, and compares
Derrida's thought with French structuralism and Lacanian psychoanalysis, this preface also emphasises the ways in which Derrida's
thought calls the authority of the western philosophical tradition
into question. Spivak is careful to emphasise that Derrida's thought
does not simply inhabit the 'truant world of relativism'[3] – a claim
that anticipates misreadings of Derrida's widely misunderstood

claim that there is nothing outside the text. Indeed for Spivak, Derrida's theory of a general system of writing or textuality – by which he means the economic and social text as well as the philosophical or literary text – enables a radical approach to reading the world. As Spivak explains: 'The world actually writes itself with the many-leveled, unfixable intricacy and openness of a work of literature'.[4] To read the world as a text, in other words, is to read the contradictions and aporia in the rhetoric of multinational finance and World Bank reports, but it is also to read the lives and histories of dispossessed, 'subaltern' groups who have no access to the dominant 'text' of globalisation.

Spivak finds in Derrida a thinker who enables her to interrogate the authority of western thought. Specifically, Derrida's reading of Rousseau and Lévi-Strauss in *Of Grammatology* provides Spivak with the conceptual tools to criticise the cultural and philosophical authority of the West. Spivak notes a 'geographical pattern' in Derrida's argument, whereby a relationship between logocentrism and ethnocentrism is 'indirectly invoked'.[5] Derrida emphasises how the coherence and continuity of western thought has been predicated on the 'debasement of writing and its repression outside "full" speech'.[6] Derrida refers to this repression of writing as phonocentric, because it privileges the voice as a transparent medium through which the subject represents *him*self as a coherent subject. Yet, as Derrida emphasises, even the physical act of speech relies on a process of writing or a system of differentiation to generate meanings. By critically inhabiting the narrow concept of writing as a transparent vehicle for speech, Derrida traces a movement of general writing that secures the production of meaning. Yet he also emphasises how this general writing cannot be understood as a positive concept or category. Indeed, it is precisely the exclusion of this general writing from representation which regulates the opposition between speech and writing, where writing is defined as a transparent vehicle for speech. As Derrida writes:

> This arche-writing, although its concept is *invoked* by the themes of 'the arbitrariness of the sign' and of difference, cannot and can never be recognised as the *object of a science*. It is that very thing which cannot let its self be reduced to the form of presence. The latter orders all objectivity of the object and all relation to knowledge.[7]

Although this 'concept' of arche-writing 'communicates with the vulgar concept of writing',[8] it cannot be known as a positive thing within western conceptuality; instead it leaves a trace of its effectivity in the liminal spaces of western discourse. As Derrida demonstrates, the systematic effacement of arche-writing in western philosophical notions of truth is also evident in western ethnographic descriptions of oral-based cultures.

In his critique of Lévi-Strauss's self-reflexive, anti-ethnocentric representation of the Nambikwara (an indigenous group from the Brazilian Amazon) in *Tristes Tropiques*, Derrida argues that Lévi-Strauss ultimately falls back on the ethnocentric trope of a 'people without writing'. Lévi-Strauss's representation of the Nambikwara employs the conventions of a colonial travelogue, where the anthropologist personifies an evil western culture that contaminates a world untouched by the violence of writing and western technology. The anthropologist, in short, constitutes 'the other as a model of original and natural goodness'.[9] Against this representation of the Nambikwara, Derrida contends that Lévi-Strauss falls back on the phonocentric opposition between speech and writing, an opposition which conceals a more originary movement of writing that is instituted prior to the anthropologist's intervention. Derrida traces this unrepresentable movement of writing in a discussion of the practice of naming among the Nambikwara.

By unravelling the layers of violence underpinning the exchange between Lévi-Strauss and the Nambikwara, Derrida suggests that the oratory of the Nambikwara articulates the differentiation of writing before it disappears into western anthropological representation. The Nambikwara's refusal to speak the 'proper names' of their enemy does not signal their authentic, self-presence within an oral tradition that is uncontaminated by writing. Rather, this refusal draws attention to the obliteration of 'the proper' in the general writing of oral-based cultures. If western, phonocentric models of writing privilege speech as the expression of a single, self-present subject, oral-based cultures emphasise the movement of speech in performance, where meanings are mediated across time and space in a differential movement between the speaker and the audience. It is implicit in Derrida's argument that oral-based cultures can also have a coercive, socially binding function that is analogous to the narrow, transparent system of western writing. The ethno-anthropological work of Lévi-Strauss is unaware of this coercive aspect of oral culture, and is therefore unable to make distinctions between the situated and constitutive employment of oral-based cultures in different social and political contexts.

Spivak makes it plain that 'the *East* is never seriously studied in the Derridean text'.[10] But she also emphasises the radical potential of Derrida's deconstruction of the European philosophical tradition for post-colonial reading. For example, Spivak asserts that there is a parallel between Derrida's deconstruction of the western philosophical tradition and her interrogation of the legacy of the colonial education system in India, which taught students to regard the western humanist subject as a universal standard of enlightenment to which non-European subjects should aspire.[11]

Spivak's critical engagement with Derrida has certainly informed some of her most well-known post-colonial readings in essays where she questions the coherence of literary and cultural narratives which privilege the western humanist subject by highlighting the ways in which these narratives are predicated on the exclusion of marginal or subaltern figures. In 'Three Women's Texts and a Critique of Imperialism', included in *A Critique of Postcolonial Reason*, Spivak contends that the economic empowerment of the eponymous heroine in Charlotte Brontë's novel *Jane Eyre* is made possible by the marginalisation of the novel's colonial sub-text. For Jane's economic empowerment is made possible by the inheritance of her deceased uncle's fortune, reaped from the profits of a Caribbean slave plantation. Spivak makes a similar argument in her reading of the white South African novelist J. M. Coetzee's *Foe* in 'Theory in the Margin', wherein she considers how Coetzee foregrounds the imperialist determinants of Daniel Defoe's *Robinson Crusoe* and *Roxana*.[12] And in 'Can the Subaltern Speak?', Spivak argues that Derrida 'marks radical critique with the danger of appropriating the other by assimilation'[13] – a claim that helps to guard against the claims of benevolent radical intellectuals to speak for the disenfranchised.

For Spivak, the critical value of deconstruction lies both in its acknowledgement that any critical enterprise runs the risk of falling prey to the object of its critique, and in its argument that a general condition of impropriety or catachresis underpins all systems of meaning. This latter condition is particularly pronounced in the post-colonial world, where political concepts such as nationhood and citizenship were invoked without an adequate historical referent, precisely because these concepts were imported from eighteenth-century Europe. This is not to suggest, however, that Spivak is uncritical of Jacques Derrida's thought. She offers a feminist critique of Derrida's reflections on the figure of woman in western philosophy and takes Derrida to task for misreading Karl

Marx's argument in *Das Kapital.* Before assessing Spivak's engagement with Marx after Derrida in more detail, the following section
considers Spivak's writings on the subaltern.

Subaltern Studies

The concept of the subaltern has a rich and complex genealogy in
Spivak's thought. On the one hand, subalternity refers to a position
of social, cultural and linguistic subordination within a particular
colonial or post-colonial society and, on the other hand, it denotes
a position that cannot be conceptualised as a positive category. This
double meaning serves to complicate political programmes that
claim to speak on behalf of the oppressed or the disenfranchised.
To further clarify the meaning of the term in Spivak's thought it
is also important to track the source of the term in the work of
the left-wing Italian thinker Antonio Gramsci and the South Asian
Subaltern Studies collective.

The term 'subaltern' is conventionally understood as a synonym
of subordinate, but it can also denote a lower-ranking officer in the
army, or a particular example that supports a universal proposition
in philosophical logic. Spivak's use of the term subaltern is primarily informed by the work of the Italian Marxist thinker Antonio
Gramsci on the rural-based Italian peasantry and the research of
the international Subaltern Studies collective on the histories of
subaltern insurgency in colonial and post-colonial South Asia. In his
Prison Notebooks Gramsci uses the term subaltern interchangeably
with 'subordinate' and 'instrumental' to describe 'non-hegemonic
groups or classes'.[14] This is not to say that the term subaltern is
synonymous with the category of proletariat, however. As the subaltern historian David Arnold explains, 'the language of subalternity
might generally be more appropriate than that of class' in societies
like India or Italy that 'had not become wholly capitalistic'.[15]

It is this sense of the subaltern – as a general category of subor-
dination – that informs the work of the Subaltern Studies collective.
Drawing on Gramsci's account of the rural peasantry in Southern
Italy, as well as the work of the British Marxist historians Eric
Hobsbawn and E. P. Thompson, the Subaltern Studies collective
use the term as a 'name for the general attribute of subordination in
South Asian society whether this is expressed in terms of class, caste,
age, gender and office or in any other way'.[16] By focusing on South
Asian history from the perspective of the subaltern, the members

of the collective have persistently sought to challenge the elitism of bourgeois nationalist historiography, which has its roots in a British colonial ideology. What is more, Subaltern Studies historians such as Ranajit Guha and Dipesh Chakrabarty rejected the characterisation of peasant consciousness as pre-political or semi-feudal in the work of elite historians, and argued instead that the 'nature of collective action against exploitation in colonial India was such that it effectively led to a new constellation of the *political*'.[17]

It was partly this theoretical approach to the histories of subaltern resistance that prompted Gayatri Spivak's critical engagement with the Subaltern Studies collective.

In an interview Spivak clarifies her own employment of the term 'subaltern':

> I like the word 'subaltern' for one reason. It is truly situational. 'Subaltern' began as a description of a certain rank in the military. The word was later used under censorship by Gramsci: he called Marxism 'monism,' and was obliged to call the proletarian 'subaltern.' That word, used under duress, has been transformed into the description of everything that doesn't fall under a strict class analysis. I like that, because it has no theoretical rigour.[18]

Like Guha, Chakrabarty and Arnold, Spivak traces how the word subaltern has become transformed by the Subaltern Studies collective into a category that is clearly distinct from the word proletariat. In this interview Spivak valorises the term 'subaltern' because it is a more flexible and situated category of political identity than the term proletarian, which conventionally denotes the masculine working-class subject of nineteenth-century Europe.

Yet this is not to suggest that Spivak is entirely in agreement with the work of Subaltern Studies historians. Spivak's formulation of the subaltern as a theoretical concept is distinct from that of the Subaltern Studies' historians in that she argues that the subaltern is a historical fiction that enables the historical claims of the Subaltern Studies historians, rather than a positive presence that can be recovered from the archives of colonialism. In 'Deconstructing Historiography', for example, Spivak's reading of the Subaltern historians project emphasises how their practice of revisionist historical writing is broadly speaking at odds with their methodology. Early writings on the history of peasant insurgency try to recover a pure subaltern consciousness that is equivalent to Marx's notion of class consciousness. Spivak argues that such an approach bestows a false coherence on the much more complex and differentiated struggles of particular subaltern groups. By doing so, the Subaltern Studies historians are thus in danger of objectifying the subaltern, and thereby controlling them 'through knowledge even as they restore versions of causality and self-determination to him'.[19] Rather than disavowing this risk of falling prey to the dominant structures of knowledge and representation, Spivak emphasises that this risk is necessary in order to address the subaltern voices and histories that are being studied. In this particular context, Spivak invokes Jacques Derrida's statement that 'the enterprise of deconstruction always in a certain way falls prey to its own work'.[20] By affirming the risk of complicity in the Subaltern Studies work (rather than disavowing it), Spivak suggests that the 'actual practice' of the Subaltern Studies historians is 'closer to deconstruction'.[21]

Spivak's critique of the Subaltern Studies' methodology is significant in terms of what it reveals about the politics of representation, a concern that Spivak addresses more explicitly in her 1988 essay 'Can the Subaltern Speak?'. In this essay, Spivak begins by offering a critique of a conversation between the late twentieth-century French intellectuals Michel Foucault and Gilles Deleuze about the relationship between the politically committed intellectual and 'oppressed' or socially marginalised groups such as prisoners or the mentally ill. Since both Foucault and Deleuze are generally critical of humanist notions of the subject, which presuppose that human subjects have agency or power over their own destiny, it may seem surprising that Foucault and Deleuze speak about the 'oppressed' as if the 'oppressed' can speak and know their own conditions. For Spivak this claim is problematic for two reasons. First, in speaking of 'the oppressed' as if they could know and represent their own conditions, Foucault and Deleuze efface the position of the intellectual who acts as a proxy for the 'oppressed' subject that it names and calls into being. Second, Spivak argues that this lapse in Foucault and Deleuze's post-representational thinking has serious ethical and political consequences when it is framed in terms of the global division of labour between the First World and the Third World: 'Neither Deleuze nor Foucault seems aware that the intellectual within socialized capital, brandishing concrete experience, can help consolidate the international division of labor'.[22]

It is partly for these reasons that Spivak suggests in 'Can the Subaltern Speak?' that Jacques Derrida's deconstructive thought provides a more ethical conceptual framework than that provided by the work of Foucault or Deleuze for engaging in a meaningful dialogue with the subaltern:

> Derrida marks radical critique with the danger of appropriating the other by assimilation. He reads catachresis at the origin. He calls for a rewriting of the utopian structural impulse as 'rendering delirious that interior voice that is the voice of the other in us'. I must here acknowledge a long-term usefulness in Jacques Derrida which I seem no longer to find in the authors of *The History of Sexuality* and *Mille Plateau*.[23]

Indeed, for Spivak, Derrida's ethical thought provides a means of unsettling the authority of the benevolent intellectual who seeks to engage with the subaltern: 'no amount of raised consciousness fieldwork can ever approach the painstaking labor to establish ethical singularity with the subaltern'.[24]

Spivak's deconstructive approach to the agency and voice of subaltern insurgency has invited criticism from a number of critics. Most famously, Benita Parry has argued that Spivak's use of post-structuralist methodologies to describe the historical and political oppression of disempowered women has further contributed to their silencing. Writes Parry, 'Spivak in her own writings severely restricts (eliminates?) the space in which the colonized can be written back into history, even when "interventionist possibilities" are exploited through the deconstructive strategies devised by the post-colonial intellectual.' In Parry's argument, Spivak effectively writes out 'the evidence of native agency recorded in India's 200 year struggle against British conquest and the Raj' with phrases like, 'The subaltern cannot speak'.[25] What such criticisms crucially overlook, however, is the precise meaning of 'speech' in Spivak's essay. In an interview with Donna Landry and Gerald McLean, Spivak argues that '"the subaltern cannot speak" . . . means that even when the subaltern makes an effort to the death to speak, she is not able to be heard, and speaking and hearing complete the speech act'.[26] To say that the gendered subaltern cannot speak, then, is to say that she is denied the agency to make public speech acts. But in marking the institutional and political conditions that prevent the gendered subaltern from making public speech acts, Spivak suggests that the post-colonial intellectual can begin to invent spaces in which the subaltern can be heard.

What is also important here is Spivak's concern with the *gendered* subaltern. Indeed, what lies behind Spivak's criticism of the subaltern studies collective is a concern that their positivist methodology

– a method which insists on the principle that all historical claims are substantiated with reference to positive archival sources – will not be adequate to trace the historical participation of subaltern women in acts of anti-colonial national insurgency. For if women's participation in acts of anti-colonial national insurgency was not recorded in historical events, this does not necessarily mean that women did not participate in such events. A good example of this problem is Spivak's account of Bhubaneswari Bhaduri's suicide, a middle-class Indian woman who 'hanged herself in her father's modest apartment in North Calcutta in 1926'. 'Nearly a decade later', Spivak contends that 'it was discovered that she was a member of one of the many groups involved in the armed struggle for Indian independence'.[27] Significantly, the historical sources upon which Spivak bases this claim are family anecdote and rumour. Although there is no official documented evidence of Bhaduri's involvement in anti-colonial insurgency, Spivak speculates that Bhubaneswari had attempted to cover up her involvement with the nationalist resistance movement through an elaborate suicide ritual that *resembled* the ancient practice of Hindu widow sacrifice or *sati*. Spivak clearly identifies the agency and voice of subaltern women such as Bhubaneswari Bhaduri despite their exclusion from the dominant historical record.

Reading Marx after Derrida

Spivak's critical engagement with the Subaltern Studies collective and her commitment to recovering the voices and histories of the gendered subaltern cannot be separated from her rereading of Marx's labour theory of value. Throughout her work, Spivak emphasises the enduring importance of Marx's labour theory of value for understanding the contemporary world economic system, and the superexploitation of subaltern women's bodies in the global South upon which that system depends. She also questions the rigor of Jacques Derrida's presentation of Marx's thought in *Spectres of Marx*, arguing that Derrida confuses the distinction Marx makes between commercial and industrial capital in *Das Kapital*.

In Marx's labour theory of value, the value of a particular commodity is calculated in the first instance by subtracting the human labour that went into the production of the commodity; the value of the commodity is then measured in relation to that of another commodity. In the exchange of two objects with different uses, there needs to be a general equivalent that is able to measure the value of an object independently of its use. Marx refers to this general equivalent as exchange value. Critics of Marx often regard the concept of use value as a sign of unalienated labour – as a sign, in other words, of Marx's romantic anti-capitalism. For Spivak, however, the category of use value in Marx's thought is a deconstructive concept that destabilises the production and circulation of surplus value or capital. This reading may seem to be particularly surprising, especially when one considers that Marx's thought is often read in terms of the dialectical thinking of the German philosopher G. W. F. Hegel. But Spivak's deconstructive reading of Marx becomes more palpable when it is considered in relation to her translations of Mahasweta Devi's writings. For Spivak's translations of Devi's fiction not only 'convey Devi's rage and irony about those – the tribal, the bonded labourer, the wet nurse, the rural minimum-wage worker – who do not achieve political equality when Indian and Pakistan declare their independence';[28] they also highlight the ways in which the subaltern woman's body is a site of exploitation in the contemporary global economy. In her reading of Mahasweta Devi's short story, 'Douloti the Bountiful', for example, Spivak argues that the final scene in the story – which depicts the tormented corpse of a female bonded labourer forced into prostitution sprawled across a map of India, which has been drawn on the ground by a schoolmaster in a rural village in India – exemplifies the global exploitation of subaltern women's bodies.

Beyond Post-colonial Studies: Transnational Literacy, Human Rights, Globalisation

Spivak's critical engagement with Marx's thought is developed further in her monograph, *A Critique of Postcolonial Reason*. In the first chapter of this book, entitled 'Philosophy', Spivak offers an illuminating reading of the figure of the native informant in the German philosophy of Kant, Hegel and Marx. Spivak considers how Kant, Hegel and Marx figure as 'remote discursive precursors' in the changing axiomatics of imperialism.[29] By doing so, Spivak reveals how each of Kant, Hegel and Marx are not merely philosophers but thinkers of the capitalist world system *avant la lettre*. In her reading of the Kantian sublime, Spivak charts the disavowal of the native informant between Kant's *Critique of Practical Reason* and his *Critique of Judgement*. Emphasising the limits of cognitive control over the rational will, Kant's analytic of the sublime worked to expand the double bind of practical reason, where the moral subject was able to think a final purpose without being able to know it. Yet, if the moral subject needed culture to define his cognitive limitations in the face of the abyssal structure of the sublime, these limitations are also marked by the narrow terms of moral subjectivity. As Spivak argues, Kant's reading of the sublime presented itself differently to people who were not constituted as human subjects within Kant's European philosophical system: 'Without development of moral ideas, that which we, prepared by culture, call sublime presents itself to man in the raw [*dem rohen Menschen*] merely as terrible'.[30]

Leading on from this discussion, Spivak proceeds to develop an argument that runs throughout her book: that relationships of colonial power cannot be structurally reversed; rather, they 'require a persistent attempt to displace the reversal [and] to show the complicity between native hegemony and the axiomatics of imperialism'.[31] In a reading of Hegel's *Lectures on Aesthetics*, Spivak considers how the classic Hindu text, *The Gita*, worked to stabilise elite forms of Indian nationalism in the twentieth century, as well as occupying a particular dialectical phase in Hegel's teleological projection of the (European) world spirit (*Weltgeist*). By rearticulating this moment in Hegel's *Lectures on Aesthetics*, Spivak spells out the implications of such a reading for elite forms of cultural nationalism in pre-independence India. If *The Gita* stands as a 'not-yet historical' text in Hegel's *Lectures*, it provides a 'supra-historical' resource for Indian nation-building.[32] The closing section of the chapter on philosophy offers an illuminating reading of the Asiatic Mode of Production (AMP) in the Marxist corpus. If the AMP signified a prehistorical space in Marx's theory of historical materialism, Spivak argues that this untheorised place can work to disrupt the constitution of the productive body as a human subject in Marx's Eurocentric narrative. Echoing her earlier reading of the raw man in Kant's *Third Critique*, Spivak notes how the property relationship defining the Asian individual in Marx's text is figured as Species-Life, but 'has not yet differentiated itself into Species-Being'.[33] Whereas Species-Life denotes the abstract human that is coded as a disembodied resource in economic relationships leading back to primitive communism, Species-Being approximates the (European) class-conscious human subject that Marx persistently describes in his critical enterprise.

For Spivak, however, Marx's elision of the Asian individual in the definition of Species-Being falls back on the Hegelian move to subordinate historical and geographical difference to a logical paradigm. As a consequence, Marx seems to define the AMP as a process without a subject. In returning to the imperialist determinants of Marx's thought, however, Spivak unhinges an asymmetry in Marx's notions of Species-Life and Species-Being that resurfaces in Deleuze and Guattari's notion of a body without organs (BwO). Situating the BwO in terms of the capital relationship, Spivak encourages us to consider how the (re)productive body of particular subaltern women is integrated into the state political or philosophical organs of the European enlightenment, as well as contemporary late capitalist circuits.

A Critique of Postcolonial Reason reframes some of Spivak's earlier arguments to interrogate the conceptual and geopolitical ground of post-colonial studies, at a time when nation states are ceding political and economic control to multinational corporations and global organisations. By doing so, Spivak attempts to change the object of politicised interdisciplinary work and to trace the historical ruptures, as well as the repetitions between the histories of colonialism and the current phase of global electronic finance capitalism, which shape contemporary cultural production.

If the trajectory of Spivak's early critical work was partly concerned with the relationship between literary and cultural studies and European colonialism, her recent work on translation, transnational literacy and subaltern rights signals a shift in the emphasis of her work. Spivak's proposal in her lecture series *Death of a Discipline* that comparative literary studies should engage with the languages of the global South, which she also names 'subaltern languages', defines a radical political task for a discipline which is conventionally concerned with reading literary texts written in different languages. For Spivak persistently argues that one must take into account the multiplicity of subaltern languages as a strategy to counter the silencing and exclusion of subaltern groups from political representation at a local, national or global level.[34]

The political dimension of Spivak's thought is also demonstrated in her essay collection *Other Asias*. In the essay 'Righting Wrongs', for instance, Spivak argues that the rural poor in India will remain an object of benevolence in human rights discourse without the recovering and training of the ethical imagination of such subaltern groups. To counter this problem, Spivak proposes a rethinking of the subject of human rights from the standpoint of the rural poor and the sub-proletariat in South Asia. Such a rethinking demands a new pedagogy that is capable of suturing the tear in the fabric of Indian society caused by centuries of class and caste oppression, as well as the transition from colonial modernity to globalisation. If 'Righting Wrongs' questions the assumption that human rights discourse can alter the disenfranchisement of the rural poor without a sustained programme of radical pedagogy that directly challenges the means by which the rural poor and the sub-proletariat have been denied a voice, 'Responsibility' considers how international civil society has failed to recognise the singular voice of the subaltern. Beginning with a discussion of Derrida's reading of Heidegger's notorious Rectoral Address in *Of Spirit*, Spivak emphasises how Derrida's reading of Heidegger identifies the ways in which enlightenment thought is complicit with totalitarianism. In so doing, Spivak demonstrates how Derrida's reading of Heidegger illuminates the ways in which deconstruction is crucially concerned with responsibility and the acknowledgement of complicity: 'This is the double bind of deconstruction, its peculiar humility, responsibility, and strength; its acknowledgement of radical contamination'.[35] The central point that Spivak makes in this essay, moreover, is that Derrida's reading of spirit in Heidegger provides a reading strategy that can enable western intellectuals to address the limitations of dominant structures of responsibility and representation, which silence subaltern voices. One example of this silencing is the presentation and mistranslation of a speech on the flood management technique of the Bangladeshi peasantry at the conference on the World Bank's Flood Action Plan in the European Parliament, Strasbourg, by Abdus Sattar Khan, 'an aging leader of the peasant movement'.[36] In Spivak's account, this elderly gentleman could be seen to act as a political representative for the cause of the Bangladeshi peasantry, whose way of life is so obviously threatened by the World Bank's policies. Yet, as Spivak emphasises, the man 'was staged as a slice of the authentic, a piece of the real Bangladesh',[37] whose speech was poorly translated and who was forced to deliver his speech at breakneck speed within the allotted time of twenty minutes. Consequently 'there was such a great gulf fixed between [Sattar Khan's] own perception of how to play his role in a theater of responsibility and the structure into which he was inserted that there was no hope for a felicitous performance from the very start'.[38] What this example illustrates is the myriad difficulties of the subaltern acting and speaking as an empowered political subject in transnational public spaces, which claim to recognise the human rights of subaltern constituencies.

Conclusion

Spivak's thought has had a major influence on post-colonial studies over the past two decades, which has tended to concentrate on her essay 'Can the Subaltern Speak?' and *A Critique of Postcolonial Reason*.[39] But Spivak's rethinking of Marx has also had a profound impact on transnational cultural studies, with thinkers such as Peter Hitchcock emphasising that Spivak is one of the few intellectuals of our time to rethink the body 'within the space of contemporary transnational capitalism'.[40] Such an argument is also important for debates in transnational feminism – for Spivak, along with leading feminist thinkers such as Chandra Talpade Mohanty and Aiwa Ong, has made a major contribution to our understanding of the position of women, the gendered body and the ideology of reproductive heteronormativity in the contemporary global economy.

Notes

1. *The Spivak Reader*, p. 17.
2. Ibid. p. 16.
3. Spivak, 'Translator's Preface', p. lxxii.
4. Spivak. *In Other Worlds*, p. 95.
5. Spivak, 'Translator's Preface', p. lxxxii.
6. Jacques Derrida, *Of Grammatology*, trans. Gayatri Chakravorty Spivak (Baltimore: Johns Hopkins University Press, 1976), p. 3.
7. Ibid. p. 57.
8. Ibid. p. 56.
9. Ibid. p. 114.
10. Spivak, 'Translator's Preface', p. lxxxii.
11. Spivak, *The Postcolonial Critic*, p. 7.
12. Spivak. 'Theory in the Margin: J. M. Coetzee's *Foe* Reading of Defoe's *Crusoe/Roxana*', in Jonathan Arac and Barbara Johnson (eds), *Consequences of Theory: Selected Papers of the English Institute, 1987–88* (Baltimore: Johns Hopkins University Press, 1990), pp. 154–80.
13. Spivak, 'Can the Subaltern Speak?', p. 308.
14. Antonio Gramsci, *Selections from Prison Notebooks*, trans. and ed. Quentin Hoare and Geoffrey Nowell Smith (London: Lawrence and Wishart, 1971), p. xiv.

15. David Arnold, 'Gramsci and Peasant Subalternity in India', in Vinayak Chaturvedi (ed.), *Mapping Subaltern Studies and the Postcolonial* (London: Verso, 2000), pp. 21–49 (33).
16. Ranajit Guha, 'Preface' to *Subaltern Studies 1* (Delhi: Oxford University Press, 1982), pp. vii–x (vii).
17. Dipesh Chakrabarty. 'A Small History of Subaltern Studies', *Habitations of Modernity: Essays in the Wake of Subaltern Studies* (Chicago: Chicago University Press, 2002), p. 9.
18. Spivak, *The Postcolonial Critic*, p. 141.
19. Spivak, *In Other Worlds*, p. 201.
20. Cited in ibid. p. 201.
21. Ibid. p. 198.
22. Spivak, 'Can the Subaltern Speak?', p. 275.
23. Ibid. p. 308.
24. Mahasweta Devi, *Imaginary Maps*, trans. Gayatri Chakravorty Spivak (London: Routledge, 1995), p. xxiv.
25. Benita Parry, 'Problems in Current Theories of Colonial Discourse', *Oxford Literary Review*, 9, 1987, pp. 27–58 (29).
26. *The Spivak Reader*, p. 287.
27. Spivak, 'Can the Subaltern Speak?', p. 307.
28. Rashmi Bhatnagar, 'Seminars on Reading Marx', *PMLA*, 123, 1, 2008, p. 237.
29. Spivak, *A Critique of Postcolonial Reason*, pp. 3–4.
30. Ibid. pp. 12–13.
31. Ibid. p. 37.
32. Ibid. p. 62.
33. Ibid. p. 80.
34. See Spivak, *Death of a Discipline* and *Other Asias*.
35. Spivak, *Other Asias*, p. 65.
36. Ibid. pp. 92–5.
37. Ibid. p. 92.
38. Ibid.
39. See the collection of essays in Rosalind Morris (ed.), *Can the Subaltern Speak: The History of an Idea* (New York: Columbia University Press, 2010), and the special issue of the post-colonial journal *Interventions*, 4, 2, 2002, on *A Critique of Postcolonial Reason*.
40. Peter Hitchcock, *Oscillate Wildly: Space, Body, and Spirit of Millennial Materialism* (Minneapolis: University of Minnesota Press, 1999), p. 15.

Major Works by Spivak

'Can the Subaltern Speak?', in Cary Nelson and Lawrence Grossberg (eds), *Marxism and the Interpretation of Culture* (Urbana: University of Illinois Press, 1988), pp. 271–313.

A Critique of Postcolonial Reason: Toward a History of the Vanishing Present
(Cambridge, MA: Harvard University Press, 1999).

Death of a Discipline (New York: Columbia University Press, 2003).

In Other Worlds: Essays in Cultural Politics (London: Methuen, 1987).

Other Asias (Oxford: Blackwell, 2008).

Outside in the Teaching Machine (London: Routledge, 1993).

The Postcolonial Critic: Interviews, Strategies, Dialogues, ed. Sarah Harasym
(London: Routledge, 1990).

The Spivak Reader, ed. Donna Landry and Gerald Maclean (London:
Routledge, 1995).

'Translator's Preface', in Jacques Derrida, *Of Grammatology* (Baltimore:
Johns Hopkins University Press, 1976), pp. ix–lxxxvii.

Suggestions for Further Reading

Morton, Stephen, *Gayatri Chakravorty Spivak* (London: Routledge, 2002).
An introduction to Spivak's thought, which assesses Spivak's contribution to debates within Marxism, feminism and deconstruction, and
looks at Spivak's style.

Morton, Stephen, *Gayatri Spivak: Ethics, Politics and the Critique of Postcolonial
Reason* (Cambridge: Polity, 2006). Examines the ethical turn in Spivak's
post-colonial thought and situates this move in relation to her engagement with Derrida and de Man, Marxism, feminism, Levinas, human
rights discourse and the Subaltern Studies collective, as well as her
recent reflections on war and terrorism. This chapter condenses and
reframes some of the arguments presented in this book.

Ray, Sangeeta, *Gayatri Chakravorty Spivak: In Other Words* (Oxford: Wiley-
Blackwell, 2009). This insightful study of Spivak's thought includes
chapters on autobiography, reading literature, singularity and gender.

Sanders, Mark, *Gayatri Chakravorty Spivak: Live Theory* (London: Continuum,
2006). This lucid introduction to Spivak's thought addresses issues such
as transnational literacy, theory in translation, Marx after Derrida, feminism internationalised, and thoughts on war and suicide; includes an
interview with Gayatri Spivak.

14

Paul Virilio (1932–)

John Armitage

A Contemporary Critic of the Art of Technology

Few French philosophers have had as significant an influence on contemporary critical theory as Paul Virilio. Born in Paris, of Breton-Italian parents, Virilio's investigations in the 1950s and 1960s took him into varied regions of enquiry, such as city planning, military space and the organisation of the Atlantic Wall – the 15,000 bunkers built by the Nazis during the Second World War along the coastline of France to repel any Allied assault. He founded with the architect Claude Parent the Architecture Principe group and the journal of the same title in 1963, studied philosophy at the Sorbonne with the phenomenologist Maurice Merleau-Ponty and, in 1969, became a professor at the École Spéciale d'Architecture (ESA) in Paris. Virilio lectured at the ESA from 1969 until his retirement in 1997. He has been a member of the editorial staff of the journals *Esprit*, *Cause Commune* and *Traverses*, became the general Director of the ESA in 1975, and was presented with France's National Award for Criticism in 1987. Virilio was designated programme director at the International College of Philosophy, Paris, in 1989. He published *Bunker Archeology*, the outcome of his study of the Atlantic Wall, in 1975, *L'insecurité du territoire*, a book on contemporary geopolitics in 1976, *Speed & Politics*, an essay on 'dromology' (the compulsive logic of speed) analysing the military and political results of the transportation and transmission revolution in 1977, and *Popular Defense and Ecological Struggles*, a volume outlining the circumstances relating to popular opposition to war, in 1978.

However, as a contemporary critical theorist, Virilio's present concern is with technology. As Virilio commented:

> When someone says to me I don't understand your position, my response is, I'll explain it to you. I am a critic of the art of technology . . . If they still don't understand, then I say: just look at what an art critic is to traditional art, and then substitute technology for traditional art, and you have my position. It's that simple.[1]

Broad tenets can be extracted from his technological theories, and the critique of the art of technology, the philosophical stance associated with Virilio, has its own distinctive standpoint on virtually any sphere of human undertaking, and particularly aesthetics. We will chiefly be contemplating Virilio's most prolonged texts on the theme of aesthetics, *The Aesthetics of Disappearance* and *War and Cinema: The Logistics of Perception*, subsequent to some general remarks regarding the critique of the art of technology instigated by Virilio.

The critique of the art of technology is a theory of technology. In particular, it is a critique of the theories of technology proposed, for example, by Marxist philosophers. Marx had highlighted a positive idea of technology, thinking of it principally as an applied area with its own task to perform in historical development. Marx's philosophy of technology established an archetypal model for how modern technology functioned, and Marxism extended that model as the foundation for its examinations of socio-cultural phenomena.[2] For Marx, for instance, modern technology served as a spur to deeply required transformations in society and culture and was an increasing incentive to revolution against the contradictions within capitalism. Technology was thus an inducement towards a new balance of the forces of production and new socio-cultural organisations that would realise the dream of humanity as communism. Marx's standpoint towards technology was in consequence ultimately optimistic since, alongside the development of human socio-cultural organisations and the human use of natural resources for economic production, it was a crucial and constructive element in the historical and material development of civilisation.

Influenced by Edmund Husserl, the German philosopher and originator of phenomenology, and the German existentialist thinker Martin Heidegger, who was preoccupied with, among other things, 'the question concerning technology', Virilio's critique of the art of technology in turn questions many of the

228

technological ideas associated with Marxism and similar critical theories.[3] Consequently, Virilio argues against Marxism's encouraging vision and philosophy of technology and against Marxism's affirmative insights into technology as a seemingly uncomplicated determinant of the meaning of modern existence, communication and history. For Virilio, the meaning of contemporary life is much more negative, and therefore Marxism's upbeat vision and philosophy of technology invariably fails to penetrate the full significance of present-day ways of life. This is because, for Virilio, works of cinematic art, for instance, contain within them uncritical conceptions of aesthetics and technology, conceptions that, today, are ever more connected through worldwide media flows and rooted in strategies designed to continually manufacture a world of terror. Virilio's theory of technology is therefore a pessimistic one, and any effort to inflict a hopeful theory or reading of technology, similar to Marxism, for example, is to be considered as the 'propaganda of progress'.[4] The critique of the art of technology aspires to expose such propaganda and challenge the pretences of all so-called 'progressive' aesthetic theories and technological systems.

Virilio's justification for his radical critique of Marxian and related contemporary modes of thinking technology is that such thought perpetually favours *only* the positive attributes of modern technology. Yet his downbeat position on technology is not merely a nostalgic one, perhaps longing for the restoration of medieval spinning wheels and water mills. Rather, Virilio's is a *hyper-critical* understanding of the characteristics of technological phenomena. Accordingly, while his view of technology is one of refusal and overflowing with alarm, Virilio is not just 'anti-technological', contrary to, for example, Marx's bright vision of technology. Nevertheless, when such a sanguine attitude towards technology as Marx's is employed in more controversial cultural ways – in society, politics, the economy, personal relations, human development, ecology, or history, for instance – his ideas and nuances become more philosophically menacing, and Virilio's critique of the art of technology confronts all such occurrences. The critique of the art of technology, unlike Marx's confirmatory perspective on and philosophy of technology, considers that questioning the *essence* or real meaning of technology is predominantly a question about what technology *is*. That is, that any critical definition of technology will understand it as something in excess of goal-seeking human activity. Technology is more than the use of tools, machinery and so on, to activate or attain human objectives.

For Virilio, such superficial socio-political and instrumental definitions of technology are founded on a sort of delusion. This delusion rests on what we might refer to as the distinction between a superficial and a more profound definition of technology, with the former usually being envisioned by Virilio as sustaining contemporary Western culture. Neither the meaning of modern existence nor the questioning of the essence of technology can be completely content with definitions of technology that only view it as part of end-seeking human endeavour. It is not enough to focus upon the purely surface aspects of particular technologies. Rather, to move beyond the surface, one must concentrate on exposing the essence of the technology under consideration. In other words, one must focus upon those sites where one can expose technology, where a more dynamic and philosophical interpretation of it ensues, and where the propaganda of progress always remains merely a facile rather than a meaningful definition of the entire technological field.

The critique of the art of technology has been very successful in the sphere of aesthetics, particularly on the topic of disappearance, a topic extremely vulnerable to its uncompromising theory of technology. From this angle, it makes perfect sense to Virilio to speak of a contemporary speeding up of cultural meanings and political interpretations as well as a critical theory aimed at tentative readings of accelerated subjectivities and cultural politics. The disappearance of appearance in contemporary aesthetics and culture, then, a form of disappearance, aesthetics and culture far-removed from the world of Marx's optimistic vision and philosophy of technology, and from any questioning of the essence of technology, renders Virilio's critique of the art of technology an activity of the utmost urgency and purpose. This is because, for Virilio, while pre-modern cultures were typified by an aesthetic of appearance, by an aesthetic founded on an enduring material or technological support for the image (wood or canvas in the example of paintings; marble in the example of sculptures; and so on), this is no longer the case. Indeed, Virilio maintains that, with the modern invention of cinematics, we entered into an aesthetic of disappearance, into an aesthetic no longer founded on a lasting technological foundation for the image. For, in our day, the cinematic image especially is utterly cognitive, that is, it only exists in the human eye, and constantly disappears, as it does on the cinema screen at twenty-four frames a second.

The Aesthetics of Disappearance

Aesthetics is therefore a key area where such theories have important repercussions. Indeed, aesthetics not only has its technologies and cinematic texts, its suppositions about the meaning of contemporary life, accelerated subjectivities and cultural politics, but also its critical analyses purportedly disclosing the aesthetic dimensions of individual cinematic works and filmmakers. Virilio leaps into such discussions in *The Aesthetics of Disappearance*, a captivating set of interventions on the meaning of modern existence and aesthetics. The book takes as its subject matter a statement of Paul of Tarsus: 'The world as we see it is passing', which develops into a theoretical demonstration of the multiple problems associated with producing reliable critical statements concerning recurrent chronological gaps or aesthetic judgements regarding unexpected temporal absences. How does one portray the aesthetic aspects of a situation where the 'senses function, but are nevertheless closed to external impressions' or, in other words, where the senses are in the process of disappearance?[5]

Virilio's answer to this question is to write of the aesthetics of disappearance. We are presented with a string of ideas relating to the senses' arrival and departure, of arrested words and actions, of temporal interruptions, of conscious and continuous time, of apparently programmed perception without obvious intervals, rather than any particular explanation of the character of aesthetics. For these abundant everyday disappearances, Virilio employs the concept of 'picnolepsy', a kind of chronic neurological disorder shaped by speed and which is derived from the Greek word 'picnos', meaning frequent. Picnolepsy is then a state of consciousness created by subjects rooted in the disappearance, in the breaks, malfunctions and accelerated imagery coursing through and characterising them. The critique of the art of technology is not an exact description of the 'picnoleptic', a person for whom nothing actually occurs, or even of what the absent instance that never survived means for present-day lifestyles. Rather, it indicates that there are holes in our theories of perception, consciousness and temporality, holes that imply that we are mistaken when making our almost child-like assumptions about the existence of events. Aesthetic works, like everyday perception, thus function according to a kind of illusion, which imagines that they transmit full information.

Questions concerning the aesthetic dimension, memory and meaning in the realm of disappearance as a consequence become questions concerning the aesthetic dimension and meaning regarding vision technologies such as cinema. And such questions direct us to a never-ending series of problems about cinema and subjectivity, cinema and picnolepsy, aesthetics and a multitude of other human activities. Certainly, Virilio argues that what precludes us from ever determining a firm starting point from which to make critical statements is our propensity to patch up our essentially fragmented visual sequences. For we repeatedly modify the outlines of visual impressions to make 'equivalents' out of what we, as 'picnoleptics', have 'seen'. But the question is: what have we 'seen' and what have we not 'seen'? What have we remembered and what have we not remembered? According to Virilio, the answer is that human vision is not a visual discourse of verisimilitude but a visual discourse of fabrication and re-creation, of picnolepsy, of indeterminate visual information or evidence which, in its turn, leads us to become doubtful of what we know of both ourselves and those around us.

The Aesthetics of Disappearance establishes not a conviction that nothing really exists or that existence cannot be described, communicated or explained to others, but how hard it is to reach any decision as to what constitutes the aesthetic dimension of disappearance. Contemporary critical theory, by which henceforth I mean the Marxian philosophical approach to the aesthetic features of disappearance and cinema that contemplates the socio-historical materialist and ideological forces and structures which create and constrict them, can only appear as the propaganda of progress to the critic of the art of technology. Virilio's opposition to Marxian ideology critique, to its attempts to unmask the difference between reality and illusion, 'true' and 'false' consciousness, is as much personal as theoretical. For not only was Virilio's father an Italian communist, whose political views he totally rejects, but Virilio also became a Christian at the age of eighteen. Taking flight from Marxian-inspired aesthetic analysis, Virilio's contemporary writings on the critique of the art of technology are as a result a Christian-inflected negative vision of technological phenomena. And it is this negation of technology that is the object of enquiry. However, Virilio has no intention of supplying a comprehensive understanding of the domain of picnoleptic uncertainty, a key to open all the doors of perception, or a theoretical machine for decoding every cinematic text. The indirect target is Marxism, which, in its use of the Marxist theory of modern technology, did appear to assure the capacity of comprehensive understanding to its supporters.

Howard Hughes and *Ice Station Zebra*

When Virilio considers real people and real works of cinematic art, in place of the difficulties of analysing them, the result is very similar, as in his contribution to discussions on the subject of the fate of the American aviator and industrialist, film producer and director, philanthropist and billionaire, Howard Hughes (1905–76). For Virilio, Hughes's life was one of two separate halves. The first half, Virilio suggests, entailed Hughes becoming, as depicted in Martin Scorsese's movie *The Aviator* (2004), starring Leonardo Dicaprio, a very wealthy man, a supreme aviator, and a leading Hollywood film producer and director. Succeeding everywhere, living publicly and flamboyantly, Hughes's otherworldly life and much desired public image was then for years overexposed in the global media, laden as it was with stories of his riches, aerial feats and liaisons with beautiful women.

And then, from age forty-seven onwards, the second half of Hughes's life involved a concealed existence as he became a man who could not bear to be seen and who in fact disappeared into hiding until his demise. Clearly no longer seeking to fulfill his individual desire for monetary acquisition, technological or industrial achievement, Hughes's only purpose for his fortune, Virilio maintains, was to buy solitary confinement. Living naked, swathed in bedsores, gaunt and bereft on a pallet in a darkened room, Hughes sought to amass not so much the power of money as the power of disappearance. Refusing to wear a watch yet proclaiming himself the 'master of time', Hughes wanted nothing less than omnipotence. Seeking to 'win' the game that is human existence, Hughes formed a contradictory division between his own individual time and that of cosmological time, with the object not only of being able to control events but also of being able to react to them immediately. For Hughes, to be was to occupy a kind of speed-space, a 'place' where his identity could merge with the void, where he could literally be no one yet simultaneously be everywhere and nowhere.

Yet, significantly, Hughes's taste for omnipresent absence was satisfied above all through his use of a variety of technological media. Not content with smashing 1930s speed records for flying around the globe, Hughes abruptly grounded his airplane, at last acknowledging that his craving for movement was actually a craving for inertia. Connected to people only by telephone, Hughes locked himself inside rooms that were identical, even if they were continents apart, thereby eradicating the sensation of travelling from one place to another, but, especially, eradicating the sensation of the *differences* between one place and another. Through Hughes's poorly lit rooms and windows no daylight could enter. Working against any unexpected image while curbing all uncertainty, Hughes wanted to be 'everywhere and nowhere, yesterday and tomorrow, since all points of reference to astronomical space or time were eliminated'.[6]

However, in all of Hughes's rooms, were a movie screen, a projector and the controls that allowed him to screen his films, or, rather, his film. For Hughes's film, like his plate for eating, was nearly always the same one: John Sturges's *Ice Station Zebra* (1968), starring Rock Hudson, a quite ordinary story of a race for a Russian satellite that crashes close to the North Pole. Yet it was a story so gripping for Hughes that he screened it to himself over 150 times.[7] Hughes's obsession with *Ice Station Zebra* does not receive an explicit analysis by Virilio. Nevertheless, Hughes's fixation on this film is illustrative of Virilio's interest in Hughes's twisted vision of unlit rooms and the absence of light, of, in fact, Hughes's yearning to be nowhere, to be no longer able to be seen, or to be next to other people. For Hughes, it was sufficient to appreciate that he had the ability to go wherever he pleased and that people would be anticipating his arrival when he got there. It is characteristic of the critique of the art of technology that what Virilio invokes is a multiplicity of obsessions of this sort that lay bare the processes of distortion and darkness, desire, disappearance, proximity and distance at work in any critical assessments concerning the nature of visuality and space, luminosity, nonexistence, inter-subjectivity and personal power. To be sure, much of *The Aesthetics of Disappearance* is involved with the questions raised for the critique of the art of technology by acts of disappearance on the part of people such as Howard Hughes.

To Hughes, *Ice Station Zebra* was identical to the cars he purchased, which were also indistinguishable. Indeed, he forever bought the same type of Chevrolet because he considered it particularly commonplace. To Virilio, however, such films reveal not so much Hughes's nonconformist habits, his business and political practices, his dishonest and secret activities, his cavalier way of behaving towards the world, or even his last collapse into slumber and death. Rather, they reveal Hughes's aesthetic of disappearance: an aesthetic wherein arrival and departure amount to the same thing. To sympathise with Hughes's account in this discussion is to attribute a precise meaning to modern existence with regard to his particular form of disappearance, in that *Ice Station Zebra* can be taken to disclose something about him to his fellow Americans: that he was a mystic, one whose approach to modern American life resembled that of a '*technological monk*'.[8] Yet, according to Virilio, what is significant about Hughes's mania for films such as *Ice Station Zebra* and its programmed representations, and perhaps with Sturges's own direction of the film, is that there is virtually no distinction between Hughes's sunless rooms atop the Desert Inn in Las Vegas and the caves of the earliest hermits who withdrew to the desert seeking spiritual communion with God and the afterlife. Hughes's form of disappearance was thus caught within a closed circuit of non-communication, a sort of desertification or self-induced misery that led to his own destruction. Here, there is only one issue, the issue not of the city of Las Vegas, of the State of Nevada, of their deserts, laws, beliefs and organisations but, rather, the issue of Hughes's itinerant yet semi-virtual existence and denial of the modern world.

It is only after considering such an issue that one can proceed to understand Hughes's practically inhuman yet priest-like activities. Virilio therefore challenges archetypal critical-theoretical discussions concerning the meaning of modern life by asking: what makes us so certain that Hughes's fascination with films like *Ice Station Zebra* was not a sign of our own sufferings? What does our own passion for leading enclosed lives within cinema auditoria, single-seater pornography film cubicles, video and computer game arcades, have to tell us about our own insanity? Moving beyond Hughes's form of disappearance and closed circuit of non-communication, Virilio invites us to contemplate instead questions essential to the critique of such absurdities. He challenges the wish for urban desertification that motivates Hughes's interpretation of the city as a wasteland of doubt, showing instead that films such as *Ice Station Zebra* may well have been produced to remind us of our own contemporary loneliness: namely, to escape, not solely the wish for urban desertification on the part of so many people today but also the desertification of the meaning of the whole of modern existence.

The Contribution of the Critique of the Art of Technology

What contribution does the critique of the art of technology make to aesthetics? First, Virilio's preliminary critique of the cultural impact of cinematics in *The Aesthetics of Disappearance* led immediately to his *War and Cinema: The Logistics of Perception*. *War and Cinema*, derived from the research Virilio conducted into the coordination of machine guns and cameras on military aircraft during the First and Second World Wars, analyses his hypothesis that military and cinematic technologies have acquired a deadly mutual dependence by way of various cinematic and military texts and photographs that incorporate facets of the aesthetics of disappearance. The absurdity of the technologies of war and cinema having attained a lethal interdependence as a hypothesis for the visual arts evokes another absurdity central to the aesthetics of disappearance, where 'images' of Hiroshima, for example, were created by the almost unrepresentable nuclear 'flash' which, as it permeated that city's badly lit corners and crevices, also engraved barely visible 'representations' of its fatalities on Hiroshima's streets.

However, *War and Cinema* is arguably less an account of the disappearance of uninterrupted sight in conflict than a deliberation on the substitution of hand-to-hand fighting by way of the distant but deadly and all-too-familiar sound-and-light show of contemporary warfare, such as the 'shock and awe' of the Iraq War of 2003. Here, there are hints of Virilio's interest in military strategy, with the replacement of face-to-face combat by the faraway and fatal noise and glow of present-day war seemingly an indication of a world dominated by the struggle between images of visibility and invisibility, of a world that simply cannot be depicted accurately. Military images and cinematic texts, like surveillance or camouflage, are for Virilio a flight into the mysteries of the 'logistics of perception', with military personnel and civilian cineastes alike becoming technologised and cinematised, militarised, and incurably reliant upon modes of perception and annihilation that are coextensive. As in *Desert Screen: War at the Speed of Light*, Virilio's compilation of newspaper articles on the Gulf War of 1990–1, and his *Strategy of Deception*, Virilio's incisive condemnation of the duplicity of the United States and its allies' Kosovo War, we discover once more not a precise analysis of the aesthetic work of cinema but, rather, a critical exploration of the conjunctions between technology and history, weaponry, photography and cinematography.

Second, in later texts, such as *The Lost Dimension, Negative Horizon* and *The Vision Machine,* Virilio's critique of the art of technology questions Marxist and other materialist ideas concerning space, speed and vision technologies. He argues that we cannot avert the emerging crisis of material or physical space. Virilio's is thus an aesthetic of technology and of the built environment anchored in a critical appreciation of the disappearance of equipment and architecture, politics, culture and society into the empire of speed such that we can no longer reveal either the real meaning of contemporary vision technologies or the real purpose of disappearance in any specific cultural milieu. The technologisation of aesthetics cannot cope with the consequences of 'progress' through computerised technologies of perception any more than the technologies of so-called 'post-industrial' production can. Perhaps we can argue that the critique of the art of technology functions to maintain the secrecy that lies at the core of our perception of the world, of our capacity to expand and to distribute images in ostensibly random historical ways and continually to generate novel aesthetic and technological results.

Yet if Virilio's critique of the art of technology is on target contemporary critical theory is in difficulty. Although not an established academic subject, the currently varied collection of scholarly traditions, texts, ideas, analytical techniques and socio-political perspectives that collectively comprise the discourse of critical theory's efforts at explanation become problematic if, as Virilio suggests in *Polar Inertia* and *The Art of the Motor,* total information concerning the recent multimedia revolution is unattainable. Obviously, critical theory had a deep impact upon aesthetics and its history in the twentieth century, not to mention its impact on Marxism as a leading theoretical perspective on the growth and wide-ranging influence of capitalism upon modern society and culture. To a critic of the art of technology, however, critical theory's search for explanations of the impact of technology can only appear as an instance of the propaganda of progress.

Bleak in its analysis for some, the critique of the art of technology is nevertheless unwavering with regard to the absolute cultural devastation produced by contemporary technologies of communication and surveillance on aesthetics and politics. Without a doubt, Virilio's aesthetics and politics could not be more evident than in his *Open Sky,* which corresponds with no prior form of radicalism, refuses to ignore the necessity of working on speed, perception and the politics of control, and most definitely shuns any acceptance of the global 'real time' of today's information and communications technologies, the harbingers of both our contemporary experience of the loss of the aesthetics of appearance and the arrival of the aesthetics of disappearance.

Conclusion

The analysis of the loss of the aesthetics of appearance is perhaps the most important feature of the critique of the art of technology and Virilio's aesthetics of disappearance, particularly since the aesthetics of appearance is of enduring interest to many contemporary critical theorists. The aesthetic belief in the need to bring about, to make appear, a political revolution that will set in motion communism all over the world is frequently taken for granted by Marxist critical theorists and, by the 1950s, Marxian-inflected critical theory had productively initiated numerous extremely significant cultural questions, artistic concerns and subjects for the development of an aesthetics of appearance. The critique of the art of technology questions the disappearance of the aesthetics of appearance, and with it many of our beliefs about what is taking place in the chaotic process Virilio calls *A Landscape of Events*. In contrast to diverse Marxian and materialist notions such as the importance of examining the connection between social class, ideologies and aesthetic forms, of particular cineastes and periodic cinematic styles and groups, for instance, the French 'New Wave' group of filmmakers of the 1950s and 1960s partly influenced by Italian 'Neo-realism' and classical Hollywood, the critique of the art of technology is much more interested in the impact of works of cinematic art on the built environment and city planning. It is thus the ability of the landscape of events and what Virilio brands *The Information Bomb* to further militarise science, to create cultural disarray and to launch 'cyberwar' on the general civilian population that concerns him rather than the study of works of cinematic art as such.

Likewise, Virilio's reaction to the aesthetics of the contemporary city, in his *Ground Zero, City of Panic* and *The Original Accident,* and similar to his reaction to disappearance, is pessimistic and involves, for example, a consideration of the seemingly inexplicable motivations, actions and anonymity of those who initiated the September 11 2001 attacks on New York City and Washington DC. For such anonymity, according to Virilio, 'merely signals, for everyone, the rise of a global covert state – of the "*unknown quantity*" of a private criminality – that "beyond-Good-and-Evil" which has for centuries been the dream of the high priests of an iconoclastic progress'.[9] Contemporary critical theorists might protest about Virilio's analytical need to explore rather than to explain such 'cities of panic' without recourse to the study of economic modes of production, for instance, those that might be recognised as late capitalist, and their multifaceted association with societies and cultural life, to diminish them to a collection of unsophisticated or limited meanings concerning modern existence in Frankfurt and Paris, Kabul, Baghdad, Mumbai or Gaza. Yet how many contemporary critical theorists are at all acquainted with Virilio's position that works of cinematic art in particular impact upon our journeys along the autobahns of Frankfurt or that the meaning of contemporary life in the city is increasingly being altered through media-driven terror campaigns? It could never be suggested that the critique of the art of technology is an aesthetic approach that consents to the burgeoning faith in security patrolled shopping malls, the constantly expanding web of state surveillance, or self-styled 'gated communities'. What the *essence* of the work of cinematic art is, for the critic of the art of technology, is a way in to the ever-more globally networked media empires that constantly manufacture a world of dread, the volatile yet radical impact of which is a concrete example of the perspective of the critic of the art of technology. In Virilio's *The Original Accident*, for instance, the viewpoint of the critic of the art of technology leads not to Howard Hughes or to *Ice Station Zebra* but to a discussion of the future, to cinematic and other texts that previously sought to depict an improved way of life for everyone. However, at present, as in Virilio's *The Aesthetics of Disappearance*, the future is a 'place' where nobody wants to go anymore, alive as it is with insecurities, hazards and fright, with an existence contained by terrorisation, natural disasters and unnatural accidents.

All the same, some contemporary critical theorists, who are themselves no strangers to the investigation of the propagandistic and radical purposes of aesthetics, artists and thinkers in contemporary societies, will not welcome cities of panic being employed as a ruse for the examination of a networked global media that continually (re)constructs our planet of fear. Nonetheless, they may be drawn to the critique of the art of technology as a critical approach to a contemporary socio-cultural regime dominated by the dual development of art and science that, as described in Virilio's *Art and Fear, Unknown Quantity, Art as Far as the Eye Can See* and, most recently, *The University of Disaster*, can only be understood as a kind of death drive on the part of humankind. For, in Virilio's blistering contemporary works, art and science are portrayed as competing with each other to obliterate humanity.

Yet the critique of the art of technology of Virilio's *Unknown Quantity*, for example, does not introduce an authoritative philosophical position founded on the critique of contemporary immaterialism and the build-up of extremes of all sorts between the general population and the 'aesthetic' if ruinous work of two World Wars and half a century of the 'balance of terror'. In fact, if the critique of the art of technology introduces any philosophical standpoint, it is that of a *hyper-critical* reaction to the contemporary creation of major industrial accidents. While some contemporary critical theorists may well be attracted to the critique of the art of technology, others, however, are liable to remain unconvinced by Virilio's *Art as Far as the Eye Can See*, by its repudiation of our new media world where the aesthetics of appearance and its materiality have disappeared into the mediated aesthetics of disappearance, into the immateriality of technology. In contrast, the critique of the art of technology does provoke us to reflect on aesthetics, and chiefly the *politics* of aesthetics, in an original manner; one concerning *The University of Disaster* or the catastrophic potential of the contemporary era where the arts are separating from artists and from their materials, where the general population, aesthetics and cinema are, as Virilio might have it, all in the clutches of the cultural devastation caused by contemporary information, communication and surveillance technologies.

Notes

1. See Paul Virilio and Sylvère Lotringer, *Pure War* (New York: Semiotexte, 2008), p. 192.
2. See Fredrick Ferré, *Philosophy of Technology* (Athens: University of Georgia Press, 1995), pp. 54–7.
3. See Edmund Husserl, *The Crisis of European Sciences and Transcendental Phenomenology* (Evanston: Northwestern Press, 1970); and Martin Heidegger, *The Question Concerning Technology and Other Essays* (New York: Harper, 1977).
4. See Paul Virilio, *Le Futurisme de l'instant: Stop-Eject* (Paris: Galilée, 2009).

5. Virilio, *Aesthetics of Disappearance*, p. 19.
6. Ibid. p. 36.
7. See Peter Harvey Brown and Pat H. Broeske, *Howard Hughes: The Untold Story* (Los Angeles: Warner Bros Books, 1998), p. 349.
8. Virilio, *Aesthetics of Disappearance*, p. 37; original emphases.
9. Virilio, *Ground Zero*, p. 82; original quotation marks and emphases.

Major Works by Virilio

The Aesthetics of Disappearance, trans. Philip Beitchman (New York: Semiotexte, 2009 [1980]).

Art and Fear, trans. Julie Rose (London: Continuum, 2003 [2000]).

Art as Far as the Eye Can See, trans. Julie Rose (Oxford: Berg, 2007 [2005]).

The Art of the Motor, trans. Julie Rose (Minneapolis: University of Minnesota Press, 1995 [1993]).

Bunker Archeology, trans. George Collins (Princeton: Princeton Architectural Press, 1994 [1975]).

City of Panic, trans. Julie Rose (Oxford: Berg, 2005 [2004]).

Desert Screen: War at the Speed of Light, trans. Michael Degener (London: Continuum, 2002 [1991]).

Ground Zero, trans. Chris Turner (London: Verso, 2002 [2002]).

The Information Bomb, trans. Chris Turner (London: Verso, 2000 [1998]).

L'insécurité du territoire (Paris: Stock, 1976).

A Landscape of Events, trans. Julie Rose (Princeton: Princeton Architectural Press, 2000 [1996]).

The Lost Dimension, trans. Daniel Moshenberg (New York: Semiotexte, 1991 [1984]).

Negative Horizon, trans. Michael Degener (London: Continuum, 2005 [1984]).

Open Sky, trans. Julie Rose (London: Verso, 1997 [1995]).

The Original Accident, trans. Julie Rose (Oxford: Polity, 2007 [2005]).

Polar Inertia, trans. Patrick Camiller (London: Sage, 2000 [1990]).

Popular Defense & Ecological Struggles, trans. Mark Polizzotti (New York: Semiotexte, 1990 [1978]).

Speed & Politics: An Essay on Dromology, trans. Mark Polizzotti (New York: Semiotexte, 1986 [1977]).

Strategy of Deception, trans. Chris Turner (London: Verso, 2000 [1999]).

The University of Disaster, trans. Julie Rose (Oxford: Polity, 2009 [2007]).

Unknown Quantity, trans. Chris Turner (London: Thames and Hudson, 2003).

The Vision Machine, trans. Julie Rose (London: BFI, 1994 [1988]).

War and Cinema: The Logistics of Perception, trans. Patrick Camiller (London: Verso, 1989 [1984]).

John Armitage

Suggestions for Further Reading

Armitage, John (ed.), *Paul Virilio: From Modernism to Hypermodernism and Beyond* (London: Sage, 2000). An important compilation of theoretical articles on Virilio dealing with the main features of his texts inclusive of polar inertia and architecture, bunkers, war, new media, speed, the accident, art and feminism.

Armitage, John (ed.), *Virilio Live: Selected Interviews* (London: Sage, 2001). Cultural and social theory, architecture, acceleration, space, politics, aesthetics, technology, accidents and conflict are the principal themes of this set of interviews conducted by an assortment of international interviewers.

James, Ian, *Paul Virilio* (London: Routledge, 2007). The second single-authored monograph on Virilio in English with an emphasis on the politics of perception and speed, virtualisation, warfare and art.

Redhead, Steve, *Paul Virilio: Theorist for an Accelerated Culture* (Edinburgh: Edinburgh University Press, 2004). The first single-authored monograph on Virilio in English highlighting acceleration, modernity and the accident.

15

Slavoj Žižek (1949–)

Matthew Sharpe

The *oeuvre* of Slovenian-born political philosopher and cultural critic Slavoj Žižek is a striking 'minority report' on today's intellectual scene. Žižek's paratactic, inviting yet perplexing style, and his prodigious ability to theoretically unpack examples (from politics to pop culture) is virtually unprecedented. His work is framed in terms of a polemical critique of other leading theorists within today's left-liberal academy (Derrida, Foucault, Habermas, Agamben, Deleuze). On a descriptive level, Žižek's Lacanian theory of ideology affords new purchase on many of the paradoxes of liberal-consumerist subjectivity, which is at once politically cynical (as the Right laments) and politically conformist (as the Left complains). Prescriptively, Žižek's work challenges his readership to ask questions about the possibility of political change – if that is what the left wants – otherwise rarely asked since 1989. Which changes? Justified by what? With what practical consequences?

Žižek was born in 1949 in Ljubljana, Slovenia, and grew up in the comparative cultural freedom of the former Yugoslavia's self-managing socialism. Here, he was exposed to the films, popular culture and theory of the non-communist West. Žižek completed his PhD at Ljubljana in 1981 on German Idealism, and between 1981 and 1985 studied in Paris under Jacques-Alain Miller, Lacan's son-in-law. In this period, Žižek wrote a second dissertation, a Lacanian reading of Hegel, Marx and Kripke. In the late 1980s, Žižek returned to Slovenia where he wrote newspaper columns for the Slovenian weekly *Mladina*, and co-founded the Slovenian Liberal Democratic Party. In 1990, he ran for the Slovenian presidency, narrowly missing office. Žižek's first published book in English (*The Sublime Object of Ideology*) appeared in 1989. Since then, he has published some two dozen books, edited several collections, debated leading global intellectuals, organised conferences, published numerous philosophical and political articles, and maintained a tireless speaking schedule. Žižek's recent work has taken an increasingly engaged political tenor, including books on September 11, the Iraq war, and his defence of the lost cause of some form of communist, post-democratic political regime.

Žižek's Ideology Critique: Disidentification, *Jouissance* and Ideological Fantasy

In 1989, when *Sublime Object of Ideology* appeared, the category of 'ideology' was in disrepute. According to the classical Marxist definition, ideologies are discourses that promote false ideas ('false consciousness') in subjects about their political regimes. Because these ideas are believed by subjects to be true, they assist in reproducing the existing status quo. To undermine an ideology, according to this position, it is enough to unearth the truth(s) it conceals from subjects. People will then become aware of the political shortcomings of their current regimes, and be moved to better them. For ideologies to have the political importance this classical Marxian theory accords to them, critics comment, subjects would have to have a level of faith in public institutions, ideals and politicians which today's liberal-cosmopolitan subjects lack. The widespread notoriety of political comics like Jon Stewart, host of the US comedy news programme, *The Daily Show* (or, in Australia, satirical comics such as *The Chaser*, most famous for dressing as Bin Laden and gaining entrance to the G8 summit), bears witness to how subjects today can know very well the awful truth concerning abuses of power, yet act as if they did not know.

Žižek proposes that in order to understand today's politics we need a different notion of ideology. He observes that, as 'ideology' since Marx has carried a pejorative sense, no one taken in by such an ideology has ever believed they were so duped. If the term 'ideology' has any meaning, ideological positions are always imputed to Others (for today's Left, for example, the political Right are the dupes of one or another noble lie about natural community or dream of perfect market functioning; for the Right, the Left are the dupes of well-meaning but utopian egalitarianism bound to lead to economic and moral collapse). For subjects to believe in an ideology, it must have been presented to them as non-ideological, as true and right. For such reasons, Žižek's bold opening claim in *The Sublime Object of Ideology* is that today ideology has less disappeared from the political landscape than come into its own. It is because of neo-liberal capitalism's marvellous success that talk of ideology has also been dismissed from polite political and theoretical opinion.

Today's typical First World subjects, according to Žižek, are the dupes of what he calls 'ideological cynicism'. Drawing on German political theorist Peter Sloterdijk, Žižek contends that the formula describing the operation of ideology today is not 'they do not know it, but they are doing it', as it was for Marx. It is 'they know it, but they are doing it anyway'.[1] Ideologies, as political discourses, are there to secure the voluntary consent of people about contestable political policies or arrangements. Yet, Žižek argues, subjects will only voluntarily agree to follow any such arrangement if they believe that, in doing so, they are expressing their freedom and might have done otherwise.

However false such a sense of freedom is, Žižek insists that it is a paradoxically essential appearance, to use a Hegelian expression. French Marxist Louis Althusser's understanding of ideological identification suggests that an individual is wholly interpellated into a place within a political system by the system's dominant ideology and ideological state apparatuses. Žižek argues that it is a mistake to think that, for a political position to win peoples' support, it needs to effectively brainwash them into thoughtless automatons. Rather, any successful political ideology always allows subjects to have and to hold a conscious distance towards its explicit ideals and prescriptions – what Žižek calls ideological disidentification, which is connected to two other central ideas in his work:

1. Žižek adapts the psychoanalytic notion that individuals are always 'split' subjects, divided between conscious awareness and unconscious beliefs, knowledge and desire. Subjects are always divided between what they consciously know about political matters and a set of more-or-less unconscious beliefs concerning the regime in which they live.
2. Žižek makes a crucial distinction between knowledge and belief. Precisely where and because subjects do not *know*, for example, what the essence of their people is, the scope and nature of their *beliefs* on such matters is politically decisive – just as in theology

Matthew Sharpe

faith is to be distinguished from knowledge or 'proof' of God's existence.

The key Lacanian caveat to these claims is Žižek's key notion that belief is always 'belief through the Other'. Although in political life individuals very often do not consciously fully understand or 'know what they do' – what their system represents, what their cause, freedom or justice is – it is decisive that they suppose there are Others who do know. Žižek contends that the key political function of holders of public office is to occupy the place of what he calls, after Lacan, 'the Other supposed to know'. Žižek often cites the Hegelian example of priests reciting mass in Latin before an uncomprehending laity, who believe that the priests know the meaning of the words, and for whom this is sufficient to keep the faith. Far from presenting an exception to the way political authority works, this scenario reveals the universal rule of how political consensus is formed.

Similarly, political authority is primarily symbolic in its nature. In Lacanian terms, the symbolic register refers to how the roles public authorities undertake are more important politically than the 'reality' of the individuals in question (whether they are unintelligent, unfaithful to their wives). The office or place an individual occupies in their political system ensures the political force of their words and the belief of subjects in their authority. Žižek sometimes puts this thought by saying that people believe through the Other, or that the Other believes for them, despite what they might inwardly think or cynically say.

Žižek follows Althusser's emphasis on the 'materiality' of ideology, its embodiment in institutions and peoples' everyday practices. Žižek's realist position is that all the ideas in the world can have no lasting political effect unless they come to inform institutions and subjects' day-to-day lives. In *The Sublime Object of Ideology*, Žižek famously cites Blaise Pascal's advice that doubting subjects should get down on their knees and pray, and then they will believe. The deeper message of Pascal's directive is that, once subjects have come to believe through praying, they will retrospectively come to see that they got down on their knees because they already believed, without knowing it.

Prior political theory has placed too little emphasis, Žižek asserts, on communities' cultural practices that involve 'inherent transgressions'. These are practices sanctioned by a culture that nevertheless

246

allows subjects some experience of what is usually exceptional to or prohibited in their everyday lives as civilised political subjects – things like sex, death, defecation, disloyalty or violence. Such experiences involve what Žižek calls *Jouissance*, another term from Lacanian psychoanalysis. As opposed to what we talk of in English as 'pleasure', *Jouissance* is an always sexualised, always transgressive enjoyment, at the limits of what subjects can experience or talk about in public. Žižek argues that subjects' experiences of the events and practices wherein their political culture organises its specific relations to *Jouissance* (for example, specific sports, alcohol or drugs, music, festivals, films) are as close as they will get to knowing the deeper Truth intimated for them by their regime's key political ideas or 'master signifiers' – 'nation', 'God', 'our way of life', 'the Party'. Žižek, like Edmund Burke and other conservatives, argues that it is such ostensibly non-political and culturally specific practices as these that irreplaceably single out any political community from its others and enemies. Or, as Žižek sometimes puts it, subjects 'enjoy (*jouis*) their Nation as themselves',[2] *Jouissance* being the basis of their political cohesion.

One implication of this theoretical account of ideology and political consent is that ideologies – as for Althusser – are political discourses whose primary function is not to make correct theoretical statements about political reality (as the 'false consciousness' model implies), but to orient subjects' lived relations to this reality. If a political ideology's descriptive propositions happen to be true (for example, 'capitalism exploits the workers', 'Saddam was a dictator'), their ideological character is not undermined. Ideology concerns how belief in certain propositions (rather than others), positions subjects on the leading political issues of the day. For Žižek, political speech is primarily performative: it is about securing a lived sense of community between subjects comparable to what Kant called *sensus communis*. If political propositions seem to describe things in the world, we nevertheless need always to understand them as Marx understood the exchange value of commodities – as a relation between people concealed behind a relation between things. Žižek sometimes cites Marx's analysis of what it is for a person to be a king in *Capital*. A king is only king because his subjects loyally think and act as if he is king. Yet, here is the Žižekian rub: the people will only believe he is king if they believe this is a sublime Truth about which they can do nothing.

This brings us to the central notion of sublime objects of

ideology. Žižek claims that regimes can only secure a sense of collective identity if their governing ideologies afford subjects an understanding of how their regime relates to what exceeds, supplements or challenges its identity. Kant's analytic of the sublime in *The Critique of Judgment*, as an analysis of an experience in which the subject's identity is challenged, is crucial for Žižek. Kant identifies two moments of sublime experience. In the first moment, the size or force of an object painfully impresses upon the subject the limitation of its perceptual capabilities. In a second moment, however, a reflective representation arises where we would least expect it, which takes as its object the subject's own failure to apprehend the object. This representation (re)signifies the subject's perceptual failure as indirect testimony to the inadequacy of human perception to attain to what Kant calls Ideas of Reason (such as God, the Universe as a Whole, Freedom, the Good).

According to Žižek, all successful political ideologies necessarily refer to and turn around sublime objects posited by political ideologies in exactly this Kantian sense. Political subjects take it that the key words of their regime's ideologies name sublime objects – extraordinary things like God, the Führer, the Nation, in whose name they will (if necessary) transgress ordinary moral laws and lay down their lives. When a subject believes in a political ideology, it does not mean that they know the Truth about the objects which its key terms seemingly name. By drawing on the parallel with Kant on the sublime, Žižek makes a more radical point. Ideologies work by (re)signifying individuals' very inability to explain the content of their political beliefs, which is testimony to just how transcendent or great is their nation, God, freedom. In Žižek's Lacanian terms, these sublime objects of ideology are Real (capital 'R') Things (capital 'T'), beyond the things and people we usually encounter.

In the struggle of competing political ideologies, Žižek argues, the aim of each is to elevate their particular perspective (about what is just, best and so on) to the point where it can lay claim to name or give voice to the political whole (for example, the Nation or People). In order to achieve this political feat, each group must succeed in identifying its perspective with the extra-political, sublime objects accepted within the culture as giving body to this whole (such as 'the national interest' or 'the dictatorship of the proletariat'). Alternatively, it must supplant the sublime objects of the previous ideologies. Žižek's adept early analysis of Stalinist ideology, for instance, turns upon the thought that the Party had this sublime political status. Class struggle in this society did not end, Žižek contends, despite Stalinist propaganda. It was displaced ideologically, from a struggle between two classes to one between the Party as representative of the People (the Whole) and all who disagreed with the Party, ideologically positioned as enemies of the people.

Žižek's adaptation of the Lacanian, psychoanalytical account of the way individuals become subject to social Law underpins his observations concerning political ideologies. On this view, the civilising of subjects is based in their founding sacrifice (castration) of *Jouissance*, enacted in the name of sociopolitical Law. To the extent that they are civilised, subjects are cut from the primal object of their *Jouissance* (the maternal Thing). To be a subject is to have to observe our societies' linguistically mediated conventions, defer satisfaction and accept sexual and generational difference in the choice of sexual partners. According to Lacan, subjects' fundamental fantasies are unconscious beliefs which allow them to accept the traumatic loss involved in this founding sacrifice. They do this by (falsely) renarrating this necessary loss as if it were an avoidable, even political, situation that might be reversed, and by providing subjects with a framework within which they can negotiate ticklish, *Jouissance*-provoking subjects like sexuality, cultural difference, political conflict and mortality.

In his key notion of ideological fantasy, Žižek applies the psychoanalytical notion of the fundamental fantasy shaping individuals' identity to understanding political groups. Each political regime has not only a body of more-or-less explicit, usually written, Laws which demand that subjects forego *Jouissance* in the name of the greater good – like the US or French constitutions. (Žižek identifies this level of the Law with the Freudian ego ideal.) In order to truly grip people, a regime's explicit Laws must also harbour and conceal a darker underside of more-or-less unspoken rules. Far from simply repressing *Jouissance*, these unwritten norms implicate subjects in a guilty, superegoic enjoyment in repression itself – for instance, in prosecuting criminals, marginalising minorities or hating enemies. Regimes' ideological fantasies encode the open secrets of those beliefs and practices which make Us who We are politically: the way the sexes relate, the way authority truly operates behind pleasing rhetoric about freedom and respect, the way we think ourselves superior to others and so on.

The split in the Law, between the symbolic and fantasmatic

registers, speaks directly to Žižek's notion of ideological disidentification. Political subjects can typically maintain a conscious sense of
freedom from the explicit norms of their culture because of their
unconscious attachment to the 'inherent transgressions' regimes'
ideological fantasies sanctify, as the way subjects can 'enjoy their
Nation as themselves'.[3] Individuals will only turn around when the
Law hails them (Žižek adapts Althusser), insofar as they are finally
subjects of the unconscious belief that the hailing 'big Other' has
access to the *Jouissance* they have lost as subjects of the Law, and
which they can accordingly reattain through political allegiance. If
only we persist in our loving identification with the Other, so the
unconscious logic runs, we might win back the *Jouissance* we have
lost. This fantasmatic notion is the passionate basis of political identification, being much more difficult to shift than any simply false
notion of the way the political system works.

The Subject and/as the Inconsistency of the Other

The key critical point for Žižek is that logics of our unconscious
individual and political fantasies are at base deeply, and demon-
strably, inconsistent. Freud famously talked of a man who returns
a borrowed kettle to its owner broken. The man adduces mutually
inconsistent excuses, united only in terms of his ignoble desire to
evade responsibility for breaking the kettle – he never borrowed the
kettle, the kettle was already broken when he borrowed it, and when
he gave the kettle back it was not broken anyway. As Žižek reads
ideologies, they function in the same way in the political field – thus
the subtitle of his book *Iraq: The Borrowed Kettle.*

The purpose of political ideologies is to secure and defend the
idea of the polity as a wholly unified community. But political strife,
uncertainty and division do occur. Regimes' ideological fantasies
operate to (re)signify this political discontent so that the political
ideal of community can be sustained. The overriding objective is
to foreclose in advance the possibility that this discontent might
show a fundamental injustice or flaw within the regime. In a kind
of political theodicy, Žižek's work thus points us to a number of
invariant, logically inconsistent ideological responses to political
discontents:

1. These divisions are politically unimportant, transient or merely
   apparent.

When this explanation fails:

2. The political divisions are contingent on the ordinary run of events, so that if their cause is removed or destroyed, things will return to normal (this is the decisive measure, for Žižek).

Or, most perilously:

3. The divisions or problems are deserved by the people for the sake of the greater good (in Australia in the 1990s, for example, we experienced 'the recession we had to have'), or as punishment for our betrayal of the national Thing, God, Virtue.

The key paradox Žižek highlights about ideologies emerges clearly in his already famous analyses of the political discontents in former Yugoslavia following the fall of communism. Each political community tends to claim that its sublime Thing ('Our Way of Life') is inalienable, utterly incapable of being understood or destroyed by enemies. Nevertheless, as chance or bitter political necessity would have it, it is simultaneously deeply fragile, even under active threat. It is under threat, invariably, by exemplars of a persecutory enemy, or as Žižek says, 'the Other supposed to Enjoy', or to be actively behind our political disunity. If only this other or enemy (the terrorist, the illegal migrant) could be removed, the ideological fantasy promises, the regime would be fully whole, and our collective 'way of life' and *Jouissance* be secured. Historical examples of such figures of the enemy include 'the Jew' in Nazi ideology or the 'petty bourgeois' in Stalinism or 'the Terrorist' in the reign of George W. Bush.

A tellingly inconsistent 'kettle logic' applies also to the way these enemies are represented in political ideologies. 'The Jew' in Nazi ideology, for example, was an inconsistent condensation of features of both the ruling capitalist class (money-grabbing, exploitation of the poor) *and* of the proletariat (dirtiness, sexual promiscuity, communism). The only consistency this figure has is as a condensation of everything in political opposition to which the Nazi ideology's Aryan *Volksgemeinschaft* ('national community') was constructed. The appearance the ideology has of describing a pre-existing reality conceals that its real function is to shape the political community's desire and sense of identity.

What then is the fundamental mystery that political ideologies

Matthew Sharpe

are there to conceal, but whose repressed Reality returns in their manifest inconsistencies – our Thing is inalienable *and* it is under Threat; the Terrorist is both inhumanly self-sacrificing *and* cowardly, insanely ascetic *and* awaiting forty virgins in paradise? Fantasy as such is always fundamentally the fantasy of (one's) origins. In Freud's 'Wolfman' case, the primal scene of parental coitus is the Wolfman's attempt to come to terms with his own origin – 'where did I come from?' The problem here is this: who could the spectacle of this primal scene have been staged for or seen by, if it really transpired before the genesis of the subject that it would explain? The only answer is that the Wolfman has imaginatively transposed himself back into the primal scene, as an impassive object-gaze, or what Žižek will call 'the gaze as love object'.[4]

So too, Žižek claims, the Act that founds a political regime is never itself legal according to the very order of Law it sets in place. Faced with this fundamental political datum, fantasy tries to renarrativise historically the founding political act as if it had been legal or noble. No less than the Wolfman's false transposition of himself back into the primal scene, the attempt of any political regime to explain away the fundamental, extralegal violence of its own origins must fail. Yet, so long as this failure is not exposed, and the founding violence remains hidden from subjects' view, the ideological myth continues to operate unchallenged, with very real consequences. Consider the fantasmatic idea of *terra nullius* in colonial Australia, for instance, a legal fiction that served first to justify and then to repress from the historical record Anglo-Saxon settlers' violence against the country's indigenous inhabitants.

In Žižek's terms, the fundamental mystery that ideological fantasy hence aims to conceal is that the big Other does not exist as a single, self-consistent, politically innocent whole. At the least, the Other has been founded on exceptional violence. Moreover, its present reproduction will depend on excluding and demonising certain 'symptomatic' political issues and groups (for example, illegal migrants, single mothers) from political debate. In practical terms, this means that however tempted we might be to claim that we are powerless, it is always potentially within our power as subjects to challenge the regimes we live within. If the 'big Others' (our political systems) did somehow exist as wholly self-consistent wholes or substances, there would not be sufficient room for any political agency. In non-Lacanian terminology, we would then be wholly socially or politically determined objects, rather than subjects. But

252

his critique of ideology and its inconsistencies shows us that this, mercifully, is not the case.

The central place Žižek assigns to a theory of subjectivity was perhaps his most radical challenge to accepted theoretical opinion when he commenced publishing in English. Žižek turned around the critiques of the subject posed by Derrida, Foucault and others by arguing that the Cartesian subject is not the fully self-assured master and possessor of nature which the post-structuralists powerfully attacked. The subject is what Žižek calls in 'Kant With (Or Against) Kant', an out-of-joint ontological excess or *clinamen* rather more like the figures of 'difference', 'otherness' or the 'liminal' central to post-structuralist theory.[5]

In *The Critique of Pure Reason*, Žižek recalls, Kant criticised Descartes's argument that the self-guaranteeing 'I think' of the *cogito* must be a thinking thing (*res cogitans*). For Kant, while the 'I think' must be capable of accompanying all of the subject's perceptions, this does not mean that it is itself a substantial object. The subject that sees objects in the world cannot see itself seeing, any more than a person can jump over her own shadow. To the extent that a subject can reflectively see itself, it sees itself not as a subject but as one more represented object: what Kant calls the 'empirical self' and Žižek the 'self' (versus the subject) in *The Plague of Fantasies*. As subjects, we know that we must have some identity, Žižek argues. But we do not and can never know *which* Thing we are 'in the Real'. This is why, moved by desire, we can only seek clues to our identity in our social and political lives, asking others the question which Žižek argues defines the subject as such: *che voui? (what do you want [from me]?)* In *Tarrying with the Negative*, Žižek reads the director's cut of Ridley Scott's *Bladerunner* as revelatory of the Truth of the subject. The main character Deckard literally does not know that he is a robot that perceives itself to be human. According to Žižek, the subject is a 'crack' in the universal field or substance of being, not a knowable thing. This is why Žižek repeatedly cites the dark passage from the young Hegel describing the modern subject not as the 'light' of the modern enlightenment but 'this night, this empty nothing'.[6]

Žižek's Lacanian 'matheme' of the fundamental fantasy $ <> a tries to represent how the subject avoids confronting this 'abyss of freedom' which is its own deepest (non)nature. The subject ($), in its fundamental fantasy, misrecognises itself as a special object (the *objet petit a* or lost object) within the field of objects it perceives. In terms which unite this psychoanalytical notion with Žižek's political philosophy, the *objet petit a* is, exactly, a sublime object. It is an object elevated or 'sublimated' by the subject to the point where it stands as the representative of the *Jouissance* the subject fantasises was taken from him at castration: if only I could get that girl/guy/job/'break', if only we could recapture that piece of territory.

The pre-eminent Lacanian illustration of the *object petit a* is the anamorphic skull at the foot of Holbein's *Ambassadors*: an example of 'the gaze as love object'. This example highlights that the 'object a' can only be seen by a subject who looks at it awry, or from a particular angle. The *objet petit a*, in this manner, is the exact opposite of the object of the modern sciences, that can only be seen clearly and distinctly if it is approached impersonally. If the *objet petit a* is not looked at from a particular, subjective perspective – or, in the words of one of Žižek's titles, by 'looking awry' at it, it cannot be seen at all.

Žižek believes this psychoanalytical notion can be used to structure our understanding of political ideologies. The sublime objects – freedom, Nation, Party – that these ideologies set up before us are only sublime, and hence politically binding, when we look at them awry: from *within* the framework or world-view the ideology sanctifies. Žižek's Lacanian critique of ideology aims to demonstrate the ideological inconsistencies (and political injustices) their sublime appearance conceals from view. In this way, it strikes a blow at the fantasmatic bases sustaining our present political identifications, asking us to step back from and relook at our pre-existing commitments. Put differently, Žižek's critical theory aims to show us how the objects most central to our political beliefs are Things whose sublime, substantial appearance reifies and conceals from us our own active subjectivity and political desire, which constructs and sustains them. The issue is for us to reflexively confront and identify with this usually repressed freedom of subjectivity, which – since it underlies the sustaining ideological fantasies of the 'big Other' of any regime – can also always undermine it, engendering new political modes and orders.

Žižek's Politics and His Critics

The question most critics have asked of Žižek's critical theory up to this date is, ironically, something very like the *che vuoi?* he identifies as the question *par excellence* of the subject. What, if anything, follows politically from Žižek's confronting, insightful descriptions of political life? Žižek's term for the process whereby we come to recognise how the sublime objects of our political regimes' ideologies are – like Marx's commodities – fetishes that conceal from us our own political agency is 'traversing of the fantasy'.[7] Traversing the fantasy, for Žižek, is at once the political subject's deepest self-recognition, and the basis for his defence of the 'lost cause[s]' of a radical politics, despite the widespread despondency or aimlessness of the Western Left. His entire theoretical work directs us towards this 'traversing of the fantasy', in the different fields on which he has written, despite today's consensus that fundamental political change is neither possible nor desirable.

Insofar as political ideologies for Žižek, like Althusser, remain viable only because of the ongoing practices and beliefs of political subjects, this traversal of fantasy must always involve an intervention which changes a regime's material, political institutions. Žižek hence speaks of traversing the fantasy in terms of an 'Act' (capital 'A'), which differs from normal human speech and action. Everyday speech and action typically does not challenge the framing socio-political parameters within which it takes place. By contrast, an Act 'touches the Real' (as Žižek sometimes says) of what a sociopolitical regime has politically repressed or which it cannot publicly avow without risking fundamental political damage. In this way, the Žižekian Act upsets the very political and ideological parameters of what is permitted within a regime. The hope and possibility thereby opened is that new institutions and norms will be brought into being in the light of which the justice of this Act will become clear retrospectively. This theory of the revolutionary Act brings Žižek close to Alain Badiou's notion of an event. Like Badiou, Žižek also turned to the Christian heritage, and the miraculous Pauline achievement of spreading Christianity throughout the Roman Empire, as a paradigm (alongside Lenin's Act in October 1917) for the political Act.

Žižek's prolific output has meant that critical literature on his *oeuvre* only began to catch up with him in the early years of the twenty-first century. Besides criticisms of his style[8] and scholarship,[9] these criticisms have focused on Žižek's politics. Žižek has been accused of incongruously 'tacking on' a 'vulgar' Marxist position to his Lacanian edifice;[10] of falsely posing as a feminist (he identifies the Act as in its essence 'feminine');[11] of falsely posing as a man of the left behind a deeply 'Left fascist' position;[12] of misreading

Matthew Sharpe

theoretical opponents;[13] or of a series of deep contradictions or antinomies.[14] Little wonder then that some critics have even sought a personal or psychoanalytical reason behind Žižek's oddly enigmatic output.[15]

The main thrust of criticism has focused on the notion of the Act. Žižek has been accused of misreading Lacan's understanding of the psychoanalytic Act,[16] and of proposing under its banner a normatively empty political decisionism. To show that we can Act is not to speak to why we should. Nor is Žižek's method of grounding political prescriptions on a model taken from the individual work of the psychoanalytical clinic propitious for supporting a strategically necessary understanding of the material weight of political institutions and cultural particularity in shaping what is politically possible. For this reason, his work tends towards the messianic prospect of completely overthrowing all habits and institutions that stand. Recently, Boucher and Sharpe have argued that the source of the political hesitations critics have seen in Žižek's work lies in an uncritical attempt to over-extend psychoanalytical categories into the political field. Žižek is aware of this possibility but tends to dismiss it by ridicule (as 'boring', 'standard') instead of by argument.[17] It is worth noting finally that in his most recent works *Parallax View* and *In Defence of Lost Causes*, Žižek has openly eschewed his earlier allegiance to the cause of radical democracy, exoterically aiming to resurrect the 'dictatorship of the proletariat' as the political alternative to global capitalism and immanent ecological catastrophe.

Notes

1. Žižek, *Sublime Object of Ideology*, Chapter 1.
2. ŽIžek, *Tarrying with the Negative*, p. 200.
3. Ibid.
4. Ibid. p. 66.
5. Žižek, 'Kant with (or against) Sade', in *The Žižek Reader*.
6. Žižek, *Tarrying with the Negative*, Chapter 1.
7. Ibid. p. 51.
8. See Justin Clemens, 'The Politics of Style in the World of Slavoj Žižek', in Sherge, Glynos and Boucher (eds), *Traversing the Fantasy*, pp. 3–22; Geoffrey Galt Harpham, 'Doing the Impossible: Žižek and the End of Knowledge', *Critical Inquiry*, 29, 3, 2003, pp. 453–85.
9. See Paul Bowman, 'The Tao of Žižek', in Bowman and Stamp (eds), *The Truth of Žižek*, pp. 27–44; Richard Stamp, '"Another Exemplary Case": Žižek's Logic of Examples', in Bowman and Stamp (eds), *The*

Truth of Žižek, pp. 161–76; Jeremy Gilbert,'All the Right Questions, All the Wrong Answers', in Bowman and Stamp (eds), *The Truth of Žižek*, pp. 61–81; John Holbo, 'On Žižek and Trilling', *Philosophy and Literature*, 28.2, 2004, pp. 430–40.

10. Ernesto Laclau, 'Structure, History and the Political', in *Contingency, Hegemony, Universality*, pp. 182–212.
11. See Sarah Herbold, '"Well-Placed Reflections": On Woman as Symptom of Man', in *Traversing the Fantasy*, pp. 125–46.
12. Claudia Berger, 'The Leader's Two Bodies: Slavoj Žižek's Postmodern Political Theology', *Diacritics*, 31, 1, 2001, pp. 73–90.
13. Ian Buchanan, 'Žižek and Deleuze', in *Traversing the Fantasy*, pp. 69–85.
14. Geoff Boucher, 'The Law as a Thing: Žižek and the Graph of Desire', in *Traversing the Fantasy*, pp. 23–44; Matthew Sharpe,'What's *Left* in Žižek? The Antinomies of Žižek's Sociopolitical Reason', in *Traversing the Fantasy*, pp. 147–68.
15. Leigh Claire La Berge,'The Writing Cure? Slavoj Žižek, Analysand of Modernity', in Bowman and Stamp (eds), *The Truth of Žižek*, pp. 9–26.
16. Russell Grigg, 'Absolute Freedom and Major Structural Change', in *Traversing the Fantasy*, pp. 183–94.
17. Matthew Sharpe and Geoff Boucher, *Žižek and Politics* (Edinburgh: Edinburgh University Press, 2009).

Major Works by Žižek

The Abyss of Freedom (Ann Arbor: University of Michigan Press, 1997).

The Art of the Ridiculous Sublime: On David Lynch's Lost Highway (Seattle: Walter Chapin Simpson Centre for the Humanities, 2000).

Contingency, Hegemony, Universality: Contemporary Dialogues on the Left, with Judith Butler and Ernesto Laclau (London and New York: Verso, 2000).

For They Know Not What They Do: Enjoyment as a Political Factor (London and New York: Verso, 1991).

The Fragile Absolute – Or, Why Is the Christian Legacy Worth Fighting For? (London and New York: Verso, 2000).

The Fright of Real Tears: Krzysztof Kieślowski between Theory and Post-Theory (London: BFI Publishing, 2001).

In Defence of Lost Causes (London: Verso, 2007).

The Indivisible Remainder: An Essay on Schelling and Related Matters (London and New York: Verso, 1996).

Looking Awry: An Introduction to Jacques Lacan through Popular Culture (Cambridge and London: MIT Press, 1991).

The Metastases of Enjoyment: Six Essays on Woman and Causality (London and New York: Verso, 1994).

'Multiculturalism, or The Cultural Logic of Late Capitalism', *New Left Review*, 225, 1997, pp. 28–51.

Organs without Bodies: On Deleuze and Consequences (New York; London: Routledge, 2003).

The Parallax View (Cambridge: MIT Press, 2006).

The Plague of Fantasies (London; New York: Verso, 1997).

The Puppet and the Dwarf: The Perverse Core of Christianity (Cambridge, MA; London: The MIT Press, 2003).

The Sublime Object of Ideology (London and New York: Verso, 1989).

Tarrying with the Negative: Kant, Hegel and the Critique of Ideology (London; New York: Verso, 1993).

The Ticklish Subject: The Absent Centre of Political Ontology (London; New York: Verso, 2000).

The Žižek Reader, ed. Elizabeth Wright and Edmond Wright, Blackwell Readers (Oxford: Blackwell, 1999).

Suggestions for Further Reading

Bowman, Paul, and Richard Stamp (eds), *The Truth of Žižek* (London: Continuum, 2007). An essential, highly critical selection on all aspects of Žižek's work, with an equally polemical response by Žižek.

Boucher, Geoff, Jason Glynos and Matthew Sharpe (eds), *Traversing the Fantasy: Critical Responses to Slavoj Žižek* (Aldershot: Ashgate, 2005). Essential collection of articles critically examining Žižek's contributions to political theory, cultural and film studies, and philosophy.

Butler, Rex, *Slavoj Žižek: Live Theory* (London: Continuum, 2004). Includes interview with Žižek.

Dean, Jodi, *Žižek's Politics* (London: Routledge, 2007). First, engaging, book on Žižek to specifically focus on his work from a political angle.

Kay, Sarah, *Žižek: A Critical Introduction* (London: Polity, 2003). Introduction to Žižek based upon his key intellectual debts to Lacan, Hegel and Marx.

Myers, Tony, *Slavoj Žižek* (Routledge Critical Thinkers) (London: Routledge, 2003).

Parker, Ian, *Slavoj Žižek: A Critical Introduction* (London: Pluto Press, 2004). Idiosyncratic, critical introduction to all aspects of Žižek's work, with an especially good framing account of his intellectual and political background in Slovenia.

Sharpe, Matthew, *Slavoj Žižek: A Little Piece of the Real*, Ashgate New Critical Thinking in Philosophy (Aldershot: Ashgate, 2004). Critical book which analyses Žižek's positions, before questioning whether he is not committed to a series of irresolvable contradictions in his politics.

Sharpe, Matthew, and Geoff Boucher, *Žižek and Politics: A Critical Introduction* (Edinburgh: Edinburgh University Press, 2009). Critical analysis of Žižek's politics which argues that Žižek's encounter with the German philosopher Schelling in the mid-1990s had a decisive effect upon his political thought.

Names index

Abbey, Edward, 110–11, 112
Adorno, Theodor, 3
Agamben, Giorgio, 4Table 1.1, 4Table 1.2, 5, 6, 7, 11, 12, 14–26, 243; *see also* subject index
Ahmad, Aijaz, 74
Akrich, Madeleine, 161
Ali, Monica, 46
Althusser, Louis, 3, 4Table 1.1, 6, 95, 106n5, 147, 148, 194, 195, 245, 246, 247, 250, 255
Anderson, Benedict, 70
Arendt, Hannah, 3, 4Table 1.1, 6, 104, 105, 155, 198, 201
Aristotle, 6, 14, 30, 97–8, 103, 200–1, 202
Arnold, David, 215
Augé, Marc, 162
Austin, J. L., 78–9, 80, 81–2

Bacon, Francis, 119–20
Badiou, Alain, 4Table 1.1, 4Table 1.2, 5, 6, 7, 11, 29–43, 100, 105, 207, 255; *see also* subject index
Barthes, Roland, 3
Baudrillard, Jean, 3
Bauman, Janina, 53, 55
Bauman, Zygmunt, 4Table 1.1, 4Table 1.2, 5, 6, 7, 11, 45–58; *see also* subject index

Beauvoir, Simone de, 78, 80, 84, 89
Beethoven, Ludwig van, 35
Benhabib, Seyla, 8
Benjamin, Walter, 6, 25, 141
Bentham, Jeremy, 56, 113
Bergson, Henri, 107n19
Bernard, Claude, 120
Bhabha, Homi K., 4Table 1.1, 4Table 1.2, 5, 7, 11, 60–73; *see also* subject index
Bhaduri, Bhubaneswari, 219
Botton, Alain de, 46
Boucher, Geoff, 256
Bourdieu, Pierre, 3
Bové, Paul, 8, 9, 10
Braidotti, Rosi, 8, 139
Brontë, Charlotte, 214
Budiansky, Stephen, 122
Buffon, Georges Louis Leclerc, Comte de, 19
Burke, Edmund, 247
Bush, George W., 251
Butler, Judith, 4Table 1.1, 4Table 1.2, 5, 7, 11, 77–89, 101, 151, 158; *see also* subject index

Callon, Michel, 161, 163
Carlyle, Thomas, 56
Castells, Manuel, 8

259

Subject index